T0322452

World Football Club Crests

BLOOMSBURY SPORT
Bloomsbury Publishing Plc
50 Bedford Square, London, WC1B 3DP, UK
29 Earlsfort Terrace, Dublin 2, Ireland

BLOOMSBURY, BLOOMSBURY SPORT and the Diana logo are trademarks of Bloomsbury
Publishing Plc
First published in Great Britain in 2018
Text copyright © Leonard Jägerskiöld Nilsson in 2018

First published by Pintxo Förlag, Sweden in 2016

Published by agreement with the Kontext Agency, Sweden

A catalogue record for this book is available from the British Library

Library of Congress Cataloguing-in-Publication data has been applied for

ISBN: HB: 978-1-47295-425-1; eBook: 978-1-47295-424-4

8 10 9

Printed and bound in China by C&C Offset Printing Co., Ltd.

MIX
Paper | Supporting
responsible forestry
FSC® C008047

To find out more about our authors and books visit www.bloomsbury.com.

Here you will find extracts, author interviews, details of forthcoming events and the option to
sign up for our newsletters.

World Football Club Crests

The Design, Meaning and Symbolism of World Football's Most Famous Club Badges

Leonard Jägerskiöld Nilsson

BLOOMSBURY SPORT
LONDON · OXFORD · NEW YORK · NEW DELHI · SYDNEY

CONTENTS

INTRODUCTION

Football clubs, their supporters and their society have always fascinated me. What is it that creates their identity, what is it that brings them together and unites them? A club's identity is expressed in various ways – through the players on the pitch and their attitude, through the colours on the shirts, through the stadium itself and through the fans. But is the club crest the most neglected factor in all this? Is it the crest that connects the fans to the board, the pubs to the dressing room, and the football stars to the autograph-hunters? The emblem is often taken for granted. It's there on the match programme and the merchandise and nobody really knows what it means and stands for.

The club crest is the key symbol for a team, and for its fans and their shared passion, which rests on local bias and tradition: the love of a club is often inherited through generations. And so too is the emblem. It's no coincidence that the demand to 'fight for your shield' or 'defend the colours' crop up within football. The club crest is all about identity, history and unity. It unites supporters on the terraces, in beer-soaked pubs, in claustrophobic, packed-out burger bars and in sun-bleached stands. The community can even reach far beyond the boundaries of football, far from the origins of many clubs. For example, the riveting hammers in West Ham's emblem are symbols of the club's roots among the iron-workers and dockers in East London. Romulus and Remus, in AS Roma's club badge, are the twins who, according to mythology, founded Rome and who have always been part of the Italian capital's collective consciousness.

Along with the industrialisation and globalisation of football, the emblem has acquired new values. Today it also represents a brand in a worldwide marketplace. And this is not without its attendant problems. In spite of the historic heritage and symbolic significance, the emblem is constantly modified, for a variety of reasons. Changes in ownership and the desire to fully exploit the brand mean that each season new and modified crests are unveiled around the world. Sometimes these changes reflect the club's history, and sometimes they don't. On the latter occasions, the real importance of the club logo is manifested in protests, even revolts, as is true of Hull City AFC: supporter groups have gone to war with the owners in the case of both the club's name and logo.

The emblem is often the source of conflict when the old meets the new, and the interests of the owners often clash with those of the fans. On one hand are the supporters who want to uphold the club's history, tradition and identity, and on the other are the owners who want to advertise a new start or reach new markets. Such was the case when Paris Saint-Germain was bought by Qatar Sports Investments in 2011. This not only demonstrated that the balance of power in French football had changed but also brought with it a new emblem for PSG. The refashioned crest was meant to demonstrate that the club was now entering a new era. In Wales, Cardiff City's owner Vincent Tan chose to exchange the blue emblem for a red one in order to establish the club in the Asian market, where red is meant to bring luck. But Tan didn't stop there. The classic bluebird disappeared from the crest to be replaced by the supposedly more popular Welsh dragon.

For several non-European owners – especially of clubs in England but also on the Continent – the value of the global market is accentuated. It's no coincidence that the pre-season tours have moved to North America and Asia. These are partly new, unexplored markets where the early birds catch the fattest worms. If a modified club emblem can help the owners on the way, the wishes of local supporters tend to be overlooked. A study of club crests is therefore as much to do with learning about the club's past as understanding its future. That's also the purpose of this book, to dive into the history of the clubs in order to conjure up an image of the future towards which they – and football in general – are heading. Not an easy process. As I discovered in my journey, the club's own archives seldom delve very deeply into this history. To my astonishment a great many clubs hadn't even saved their earlier logos, and among those with proper archives were clubs that preferred a revisionist version of their own history. They have censored their earlier crests, no longer wanting to acknowledge them. This spurred me on even more as I wrote this book. If the clubs don't take care of their historic heritage, I will.

The emblems of football form their own universe, infinite and impossible to reflect fully, so we have been forced to make a selection. The most interesting club crests are illustrated in this book, and the most important changes to the emblems are highlighted. Unfortunately, I approached some clubs, that refused to cooperate, but this does also mean that all the clubs in the book want to be part of this project. Here are giants like Real Madrid, classic teams like Wolverhampton Wanderers and cult teams like St. Pauli. Wherever they are found in the hierarchy of football, they are united by the fact that their emblems have an exciting story to tell.

Leonard Jägerskiöld Nilsson

ENGLAND

ARSENAL

FOOTBALL FIREPOWER

Arsenal football club's rich heritage is proudly displayed in the iconic crest – there's no mistaking that these are the Gunners.

Dial Square, the club that became Arsenal, was founded in 1886 by workers at the Royal Arsenal armaments factory in Woolwich, in southeast London. Its first crest was heavily based on the local council's coat of arms: reflecting the area's strong military connections, it featured three cannons.

In the following years the club changed its name to Royal Arsenal and then Woolwich Arsenal. In 1913, it made a surprise move north, across the city, to Highbury in Islington. That could have been the moment for a complete rebrand, but in fact it also took the name Arsenal, along with the Gunners nickname acquired due to the association with the factory, and the cannon symbol, which continued to appear on badges throughout the 1920s.

Legendary moderniser Herbert Chapman took over as Arsenal manager in 1925. He led the team to two league titles and one FA Cup triumph, as well as laying the foundations for the golden era of the 1930s, when the club won the league five times. He was also instrumental in developing the distinctive Art Deco design – more a logo than a crest – which was based on the club's initials, and graced the stadium in Highbury for several decades. Apart from one cup triumph and two league titles, the post-war period did not bring the same successes until the Double-winning year of 1971. The club's badge, now in colour and with the addition of the Islington coat of arms, still featured a prominent cannon to reinforce the Gunners moniker.

Of course, there have been other nicknames: in the 1970s and 1980s 'Boring, Boring Arsenal' alluded to the team's dull but efficient style of play; and in the early 2000s manager Arsène Wenger's unbeaten team were known as 'the Invincibles'. However, 'the Gunners' is a name that has stuck – reiterated by the cannon that endure on the crest.

CLUB: Arsenal FC
NICKNAME: The Gunners
FOUNDED: 1886
STADIUM: Emirates Stadium, London (59,867 capacity)
HISTORIC PLAYERS: David O'Leary, Ian Wright, Dennis Bergkamp, Tony Adams, Patrick Vieira and Thierry Henry

1. 1888–1913. Two years after the birth of the club, the team's first emblem was created. Under the name Royal Arsenal, the club's emblem was inspired by Woolwich's town crest. The three columns are cannons, each with the head of a lion. Cannons are closely linked to Woolwich because the area has a strong military history. This emblem was taken up by the club when it moved to North London.

2. 1922–1925 and 1925–1949. After the moves and the change of name in 1913, it took almost 10 years before a new official club emblem was produced. The one on the left is taken from the 1922/23 season's first match programme. It was updated three years later, when the gun was turned to the left. Both emblems carry the club's nickname.

3. 1949–2002. The end of the '40s saw the club's first emblem in colour. Red and white reflected the team's kit, which in turn had been inspired by Nottingham Forest because two of the club's founders had played there. In the new emblem, Arsenal was written in the Gothic style and the town crest of Islington, the local borough, was introduced. Furthermore it included the Latin motto *Victoria Concordia Crescit*, which means 'Victory comes from harmony' and was suggested by Harry Homer, the editor of the match programme. The crest was modernised over the years.

4. 2002–present. Arsenal ran up against problems when they wanted to patent their earlier crest and so they created a completely new emblem. The cannon was retained but this time turned back to the right. An important element of the new crest was to look forward to the club's future home, the Emirates Stadium (2006), which had already been planned when the new emblem was introduced.

1.

2.

3.

5. Arsenal have also used this Art Deco emblem, which was above the main entrance of their old stadium at Highbury. This is not just a club crest but also a piece of wordplay created by Herbert Chapman. The symbols in the hexagon are the letters A and C plus a football, which together form the club's initials (AFC). This symbol from the '30s can still be seen on souvenirs.

4.

5.

Arsenal's all-time top goalscorer Thierry Henry pats the Gunners crest after scoring the winning goal in an FA Cup match against Leeds United in 2012. The 2011/12 season was marked by a 125th-anniversary crest design which used laurel elements from the original club crest.

ASTON VILLA

THE SCOTTISH LION OF THE MIDLANDS

The Scottish lion and the word 'Prepared' have been part of the Aston Villa crest since the club's foundation in 1874 and modifications have been few.

Historically, Aston Villa is one of England's most important football clubs. The team from Birmingham was, in fact, one of the 12 first participants in the English League, though it took until 1894 before Aston Villa won their first League title. The club chairman William McGregor played an important role both for the club and for English football in general. During his time in charge, Villa won six league titles and took the FA Cup home four times – the most brilliant period in the club's history. McGregor also founded the country's top division, in 1888, and carried through reform on a national level, which resulted in the professionalisation of the game. Thanks to McGregror, English players were now able to earn money from their sport.

McGregor had been enticed to Aston Villa in the first place by a strong connection to Birmingham's Scottish community. McGregor was himself Scottish and felt a kinship with Villa, so in 1877 he chose to work for them. The Scottish identity assumed its greatest importance when he decided the lion from Scotland's royal crest should be the emblem of Aston Villa. Thus for over a hundred years the Scottish national crest has symbolised one of England's most successful clubs.

After McGregor's death in 1911, Aston Villa never quite reached the same heights again, even if the club did develop into one of England's strongest brands. The victory in the European Cup in 1982 was their greatest achievement – a title that was, incidentally, won with four Scottish players in the squad.

1. 1973–1992. The rampant lion from Scotland's national crest was Aston Villa's first emblem and has never been replaced. Prior to this badge the lion could be seen without the surrounding shield as well.

2. 1992–2000. The original lion was red, but during the 20th century there were white, claret and light-blue variations until this one was introduced in 1992. Since then, Villa's lion has been yellow.

3. 2000–2007. With the arrival of the new millennium the lion was modernised and the abbreviation F.C. was dropped. The claret and light-blue stripes symbolise the colours of the shirt, which haven't changed since 1887.

4. 2007–2016. On August 14th, 2006 the American Randy Lerner bought Aston Villa for £62.6 million. To symbolise the beginning of a new era, this emblem was introduced the following year. The white star reflects the victory against Bayern Munich in the 1982 European Cup. The motto Prepared has been used since 1878.

5. 2016–present. In the spring of 2016 Aston Villa completed an historically poor season. The team came bottom of the Premier League and were relegated. In the midst of all this, the club introduced a new emblem costing around £100,000 – a huge sum for minor alterations like the lion's acquisition of a more heraldic look... and claws. On top of this the motto 'Prepared' was removed to make the lion bigger.

CLUB: Aston Villa FC

NICKNAME: Villa, Villans and The Lions

FOUNDED: 1874

STADIUM: Villa Park, Birmingham (42,682 capacity)

HISTORIC PLAYERS: Harry Hampton, Charlie Aitken, Peter Withe, Dennis Mortimer, Dwight Yorke, Gareth Barry and Olof Mellberg

1.

2.

3.

4.

5.

Gordon Cowans sporting Aston Villa's roundel club crest which was introduced in 1973. The design decorated the kit for the 1981 League Championship, 1982 European Cup and a European Super Cup – Villa's most successful period in the modern era.

BLACKBURN ROVERS

SKILL AND HARD WORK

Arte et Labore, the Latin phrase that adorns the crest of Blackburn Rovers club, translates as 'By skill and hard work' – two qualities required to succeed in football. The words come from Blackburn's town crest, and so have an historic meaning for both the club and the town.

The people of Blackburn have always worked hard. The town was situated in the centre of the Industrial Revolution, which changed not just England but also Europe in the 18th and 19th centuries. In 1764, in nearby Oswaldtwistle, the weaver James Hargreaves invented the spinning jenny, a machine that brought a new efficiency to the textile industry and thus contributed to Blackburn's growth.

More than a hundred years later, the Lancashire cotton industry had almost run its course and the area was afflicted by high levels of unemployment. The locals looked for comfort to their football club, Blackburn Rovers. Formed in 1875, it won the League in 1912 and 1914 and took the FA Cup home five times between 1884 and 1891. But the club's greatest success was a long time coming. In the 1994/95 season, and with financial backing from local multi-millionaire Jack Walker, Blackburn Rovers won the Premier League – a great surprise even though this was a team that was managed by Kenny Dalglish and which included stars like Alan Shearer, Chris Sutton, Graeme Le Saux and Tim Sherwood. The club had worked hard to win the title; it was their first trophy in 67 years.

1. 1875–1878. John Lewis and Arthur Constantine, the two founders, were former students of the local public schools which were strongly associated with the Maltese cross. As a result, Rovers wore the Maltese cross on their shirts.

2. 1928 and 1960. For the FA Cup finals in 1928 and 1960, Rovers wore the city's coat of arms, which symbolizes the town motto 'By skill and hard work'. The bees represent the industrial history of the city while the white field represents the calico industry. At the top of the crest, a dove is perched on a weaver's shuttle, which also has a strong historical bond to the city.

3. 1989–present. It wasn't until 1974 that they started to use an emblem continuously. This is how the red rose of Lancashire, their county, became synonymous with the club. Fifteen years later, the emblem was updated. The rose also represents divine love and motherhood, and was centrally placed. The name and the year of the club's formation appeared in a blue circle, blue being a colour that has followed Blackburn since the beginning in 1875.

CLUB: Blackburn Rovers FC
NICKNAMES: Rovers, The Blue and Whites and The Riversiders
FOUNDED: 1875
STADIUM: Ewood Park, Blackburn (31,367 capacity)
HISTORIC PLAYERS: Billy Bradshaw, Derek Fazackerley, Tim Flowers, Tim Sherwood, Simon Garner, Chris Sutton, Alan Shearer and David Dunn

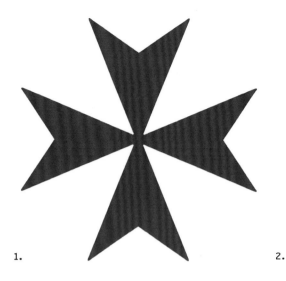

1.

2.

3.

Steve Archibald played on loan for Blackburn Rovers in the 1988/89 season and made 20 appearances. The club's crest between 1974 1989 was based on the Lancashire red rose and carried the club initials below in red.

BRIGHTON & HOVE ALBION

THE SEAGULLS

Brighton & Hove Albion was founded in 1901, joining the Southern League. However, apart from a victory in the FA Charity Shield over Football League champions Aston Villa in 1910, successes were slow to materialise. In fact, it took all of 78 years for Brighton to reach the top division; they were finally promoted to the First Division for the 1979/80 season. Their stay was brief and after four seasons in the top flight they were relegated in the same year that they reached their one and only FA Cup Final, against Manchester United. Brighton finally returned to the top flight in 2017/18.

After 1983, Brighton's fans experienced a period of turbulence, spending four spells in the third division, the most recent in 2011. Added to that, financial problems and postponed building plans meant that the club had no home ground between 1997 and 2011. Instead, they first had to share a stadium with Gillingham, 110 kilometres (70 miles) away, and then had to accept as their temporary home the use of Withdean Stadium, the athletics arena in Brighton. Thanks to owner Tony Bloom, who took over the club in 2009, things have been looking up for Brighton & Hove Albion. Since promotion to the Championship in 2011, the team have played at the newly constructed American Express Community Stadium, and in the spring of 2017, for the first time ever, the club secured a place in the Premier League.

The club's crest originally depicted a traditional coat of arms representing the twin towns of Brighton and Hove, and in the 1950s a club monogram motif was worn. For a time, the club was known as the Dolphins, but this was short-lived. In the 1977 season they adopted the nickname of the Seagulls and the club crest has reflected this ever since.

CLUB: Brighton and Hove Albion FC
NICKNAMES: The Seagulls and The Albion
FOUNDED: 1901
STADIUM: American Express Community Stadium, Brighton (30,750 capacity)
HISTORIC PLAYERS: Des Tennant, Charlie Oatway, Peter Ward, Mark Lawrenson and Bobby Zamora

1. 1946–1974. In the middle of the 20th century the first club crest club was introduced and it portrayed the twin cities' coat of arms. Brighton's to the left and Hove's to the right. This badge was first worn on the shirts in 1948 and remained until 1974.

2. 1956–1959. By the end of the 1950's Brighton and Hove Albion used a monogram badge which was customary back then.

3. 1975–1976. This Brighton crest shows a dolphin, so it was no surprise that the team was nicknamed The Dolphins. A dolphin emblem was adopted from 1975, but it was not popular and never made it to the team shirts.

4. 1977–1998. Legend has it that the club's now classic seagull was created by the fans. Before a home match with arch-rivals Crystal Palace, their supporters were cheering on their team by screaming, 'Eagles! Eagles!'. The Brighton & Hove fans responded by chanting, 'Seagulls! Seagulls!' – and the club found itself with a new nickname!

5. 1998–2011. In the mid-1990s Brighton & Hove Albion was nearly bankrupt. In 1997, after two years of infighting within the club, the supporter and businessman Dick Knight became the new chairman. To mark the event and to clearly distance himself from the earlier club leadership, he introduced a new crest.

6. 2011–present. In 2009 the professional poker player Tony Bloom bought a majority stake in the club and secured the funding for the construction of the new stadium. At the same time a new, more up-to-date badge was introduced in 2011, to coincide with the inauguration of the new stadium and the club's return to the Championship. Note that the direction of the bird's flight was modified.

1.

2.

3.

4.

5.

Brighton & Hove striker Peter Ward rides a challenge at the Goldstone Ground in the 1979. In his five years at the club he scored 79 times in 178 appearances. A fan favourite, in the 1976/77 season, he scored a club record of 36 goals.

6.

CARDIFF CITY

THE BLUEBIRD DEFEATS THE DRAGON

It isn't easy to run a football club. Just ask Cardiff City's Malaysian owner Vincent Tan. Although it was Vincent Tan's money that took the team to the top flight of English football, and although he was the man who sorted out the club's finances, he couldn't do what he wanted with it.

In the summer of 2012, Tan and the Malaysian consortium of which he was a part, decided to revamp the brand of Cardiff City FC. The club's colours changed from blue to red and a new emblem was launched: the bluebird was pushed aside by the Welsh dragon. The dragon had certainly been a part of Cardiff throughout much of the 20th century, but it had never before taken up more space than the bird. Tan's logic was that this would expand interest in the club outside Wales. The supporters, however, were incandescent.

Organisations including Cardiff City Supporters' Trust, Cardiff City Supporters' Club and Bluebirds Unite got together and protested furiously against the decision. The promotion to the Premier League in the spring of 2013 gave Tan a bit of breathing space, but he was finally forced to surrender. The club regained its blue strip halfway through the 2014/15 season, and in March 2015 another new emblem was introduced.

CLUB: Cardiff City FC
NICKNAME: The Bluebirds
FORMED: 1899
STADIUM: Cardiff City Stadium (33,280 capacity)
HISTORIC PLAYERS: Phil Dwyer, Len Davies, Robert Earnshaw, Peter Whittingham and Craig Bellamy

1. 1988–2003. Before the club created its own emblem, the team jerseys were adorned with the city shield of Cardiff. These were also the shirts worn by Cardiff in 1927, when they became the first team from outside England to win the FA Cup – the only time to date. At the time of this victory, the team was called *The Bluebirds* after the popular play The Blue Bird by the Belgian playwright Maurice Maeterlinck. The nickname has shaped the club's emblem ever since. In this version you also find the Welsh dragon and a daffodil, the national flower of Wales.

2. 2003–2008. At the start of the new millennium, the club adopted another Welsh symbol in their crest, namely the cross of St. David. The yellow cross against a black background symbolises Wales's patron saint and is used as an alternative national flag.

3. 2012–2015. Vincent Tan changed the colour from blue because in East Asia the colour red is considered lucky. He also chose to single out the Welsh dragon on the shield because it is a symbol more recognisable in the Asian market – and thus easier to sell. The slogan 'Fire & Passion' was given great prominence. Everything was designed to maximise the possibility of profit from other parts of the world – but in reality created of displeasure among home fans.

4. 2015–present. Even if the latest crest is blue, like the shirts, it is still a compromise. Vincent Tan has kept the red details – but though the dragon retains the same position as the original, it is now Asian. Except for the traditional bluebird, the shape of the emblem is taken from what was worn during the FA Cup victory in 1927.

1.

2.

3.

4.

Cardiff City striker Craig Bellamy gestures to the crowd in 2014. The Welsh club's dragon crest was shortlived and after pressure from home fans Cardiff City reverted to the traditional bluebird design the following season.

CHELSEA

LIONS AND WAR VETERANS

Chelsea's emblem has existed in five different guises since the club was founded in 1905 and, apart from the four big alterations, has been modified a number of times to adjust to the market, and the tastes and fashions of the day.

What few may know is that Chelsea's crest has a close relationship to the British military. Today's lion is a relatively late idea and wasn't introduced until 1953. Until then, an image of a Chelsea Pensioner represented the club. The Royal Hospital Chelsea was founded in 1682 for veterans of the British Army, and Chelsea FC chose to honour the institution – leading to the club's first nickname, the Pensioners. In the early days, the emblem did not appear on the shirts but only on the match programmes.

The Pensioner represented the club until 1952, when a temporary solution replaced the original before making way for today's blue lion, an emblem, among others, inspired by the Abbot of Westminster (hence the staff). This emblem remained until 1986, when the legendary owner Ken Bates, who led Chelsea to great triumphs in the 1990s, both simplified and modernised the lion. Roman Abramovich's arrival at Chelsea in 2003 saw the return of the traditional lion.

CLUB: Chelsea FC

NICKNAMES: The Pensioners and The Blues

FOUNDED: 1905

STADIUM: Stamford Bridge, London (41,631 capacity)

HISTORIC PLAYERS: Peter Bonetti, Peter Osgood, Pat Nevin, Gianfranco Zola, Frank Lampard, John Terry, Fernando Torres.

1. 1905–1952. The Chelsea Pensioners are honoured to this day. When the club won their first league title under Abramovich, the Pensioners stood to attention as a sign of respect for the players and their manager. This ritual was repeated in 2010. And, in turn, the red detail on the collar of the players' jerseys in the 2010/11 season honoured the Pensioners.

2. 1952–1953. While waiting for the new emblem, which was launched in 1953, this temporary solution was used: the club's initials against a blue background, which was suggested by the newly appointed manager Ted Drake. It was during this period that the club's nickname the Blues began to take hold.

3. 1953–1986. The lion symbolising Chelsea today was originally taken from the family crest of the then-club president Earl Cadogan. The lion's staff comes from the Abbot of Westminster and the roses represent England. The emblem has been modified several times through the years.

4. 1986–2005. In 1982 Ken Bates bought Chelsea for £1 and pushed through a number of changes. Among them were this updated lion, introduced in 1986. The lion changed colours during the 1990s but was around to share the golden days with, among others, Gianfranco Zola, Gianluca Vialli and Dennis Wise.

5. 2005–present. In the early days of the Roman Abramovich era, the club celebrated its centennial. This was marked by the reintroduction of the emblem from the 1950s, albeit in a modernised version, which makes it the emblem that has represented the club during its most successful period.

1.

2.

3.

4.

5.

Didier Drogba wearing the 2004 version of the Chelsea club crest. The Ivory Coast striker made 381 appearances and scored 165 goals, helping the west London club win the Premier League and FA cup four times each and the Champions League for the first time.

CRYSTAL PALACE

THE EAGLES FROM SOUTH LONDON

Crystal Palace FC got its name from the enormous glass structure that was erected to house the Great Exhibition of 1851. After the exhibition finished, the 'Crystal Palace' was moved to Sydenham Hill in South London, to the area that was then named after it. The football club was founded there in 1905, its early crest depicting the namesake structure.

Palace spent their early years in the lower divisions, reaching the top flight for the first time only in 1969. There they stayed for four years, but after Malcolm Allison took over as manager in 1973 they were relegated twice in consecutive seasons. His impact on the playing fortunes of the club may not have been positive, but he did make considerable changes to its image. Allison changed the nickname to the Eagles, following in the footsteps of Portuguese club Benfica, and also switched the club kit to red and blue stripes in homage to Spanish giant Barcelona. As a result, the eagle was adopted as the crest's motif. When Allison left in 1976, Terry Venables took over and led the club back up to the First Division in 1979. Palace then spent the next 30 years yo-yoing between the top two divisions and twice went into administration.

In 2010 businessmen Steve Parish, Martin Long, Stephen Browett and Jeremy Hosking bought the club. The new owners sorted out the finances and thus began the club's climb up the table. Like the fabled phoenix (a mythological bird that has been compared to the eagle on the team's badge), Palace rose from the ashes and returned to the Premier League just three years after bankruptcy had threatened. This was secured after a play-off final against Watford at Wembley in May 2013 – a fitting journey for a club whose historic model, the Crystal Palace, famously burned down in 1936.

CLUB: Crystal Palace FC
NICKNAME: The Eagles
FOUNDED: 1905
STADIUM: Selhurst Park, London (26,309 capacity)
HISTORIC PLAYERS: Jim Cannon, Peter Simpson, Nigel Martyn, Julián Speroni, Ian Wright, Mark Bright and Alan Pardew

1. 1955–1972. Although the club was founded in 1905, it wasn't until the end of the 1940s that an official crest was introduced. At that point the club was represented only by an image of the historical glass palace from which the club derived its name. In 1955 the emblem was updated to achieve a better likeness of the building.

2. 1972 – 1973. During only one season this crest was used. The claret and blue colours was the main motive along with the initials of the club in a modern fashion. The traditional nickname 'the Glaziers' was included in the rebranding.

3. 1973–1994. On March 31, 1973 Malcolm Allison was hired as the club's new manager, a decision that helped shape Palace's history. Over and above the changes he made on the pitch, Allison pushed through a programme of radical changes throughout the club. The first of these was a change of the nickname from the Glaziers to the more imposing moniker The Eagles. He followed up by changing their colours to red and blue – after 68 years of claret and light blue. Both of these changes were clearly illustrated in the new crest that Allison also introduced. In 1987 the badge was redesigned to rebrand the club and for the first time in history the eagle, perched onto a football, was seen together with the palace.

4. 1994–2013. In the middle of the 1990s the owner Ron Noades wanted to spruce up Palace's profile. Among other things he felt that the eagle on the crest looked too like a phoenix, so he changed it to a sharper and more aggressive eagle.

5. 2013–present. Three years after the new owners had saved the club from bankruptcy, a new emblem was introduced. Inspired by the logo from the early 1970s, the palace regained its early shape and the eagle reclaimed its old position. In 2010 the eagle Kayla was unveiled as the club mascot, like the corresponding birds at Benfica and Lazio.

1.

1.

2.

3.

3.

4.

5.

Ian Wright socred 90 goals in 225 appearances for Palace. He was also part of the team that reached the FA Cup final in 1990.

DERBY COUNTY

THE SNORTING RAM

One of the original members of the Football League, Derby County FC was founded in 1884 as part of Derbyshire County Cricket Club. Their nickname, the Rams, was established at the same time the club was founded and has been a mainstay of the crest ever since. The nickname came from a local regiment whose official song was 'The Derby Ram', reflecting the county's connection to the wool industry.

Their first major trophy came when they won the first FA Cup to be held after the Second World War. Their victory in 1946 remains their only FA Cup win. Their golden age, in the 1970s, happened under legendary manager Brian Clough. Taking over in 1967, he led them to the top division in 1969, and to their first ever League title in 1972. In the following season, the club reached a European Cup semi-final. After Clough departed in 1973, Don Mackay took over and led them to their second League title in 1975.

Recent times have not been so kind to Derby and they have suffered various indignities, none more so than in the 2007/08 season. Then they finished bottom of the Premier League table having secured just 11 points, a record low in the Premier League. They also became the earliest team to be demoted, relegation being confirmed as early as March. The fact that they managed to win only a single match made it all even worse.

CLUB: Derby County FC

NICKNAME: The Rams

FOUNDED: 1884

STADIUM: Pride Park, Derby (33,597 capacity)

HISTORIC PLAYERS: Stephen Bloomer, Kevin Hector, Colin Todd, Ron Webster, Roy McFarland, Stefano Eranio and Paulo Wanchope

1. 1946–1968. Set within a shield and showing the famous ram as well as the club's initials, this crest was introduced after Derby's victory over Charlton in the 1946 FA Cup final.

2. 1971–1979. Before the 1971/72 season, Derby's kit was changed to look more like that of the English national team. At the same time they introduced a new club emblem, this time with a snorting ram. This would herald a new era of more attacking football, bringing them their first league title in 1972, under Brian Clough.

3. 1997–2007. For a period in the 1980s and '90s, the ram was turned to the right rather than the left. This emblem instead of the above, now once more facing left and featuring the club name on the banner, was unveiled when they moved to their new stadium, Pride Park, in 1997.

4. 2007–2009. In the autumn of 2007 Derby were back in the Premier League for the first time in five years. They celebrated by framing the ram in this crest. The gold lettering was a nod to the club's earliest colours in the 1880s. The emblem was criticised by the fans because the earlier colours were white, light blue, black and brown — all absent from this badge. The club corrected this error in 2009, offering the same logo in simple black and white.

5. 2012–present. The logo from the 1970s, much loved by the fans, made a comeback in the autumn of 2012, with some modifications. The emblem is now black instead of blue, and the eye of the ram is no longer clearly marked. The reason for the ram representing the club in the first place is Derbyshire's strong association with the textile industry.

1.

2.

3.

4.

5.

In the 1960s and '70s, local-born defender Ron Webster played 455 games for Derby County, the second highest in club's history.

EVERTON

THEO KELLY'S TIE

Everton was initially an early adopter of an emblem on match shirts. In 1920 they had the club's initials in white against a blue background, but this emblem was short-lived and for the next for 40 years Everton became known as a club that played without a club crest on their kit. The club did not, however, lack a proper emblem.

Everton's logo today reflects their local roots, and dates all the way back to 1938. That is when the club secretary, Theo Kelly, was given the task of designing an emblem to adorn the ties worn by club employees. It took him four months to create the design that would represent the club for decades to come. Kelly had decided that the main motif should be Prince Rupert's Tower, the rounded building known locally as the Everton Lock-Up. This important landmark in the Everton area of Liverpool was erected to house drunkards and criminals. Kelly chose also to include two laurel wreaths, since they are symbols of victory. The Latin motto *Nil Satis Nisi Optimum*, which translates as 'Nothing but the best is good enough', also made its debut.

The tie was worn by Kelly himself at the first match of the 1938 season. This was now the club's official emblem, but 40 years passed before it appeared on match shirts in 1978. Since then, it has been redesigned six times – but every version has included the tower.

An infamous redesign in 2013 met with enormous criticism from the fans, who missed the Latin motto and the laurel wreaths. The club was accused of having succumbed to the will of the equipment moguls and the fans organised a petition, which amassed 22,000 signatures. In response, Everton issued an official apology and invited fans to help design the new version. The crest from the next season was approved by 80 per cent of fans and has been worn by players from the 2014 season onwards.

1. 1983–1991. Theo Kelly's historic emblem was simplified so that it could be more easily embroidered onto the team shirts. The Latin motto disappeared and the club initials were given more space. Both the tower and the wreaths were there during the period that would be Everton's most successful: two league titles, one FA Cup and one League Cup triumph.

2. 1991–2000. At the start of the 1990s the original emblem was recreated, now only in blue and white. The club name was removed and replaced with the Latin motto which, with the exception of one year, has remained ever since.

3. 2013–2014. The world of football was being modernised and Everton wanted to keep up. Thus, they unveiled this emblem for the 2013/14 season – to a storm of criticism from fans.

4. 2014–present. On October 3, 2014, Everton introduced three different emblems and asked the fans to choose their favourite. Eighty per cent of the club's registered members took part in the vote and this design was the clear winner. With the motto and laurel wreaths back in place, Theo Kelly's design is still going strong.

CLUB: Everton FC
NICKNAMES: The Toffees, The People's Club, The Blues
FOUNDED: 1878
STADIUM: Goodison Park, Liverpool (39,572 capacity)
HISTORIC PLAYERS: Neville Southall, Duncan Ferguson, Dixie Dean, Graeme Sharp Kevin Sheedy, Kevin Ratcliffe and Wayne Rooney

1.

2.

Graeme Sharp, skipper Kevin Ratcliffe and Neville Southall do a lap of honour after securing the 1984/85 first division league title.

3.

4.

FULHAM

THE FAMOUS HUNTING LODGE OF CRAVEN COTTAGE

Founded in 1879 as Fulham St. Andrew's, a church youth club, they were renamed Fulham FC within 10 years and in 1896 moved to their current home, Craven Cottage. Having spent most of their time in the lower divisions, they established themselves in the First Division in the 1960s with a side that included England internationals such as Johnny Haynes and World Cup winner George Cohen.

During the next two decades, Fulham slipped further down the league, reaching almost rock bottom in 1996 at the foot of the Fourth Division. The club was bought by Harrods' owner Mohammed Al-Fayed in the summer of 1997, and their journey to the Premier League began. Fulham were then languishing in the lower echelons of English football, having just secured promotion to the third tier. It was unthinkable even to mention the Premier League – unthinkable for everyone apart from Al-Fayed. When he took over the club, he vowed that he would take Fulham to the highest division within five years – a promise that he kept.

2001 saw Fulham's debut in the Premier League with such interesting players as Dutch goalkeeper Edwin van der Sar in the squad. The team ended up 13th in the League, and after another couple of seasons were firmly established in the top flight of English football. Their greatest achievement was coming seventh in the League in 2009 under the guidance of Roy Hodgson. The following year came that historic Europa League final where Fulham narrowly lost 2-1 to Atlético Madrid.

The club is famous for the cottage adjoining its riverside ground, and this was depicted on club's crest of the 1930s. In later years, the crest has drawn heavily from local heraldry, but since 2001 it is a typographic shield that has adorned the team's famous white shirts.

CLUB: Fulham FC
NICKNAMES: The Cottagers, The Whites and The Lilywhites
FOUNDED: 1879
STADIUM: Craven Cottage, London (25,700 capacity)
HISTORIC PLAYERS: Johnny Haynes, Bobby Robson, Edwin van der Sar, Danny Murphy and Clint Dempsey

1. 1898. Even though Fulham was founded in 1879, under the name of St. Andrews Cricket & Football Club, the club had to wait 19 years for this crest to show. It was inspired by the See of London which the crossed swords represent.

2. 1931–1939. Even if Fulham's first emblem was inspired by London's crest this version is perhaps the real classic in the club's history. In Fulham's stadium, Craven Cottage, there really is a cottage of that name, a symbol that has become synonymous with the club and which was represented in their crest during the 1930s. The original Craven Cottage was built in 1780 on land that was said to have been Anne Boleyn's hunting ground.

3. 1972–1977. After almost thirty years with the coat of arms of the London Borough of Fulham as a crest this monogram was introduced in the beginning of the 1970's. It lasted for five years and was the historical inspiration to the crest of today. It was later replaced by a simplified version of the Hammersmith & Fulham coat of arms.

4. 1995–2001. After the end of the Second World War a crest was introduced which was almost identical to that of Hammersmith, the area where Fulham is situated. This emblem was modified over the years and in 1995 this version was unveiled. The sword, shield and helmet are taken from the Hammersmith crest, while the blue and white stripes stand for the Thames which flows past Craven Cottage.

5. 2001–present. In conjunction with Fulham's debut in the Premier League at the start of the new millennium this crest was introduced. The initials suggest the emblem that the club used in the 1970s. The press release from the club announced, 'The emblem emphasises our origins.'

1.

2.

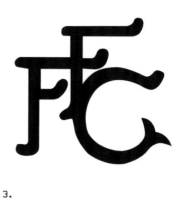

3.

4.

5.

Few have a greater association with Fulham than Jimmy Hill. He joined the club in 1953 as a player and was later chairman. Shown here in 1973, the club crest at this time draws inspiration from the heraldry of the local area.

HULL CITY

THE BATTLING TIGERS

Established in 1904, Hull City soon adopted the nickname of the Tigers because of their amber and black shirts. In 2008 they finally reached the top division for the first time in their history thanks to a goal from Dean Windass which won the Championship Play-Off final.

On 20 June, 2014, Hull City AFC changed its emblem for the seventh time in the club's history – a change that met with strong criticism from the fans. The new emblem did keep with tradition in displaying the classic tiger head that has become synonymous with Hull, but it lacked the name of the club, Hull City AFC. This was a bold decision in an already sensitive affair.

The businessman Assem Allam had long wanted to change the name of the club from Hull City AFC to Hull Tigers. He felt both that the name City was too commonplace and that the nickname Tigers would be easier to market on the continent. The fans, led by the organisation City Till We Die, opposed the plan and handed in petitions to the FA. English football's governing body now acted as judge and jury, and in April 2014 denied Allam permission to change the club's name.

It was a victory for the protesting fans. But Allam didn't give up. and two months later he changed the emblem without consulting the fans, and reneging on the promise announced in a press release in August 2013. This further enraged the supporters. City Till We Die released the following statement: 'We are deeply disappointed that the club has changed the emblem without consulting us. There is no reason to change a badge which has been worn proudly by the club's players, which has taken part in four promotions, played in the Premier League and an FA Cup final.

CLUB: Hull City AFC

NICKNAME: The Tigers

FOUNDED: 1904

STADIUM: KCOM Stadium, Kingston upon Hull (25,450 capacity)

HISTORIC PLAYERS: Andy Davidson, Chris Chilton, Ken Wagstaff, Dean Windass and Geovanni

1. 1935–1947. Although the club was founded in 1904 it wasn't until 1935 that the first emblem was introduced. As Hull City AFC was the only football team in town, the club's badge was inspired by Kingston upon Hull's crest. The origin of the three crowns is unclear, but there is speculation that they symbolise the three wise men. This emblem was worn only during the 1935/36 season but came to symbolise the club for a long time thereafter.

2. 1947–1975. Hull's nickname, the Tigers, was established long before the tiger itself appeared in their emblem. It originates from the orange and black worn by the team ever since the club was founded. In 1947 the club's then board wanted to emphasise the connection by introducing Hull's first tiger emblem. The shield around the tiger disappeared in 1957, but the tiger head remained until 1975.

3. 1998–2003. Between 1975 and 1998, Hull tested out a number of variations on the emblem. For a couple of seasons the team was represented simply by the club initials: HCAFC. At the end of the 1990s a new logo was introduced, one that had been designed by the student James Hinchcliffe, the son of one of the club's earlier owners. It emphasised the club's connection to the area, reinstating the three crowns and now including the landmark Humber Bridge.

4. 2003–2014. In spring 2003, Hull City left its old stadium, Boothferry Park, and moved into the newly built KCOM Stadium. To mark the event and to illustrate the modernising of the club, this emblem was launched, which includes both the club's name and its nickname. In summer 2013, AFC was removed from the emblem – much to the displeasure of the fans.

5. 2014–2019. Hull had just played their first FA Cup final (losing 3–2 to Arsenal) and so qualified for European football for the first time. Away from the pitch, the owner Assem Allam lost the battle for the club name. He responded by erasing the club name in the updated crest. The first season with this new emblem didn't work out too well, ending with the club's relegation from the Premier League.

6. 2019–present. In 2019 the club reintroduced the name 'Hull City' above the tiger's head. The new badge was created in consultation with the supporters in a process involving 7000 fans.

1.

2.

3.

4.

5.

6.

Hull City player Raich Carter in 1952 with the first tiger club crest. In addition to making 136 appearances for the club, the inside forward later managed the team, leading them to the Division Three North title. Carter was also a talented county cricketer.

LEEDS UNITED

RICH TRADITIONS – EVOLVING CREST

In 1919, Leeds United were formed from the ashes of the disbanded club Leeds City. They enjoyed their most successful period in the early 1970s, when they became one of the strongest clubs in England. Under Don Revie they were promoted back to the First Division in 1964 and within the next 10 years had won two league titles, an FA Cup and two Fairs Cups (predecessor of the UEFA cup and the current Europa League). Revie was also responsible for changing the team's colours from blue and yellow to all white (à la Real Madrid) and introducing a new crest.

Over the years, the team sheet has been graced by such iconic names as Billy Bremner, Jack Charlton and Eric Cantona and as late as 2001 the club played in a Champions League semi-final. In 1992, the year before the advent of the Premier League, they added a third League title with Howard Wilkinson in charge. He remains the last English manager to win the top division in England. Today, the reality is rather different. The Yorkshire club has been leading a life of footballing anonymity in the second tier of English football, and as recently as 2010 found themselves in the lowly League One.

There are several reasons for this calamitous decline, but the man who is probably the most culpable is Peter Ridsdale. As chairman, he left the club with debts in excess of £100 million. Ridsdale is as unpopular as Massimo Cellino, who became the target of the fans' anger during his tempestuous spell in charge. The turbulence that has marked Leeds' recent history has been reflected in the story of the club emblem, which has undergone a number of radical changes. In early 2018, the club's propensity to shoot themselves in the foot was perfectly illustrated by the unveiling of a new badge, which lasted less than a week; the club was swamped by protests.

CLUB: Leeds United FC

NICKNAMES: The Whites, United and The Peacocks

FOUNDED: 1919

STADIUM: Elland Road, Leeds (37,890 capacity)

HISTORIC PLAYERS: Jack Charlton, Billy Bremner, Peter Lorimer, Lee Chapman, David Batty, Eric Cantona, Tony Yeboah and Harry Kewell

1. 1965–1972. An owl in blue and white looks more like something that should be worn by Sheffield Wednesday (the Owls), but this is, in fact, the first emblem to adorn Leeds' match shirts after decades when the town crest had served as the club symbol. The city crest features three owls, hence the club logo. Manager Don Revie believed that birds mean bad luck, so in 1972 the design of the emblem was changed to display only the club's initials.

2. 1973–1981. This image, generally referred to as 'smiley', became widely popular, not least because it coincided with the club's golden age. After three years, the colours were inverted and then, at the end of the 1970s, it was expanded with the addition of a ring around 'smiley'. This logo is a strong seller to this day as one of the club's retro products.

3. 1981–1984. When Umbro took over as kit supplier in 1981, the emblem was changed. The inspiration for the central motif here is the club nickname the Peacocks, which itself derives from the original name of Elland Road: the Old Peacock Ground.

4. 1984–1998. This fusion of the white rose of York and a football was popular with fans. This was partly because of the symbolic regional association of the rose, which stood for the House of York during the Wars of the Roses in the 15th century, and partly because Leeds won its last league title wearing this emblem.

5. 1998–present. At the end of the 1990s, Leeds produced a new, more modern emblem. It was, however, criticised, and was seen by the fans as lacking in any sense of history. The next year, in order to win over the angry fans, the club made space for the earlier emblem in the top centre. The club's initials are written in the same style used for the emblem that adorned the shirts in the 1972/73 season.

1.

2.

3.

4.

5.

Leeds United '90s striker Tony Yeboah
models a simplified 1960s/'70s-inspired
shirt crest, with the club initials running
at a diagonal.

LEICESTER CITY

THE FOXES FOR WHOM NOTHING IS IMPOSSIBLE

Originally known as Leicester Fosse when founded in 1884, the team did not become City until 1919. At this time they also became known as the Foxes in recognition of the fact that Leicestershire is considered to be the traditional home of fox hunting. Leicester City's outlandish triumph in 2016 was not only their greatest success by some distance but also brought them global attention. The whole thing was impossible. . .

Little Leicester City couldn't win the Premier League. The smart money was stacked against them – as were the odds of 5,000 to 1 – and the club was languishing at the bottom of the table. But this team set out to show that money isn't everything.

Before this gilded season, the club's preparations were temporarily derailed by a scandal that resulted in the dismissal of three players and the manager. The road to success is rarely a straight one, especially not Leicester's.

Despite these setbacks, things couldn't have worked out any better. Claudio Ranieri, who had left his job as Greek national coach after his failed tenure, revitalised the team, and players such as Riyad Mahrez, Jamie Vardy and N'Golo Kanté stepped up to become the League's biggest stars. On 2 May, 2016, Leicester City became the sixth club to win the Premier League – and in doing so produced the greatest surprise in the history of English football, possibly the world. It's a victory which proved that nothing is impossible.

CLUB: Leicester City Football Club

NICKNAME: The Foxes

FOUNDED: 1884

STADIUM: King Power Stadium, Leicester (32,262 capacity)

HISTORIC PLAYERS: Graham Cross, John Sjoberg, Keith Weller, Gary Lineker, Emile Heskey, Steve Walsh, Jamie Vardy and Riyad Mahrez

1. 1950–1972. The earliest club crest showed the head of a fox and appeared on Leicester's shirts when British football resumed in 1946 after the end of the Second World War. The fox's head inspired the club nickname the Foxes. The emblem was changed in the early '50s when it became more sophisticated: the whole club name was spelled out, the fox was redesigned and two whips were added, the latter reflecting the British tradition of fox hunting. Several different versions of this emblem appeared with different shapes of shield and variations in colour.

2. 1983–1992. The crest was radically altered in 1983, when the fox was given exclusive space in the design. It was produced in blue against a white background – and vice versa.

3. 1992–2009. During the early '90s Leicester City revised their club crest. The head of the fox was reintroduced, albeit with a more modern look, against a background of a five-petalled flower, taken from Leicester's city crest.

4. 2010–present. When the club reached its 125th anniversary, it presented a special jubilee version of the emblem in which the fox was no longer in monotone. The change was retained in the crests that followed the club from the middle of the Championship to the top of the Premier League.

1.

2.

3.

4.

Gary Lineker, the famous son of Leicester, began his stellar career at his beloved home club. Seen here playing in 1984, he scored 95 goals in 194 games for the Foxes.

LIVERPOOL

THE ETERNAL FLAME

Liverpool's rise to being one of the most successful football clubs in the world has been watched over by a mythical bird since 1901. Splitting from Everton FC in 1892, the Reds adopted the city's symbol, the liver bird, a few years later – and it has remained on the crest ever since.

The bird also adorns buildings in the city, though it is not clear what species it might be. The bird holds a branch in its beak in a nod to the port city's maritime heritage.

Liverpool has had its fair share of troubles, from its near bankruptcy in 2010 to the disasters of Heysel Stadium in 1985 and Hillsborough in 1989 – the latter remembered by an eternal flame burning at Anfield.

The Heysel Stadium disaster of 1985 led to the deaths of 39 Italian fans at the Liverpool v Juventus European Cup final in Belgium.

Four years later came the tragedy of Hillsborough. Few clubs have been so defined by a single event. It took 96 lives, and was more than an accident; it was a national catastrophe. The security arrangements before the match between Liverpool and Nottingham Forest were unsatisfactory and contributed to the disaster. The 96 who perished were accused of having caused their own deaths; many had been crushed to death, and the fans were held responsible for massing into the overcrowded pens – even though it was the police who had ordered a gate to be opened. 'Justice for the 96' became the motto for the families and supporters, who fought for more than 25 years for justice. On 26 April, 2016, 27 years after the tragedy, the judgement that the whole of Liverpool had been waiting for was finally delivered. The police were responsible, not the fans.

Liverpool is one of England's most successful clubs: it has secured many victories in the League and achieved a remarkable turnaround in the 2005 Champions League final against AC Milan.

CLUB: Liverpool FC
NICKNAME: The Reds
FOUNDED: 1892
ARENA: Anfield, Liverpool (54,000 capacity)
HISTORIC PLAYERS: Ian Callaghan, Kenny Dalglish, Ian Rush, John Barnes, Jamie Carragher, Michael Owen and Steven Gerrard

---

1. 1892–1939. Liverpool's club crest has always portrayed the mythical liver bird. The club's first emblem was a copy of the city crest, which features several marine symbols since Liverpool is a port. In the middle is a cormorant with seaweed in its beak, a bird that has morphed over the years into the liver bird. The bird is flanked by two mythological gods, Neptune and Triton. The Latin motto *Deus nobis haec otia fecit* means 'God gave us this rest'.

2. 1947–1970. Soon after the Second World War, the club emblem used on the match programme was changed for this one, apparently because they could no longer use the city crest.

3. 1955–1969. The liver bird was worn on match jerseys for the first time in the 1950 FA Cup final. Five years later it became a recurring symbol on home shirts. After that it was developed in a number of different versions.

4. 1970–1992. For more than two decades, these were among the club's official emblems. They appeared on souvenirs and match programmes while the bird often stood alone on the jersey. Liverpool has used a number of crests in parallel, which means that accurate dating can be a problem.

5. 1992–1993. At Liverpool's centenary, the emblem was changed to celebrate the club's glorious history. The Shankly Gates, an Anfield entrance named after the legendary manager Bill Shankly, are seen above the shield. The club anthem 'You'll Never Walk Alone', a song from Rogers and Hammerstein's *Carousel* which became a pop hit in the 1960s courtesy of Gerry and the Pacemakers, is also incorporated into the club crest.

6. 1993–1999. The year after the centenary, the emblem was updated with the addition of the eternal flame, a memorial to the 96 who died at Hillsborough. The monument can be found outside Anfield, flanked on both sides by the shield.

7. 1999–present. Just before the new millennium, the club crest was modernised, but the central elements of the flames, the gate and the liver bird remained.

8. 2012–present. Today Liverpool carries on its tradition. The liver bird made a comeback on the match shirt as a reminder of the club's golden era during the 1970s and '80s.

1.

2.

3.

4.

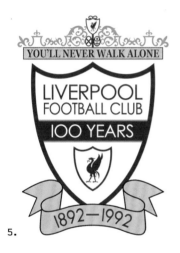

5.

6.

7.

8.

MANCHESTER CITY

THE BRILLIANT SKY BLUES

The Manchester City brand continues to grow. Since Abu Dhabi United Group bought the club in 2008 and invested hundreds of millions in it, the light blue Manchester team has slowly but surely got closer to the elite of world football. In this period the club have won the Premier League three times, the League Cup three times, and the FA Cup, and have made their debut in the Champions League. All this with the help of world-class players like Sergio Agüero, Yaya Touré and Carlos Tévez, players who only 10 years ago would have looked like wildly unrealistic purchases.

Just before the Abu Dhabi Group bought Manchester City in 2008, the future of the club was uncertain: the assets of the then owner Thaksin Shinawatra had been frozen due to political problems in Thailand. Ten years earlier in 1998, the situation had been even worse. The club had reached their lowest point: for the first time since they were founded as St. Mark's, the first time in almost 120 years of existence, they had been relegated to the third tier of English football. Manchester City returned to the Premier League within three years of their nadir, but the unrivalled period of success which followed was entirely unexpected.

The post-2008 period is not, of course, the only successful one in the club's history. Manchester City had earlier been a real force in English football, their achievements including two league titles in 1937 and 1968, four victories in the FA Cup, two League Cup wins and a Cup Winners Cup triumph. The club has long lived in the shadow of arch-rivals Manchester United, but times have now changed. City have won three Premier League titles in the last seven years, compared to United's solitary title in 2013.

CLUB: Manchester City FC
NICKNAMES: City, The Citizens and The Sky Blues
FOUNDED: 1894
STADIUM: Etihad Stadium, Manchester (55,097 capacity)
HISTORIC PLAYERS: Eric Brook, Bert Trautmann, Mike Summerbee, Shaun Goater, Richard Dunne, David Silva and Sergio Agüero

1. 1894–1964 and 1976–1981. The antagonists Manchester City and Manchester United have both used their city's crest over the years. For City, this was mainly true in the first half of the 20th century.

2. 1965–1972. In the mid-1960s, they reverted to the shield of the city crest, even if it wasn't seen on match shirts until the 1971/72 season. The diagonal stripes are those of the Grelley family, feudal rulers of Manchester. The ship refers to the city's historical trading activities.

3. 1972–1976 and 1981–1997. In 1972, the emblem was modified, with a change of colours and the Lancashire rose replacing the diagonal stripes. This emblem became popular with the fans and would inspire the logo that was unveiled in 2015.

4. 1997–2016. The club's two previous emblems could not be protected by copyright because of their similarity to the city crest. Therefore this emblem was introduced in 1997. The golden eagle is an old heraldic symbol for Manchester. The three white stripes represent the city's three rivers: Irwell, Irk and Medlock. The Latin motto means 'Pride in Battle', while the stars are simply decorative additions. This emblem was never popular with fans despite the successes achieved in its time.

5. 2016–present. On 15 October, 2015, after several years of criticism from the fans, the club announced that a new crest would be created with their help. Thanks to them and to the football historian Gary James, this emblem was introduced on Boxing Day after a much publicised advertising campaign. The round form is back, as is the rose and the club's full name. This emblem, the first to give the year of the club's founding, was used from the summer of 2016.

1.

2.

3.

4.

5.

Sergio Agüero celebrates after scoring the goal that secured the league title for Manchester City for the first time in 44 years. They won the title on account of finishing higher than local rivals Manchester United on goal difference.

MANCHESTER UNITED

THE RED DEVILS FROM MANCHESTER

The club started life as Newton Heath in 1878, becoming Manchester United only in 1902, when their red and white kit was created. United have become one of the world's biggest clubs, although the team will always be associated with the tragedy of the Munich air disaster. Among the 23 people who died were 8 players, including Duncan Edwards and club captain Roger Byrne.

The disaster forced the club to start from scratch. Among the survivors were Bobby Charlton and the manager Matt Busby. Both would be part of Manchester United's European Cup final team 10 years later in 1968, when they beat Benfica, winning their first trophy in the tournament – and indeed the first for any English club. It was proof that the club had fought their way back. Without Matt Busby, United might never have picked themselves up after Munich. The legendary manager laid the foundations for the great club that Manchester United is today.

It was a great club, and grew still greater under Alex Ferguson. Indeed, it became synonymous with him. The Scot took over the team in 1986, when they were second to bottom of the table. After he had saved the club from relegation, results deteriorated again and in the winter of 1989 some fans were calling for his dismissal. United, however, were patient and Ferguson went on to reward this patience by leading them to 38 trophies in 26 years. Among them were an unprecedented 13 league titles, five FA Cups and two Champions League titles, an inheritance worthy of Sir Matt Busby. After Ferguson had said his farewells in 2013, a number of great names have tried to take United back to the top of the table, but the board has not yet shown them the same forebearance as they did to Ferguson.

CLUB: Manchester United FC
NICKNAMES: United and The Red Devils
FOUNDED: 1878
STADIUM: Old Trafford, Manchester (74,994 capacity)
HISTORIC PLAYERS: Bobby Charlton, George Best, David Beckham, Paul Scholes, Ryan Giggs, Wayne Rooney, Cristiano Ronaldo and Paul Pogba

1. 1948–1969. Oddly enough Manchester United have shared an emblem with their arch rivals Manchester City. Like many other clubs, United didn't have their own emblem but like their neighbours they used the city crest on occasions such as FA Cup finals.

2. 1969-1970. At the end of the 1960s, United created their first club crest, one inspired by the city crest. The ship symbolises the trade that has been conducted in the city. The diagonal stripes originated from the regional feudal family, the Grelleys. For some reason, the club chose white for the roses – like those of Yorkshire, although Manchester is in Lancashire. The logo was never transferred to match jerseys, but was the club's official emblem up to 1970. There are various suggestions for the date when it was first used.

3. 1970-1978 and 1979-1998. The club's nickname, the Red Devils, was coined by Matt Busby himself and became an important part of the emblem in the early '70s. The devil replaced the earlier shield and the roses were replaced by footballs. This emblem was temporarily rested during the centennial in 1978/79.

4. 1998–present. To the great annoyance of the fans, 'Football Club' was removed from the badge just before the new millennium. This was done to make the brand more internationally viable and simpler to print. Ironically enough, Ed Woodward, vice chairman, has said that owners Avram and Joel Glazer may consider reinstating 'Football Club' in the crest because 'Manchester United is a football club and not a company.'

1.

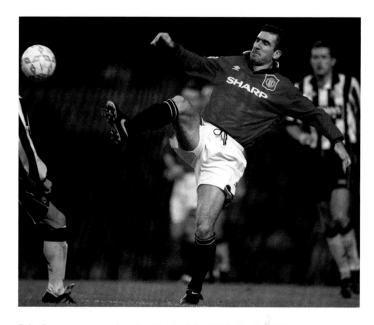

Eric Cantona stretches for the ball in 1994. Sir Matt Busby was responsible for the club's Red Devils nickname and therefore its subsequent incorporation into the club crest. He thought it would be intimidating to opponents.

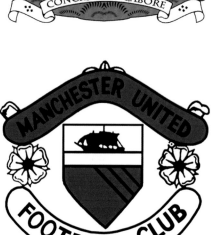

2.

3.

4.

MILLWALL

IN THE LIONS' DEN

Originally founded in 1885 on the Isle of Dogs in East London and nicknamed the Dockers, Millwall only became known as the Lions at the beginning of the 20th century. When they moved to a new ground in 1910, it was appropriately named the Den because the fans have a reputation for being amongst the most fearsome in British football. The tough image associated with the club is characterised by their uncompromising chant of 'No one likes us, we don't care.'

Millwall have spent the majority of their history in the lower divisions, but in 1988 they reached the top flight for the first time in their history, winning the Second Division Championship under manager John Docherty. This achievement briefly ushered in the most successful period in the club's history, when the dual strike force of Teddy Sheringham and Tony Cascarino were one of the most formidable in the First Division. The club finished 10th in their first season.

However, they were relegated the following season and have not returned to the top tier since then. When they reached the FA Cup final in 2004, they became only the second team from outside the top division to do so since 1982. Despite their 3-0 loss to Manchester United, this marked the greatest single achievement in their history. In the last two decades they have been close to promotion back to the top flight, only to lose out in the play-offs – in 1991, 1994 and 2002.

CLUB: Millwall FC
NICKNAMES: The Lions and The Dockers
FOUNDED: 1885
STADIUM: The Den, London (20,146 capacity)
HISTORIC PLAYERS: Barry Kitchener, Keith Stevens, Teddy Sheringham, Neil Harris and Tim Cahill

1. Millwall's original nickname, the Dockers, referred to both the club's origins and its fans. After the team created a stir in the FA Cup in the 1899/1900 season and knocked out the giants Aston Villa, Millwall were called 'the Lions of the south', a nickname that stuck and inspired the club's first emblem: a lion rampant. It was also during the early 1900s that the motto 'We fear no foe where e'er we go' began to be used. The exact year for this emblem has not been confirmed.

2. 1936–1956. It took until 1936 before the emblem was seen on Millwall jerseys. This was introduced by the then manager Charlie Hewitt, who also changed the club's colour from navy blue to royal blue. The red lion looks like Scotland's national crest, which has led to the misapprehension that this was the inspiration for the badge.

3. 1956–1974 and 1990–2007. The Millwall crest has existed in various guises, but this one lasted longer than most. In the mid-1950s the one lion became two. This design proved popular with the fans and was taken up again during the era of chairman Theo Paphitis, some 25 years after it was introduced. Millwall players wore this badge at the club's greatest success to date: the FA Cup final of 2004, which they lost 3-0.

4. 1978–1999 and 2007–present. This emblem of the attacking lion, the longest lasting (in various guises) in Millwall's history, was unveiled in 1979. Over the years, the lion has changed colour, has stood alone, has been flanked by the club initials, and has been encircled like today's variation, used since 2014.

1.

2.

3.

4.

Eamon Dunphy sports the 1967 incarnation of club crest. The Irishman was considered an intelligent and skilful midfielder, and was a member of the 1971 Millwall side that failed by just one point to gain promotion to the First Division.

NEWCASTLE UNITED

WORN WITH PRIDE

Not many clubs can date their official badge to one of their greatest victories, but Newcastle United can pinpoint its triumphant 1969 Inter-Cities Cup Final against Újpesti Dózsa as the date the city's crest formally appeared on team shirts for the first time. Over the years the badge has changed with fashion, but history and tradition have remained integral.

In fact, today's crest still features a version of Newcastle upon Tyne's coat of arms. Since the mid-1970s it has gone through three modifications, but, much to the joy of the city's inhabitants, the local connection has been retained in the emblem. The port, with its old ship-building industry, and the castle are both important for the city, and both are reflected in the emblem – significant symbols for the club's loyal supporters.

Although recent successes have been few and far between, St James' Park attracts average attendances of more than 50,000, one of the highest figures in English football. In former times, faithful fans could relate to home-grown talent like Jackie Milburn, Peter Beardsley and Paul Gascoigne. The current emblem reminds everyone of Newcastle United's rich roots.

1. 1892–1976. From its founding in 1892, the club used Newcastle Upon Tyne's city coat of arms for cup finals as well as on tickets and on match programmes. The latin motto Fortiter Defendit Triumphans means 'Triumphing by brave defence'. It wasn't until 1969 that the crest was transferred onto match shirts.

2. 1976–1983. In the mid-1970s a new emblem was introduced. Vital symbols of the city's history, such as the River Tyne and the Norman castle, featured prominently. The club's nickname, the Magpies, was also given a central role. The nickname was inspired by the club's famous black and white kit.

3. 1983–1988. In 1983 a modern, streamlined design, featuring the club's often-used 'NUFC' lettering in a style that suggested a football, was launched. The only local symbol retained was the magpie. This emblem was worn on the club shirts for the next five years.

4. 1988–present. A brand-new crest was introduced by the end of the 1980s, the club found its way back to its roots with the reintroduction of the city crest to its emblem. The seahorses symbolise Newcastle's historically significant port. The tower above the shield represents the Norman castle which William the Conqueror's son, Robert Curthose, erected in 1080 with the name 'New Castle'. The lion is grasping a flag with a version of the cross of St. George. The shield represents the famous black and white stripes from the kit.

CLUB: Newcastle United FC
NICKNAME: The Magpies
FOUNDED: 1892
STADIUM: St. James' Park, Newcastle (52,405 capacity)
HISTORIC PLAYERS: Jackie Milburn, Peter Beardsley, Paul Gascoigne Nolberto Solano, Alan Shearer, Shay Given and Fabricio Coloccini.

1.

2.

3.

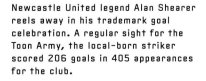

5.

Newcastle United legend Alan Shearer reels away in his trademark goal celebration. A regular sight for the Toon Army, the local-born striker scored 206 goals in 405 appearances for the club.

QUEENS PARK RANGERS

WEST LONDON ROYALTY

Queens Park Rangers was founded in 1882 after a merger between two clubs and was named after the nearby Queens Park. Their most successful period came in the early 1970s under manager Dave Sexton with players such as Gerry Francis and Stan Bowles. In the 1975/76 season they were challenging for the First Division title, eventually losing out by a solitary point to Liverpool. They have not been as close to glory again and have spent most of the last 30 years in the second tier.

A new era began when the Formula 1 duo of Flavio Briatore and Bernie Ecclestone bought a majority share in the club in 2007. In December of that year they were joined by Lakshmi Mittal, then the second richest person in the world, who had bought a share of this working man's club. Along with the salvation they brought, the newcomers seemed to be transforming the identity, even the very reality of the club.

It proved to be a time of upheaval, with Flavio Briatore firing six managers in two-and-a-half years. Despite this QPR managed to secure promotion to the Premier League in 2011, whereupon Briatore and Ecclestone sold their shares in the club to Tony Fernandes, owner of Air Malaysia.

Since the introduction of the club's first crest in 1953, the design has undergone various incarnations, ranging from emblems heavily influenced by the crest of Hammersmith through to ornate monograms displaying the club initials. The crest adopted for the 1970s and early 1980s – QPR's most successful era – also incorporates bands reminiscent of the team's famous blue and white hooped shirt.

CLUB: Queens Park Rangers FC

NICKNAMES: The Hoops and The Rs

FOUNDED: 1882

STADIUM: Loftus Road, London (18,439 capacity)

HISTORIC PLAYERS: Gerry Francis, Rodney Marsh, Phil Parkes, Alan McDonald, Mark Hateley, Ray Wilkins, Trevor Sinclair and Les Ferdinand

1. 1953–1972. The club's first emblem was introduced relatively late, not until the 1953/54 season, taking inspiration from the crest of Hammersmith, the London district where QPR is based. The crest was used up to the 1970s, though it disappeared from the jerseys in 1959.

2. 1972–1982. In 1972, QPR unveiled a new emblem featuring a football depicted against the club's blue and white stripes, or hoops. Often it was only the ball with the club initials that was transferred to the team kit. The main reason for getting a new crest was that the three horseshoes in the earlier version were thought to bring bad luck – in spite of the fact that until then the club's only triumph had come in the League Cup in 1967, when the horseshoes were present.

3. 1982–2008. This emblem was created to coincide with Queens Park Rangers' centenary, and is also the most classic of all the designs. The three intertwined letters and the band with 'Loftus Road' represented the club during its most successful period ever. Between 1983 and 1996, the team was a constant presence in the top tier of English football.

4. 2008–2016. When Briatore, Ecclestone and Mittal bought QPR, a new emblem was needed to mark the new era. The shape of the shield from the original crest was reintroduced. In spite of the historic reference, this emblem was loathed by the supporters because it was connected with the chaos created by Briatore. The fans demanded a new emblem.

5. 2016–present. The new owner Tony Fernandes listened to the supporters and accepted their help in voting through the club's new emblem. Between July 2015 and January 2016, the fans were able to inform themselves about the history of the club's crest before then voting for the elements they wanted in the new crest. This emblem reverted to an earlier look in terms of the shape and the team's initials.

1.

2.

4.

3.

5.

SHEFFIELD WEDNESDAY

THE OWLS FROM THE CITY OF STEEL

In 2016 Sheffield Wednesday came full circle by readopting its original crest from the 20th century. Used from 1956 to 1973, though not on players' kit, the official crest in a heraldic style was slightly modified in 2016, when the new owners wanted to reconnect with the famous club's roots.

Nicknamed the Owls after the Owlerton area of Sheffield, Wednesday kept the owl as the centrepiece of its logo for decades. From 1973 to 1995, the club went minimalist with a badge designed by a 19-year-old student who had won the club's competition. The owl was named Ozzie.

From 1995 to 1999, the club returned to a shield reminiscent of the original crest, in which the rose also returned and the name of the club's stadium, Hillsborough, was spelled out. The turn of the millenium saw Ozzie return in a shield-shaped crest, to which the club's founding year, 1867, was added.

The Wednesday, as the club was called, was founded in 1867 in Sheffield, famous for its steel industry and today the fourth biggest city in England with a population of 563,000. As the club was one of the first in the country, it enjoyed relatively early success. Around the turn of the century, it won both the League and the FA Cup, achievements that confirmed Wednesday as one of the country's greatest clubs. During the greater part of the 20th century, the club played in the top flight and enjoyed their most recent successes as late as the 1990s. In 1991 they won the League Cup, the year after they had come third in the old First Division, and in 1993 they reached both domestic cup finals. Relegated from the Premier League in 2000, since then Wednesday have been scrabbling around in the peripheries of British football, a position unworthy of a club with such an illustrious history.

CLUB: Sheffield Wednesday FC
NICKNAME: The Owls
FOUNDED: 1867
STADIUM: Hillsborough, Sheffield (39,732 capacity)
HISTORIC PLAYERS: Andrew Wilson, John Fantham, Chris Waddle and Benito Carbone

1. 1956–1973 and 2016–present. Sheffield Wednesday's nickname the Owls inspired the club's first emblem, introduced in 1956. The nickname came from the district of Owlerton to where the club moved in 1899. Oddly enough, Wednesday had been known as the Blades, the same nickname used today for their arch-rivals Sheffield United. By the head of the owl are the club initials, and at the bottom of the shield is the white rose of York. The Latin motto *Consilio et Animis* means 'Through Wisdom and Courage'. The emblem was readopted in 2016, when the new owner Dejphon Chansiri wanted to reconnect with the club's roots.

2. 1973–1995. To be able to copyright the emblem, the club decided in 1973 to run a competition to create a new crest. Student Robert Walker won with his Ozzie. The new club crest was modified over the years as the club's initials and the colours of yellow and blue were added.

3. 1995–1999. In the mid-1990s a new crest was designed, reminiscent of the original one with the owl on its bough.

4. 1999–2016. The much-loved owl Ozzie made a comeback in time for the millennium, now on a shield. For the first time, the year of the club's founding was added.

1.

Wednesday's Chris Waddle in action against local rivals Sheffield United in the 1993 FA Cup semi-final. The Owls came out on top with a 2-1 victory.

2.

3.

4.

SOUTHAMPTON

THE SAINTS ON THE SOUTH COAST

Gareth Bale, Adam Lallana, Theo Walcott, Luke Shaw, Alex Oxlade-Chamberlain and Calum Chambers have one thing in common: they were trained in Southampton's youth academy, where former national stars Alan Shearer, Matthew Le Tissier and Wayne Bridge also received their footballing education. The fact that Southampton managed to get back to the Premier League in 2012 after many difficult years is very much down to the club's much admired academy.

Southampton's nickname, the Saints, derives from their original foundation in 1885 as a church club, St. Mary's, and these roots inspired the naming of their new ground in 2001. Southampton's FA Cup success in 1976 under manager Lawrie McMenemy was their first major trophy and the most memorable day in their history. As a Second Division side at the time, they upset firm favourites Manchester United and are one of the last clubs from outside the top division to win the FA Cup.

After 27 consecutive seasons in England's top flight, Southampton were relegated to the Championship in the spring of 2005. Financial turbulence and internal strife followed and shook the once stable club, which led to relegation to League One after four seasons in the Championship. Then the recovery began. With talents like Lallana and Oxlade-Chamberlain, they were promoted from League One after two seasons, and then gained a second successive promotion back to the Premier League in 2012. Southampton's renaissance was thanks to the money made from sales of players nurtured by the club – deals which, since the relegation in 2005, had brought in around £36 million.

CLUB: Southampton FC
NICKNAME: The Saints
FOUNDED: 1885
STADIUM: St. Mary's Stadium, Southampton (32,505 capacity)
HISTORIC PLAYERS: Terry Paine, Mick Channon, Derek Reeves, Alan Shearer, Francis Benali, Matthew Le Tissier and Gareth Bale

1. In the beginning Southampton took their inspiration from the city crest. The red roses symbolise the house of Lancaster, the white the house of York, the two families who fought the Wars of the Roses (1455–1485). Unfortunately there are no exact years for when this crest was in use.

2. The town crest appeared in one other version before the club decided to strengthen their identity through an emblem created with input from their supporters. Neither this nor the previous version were ever used on match jerseys. As with the original crest, there are no exact dates for this one.

3. 1974–1995. In 1974, the Southampton fan Rolland Parris won the competition to design the new emblem. The new crest soon became popular thanks to the numerous local elements. The halo on top refers to the club nickname, the Saints; the scarf represents the club colours; the oak tree is a nod to the New Forest in Hampshire and to Southampton Common, a park in the city centre; the water symbolises Southampton's importance as a port; and the white rose comes from the city crest.

4. 1995–present. In the mid-1990s, the crest was lightly modified, the old classic football being replaced by a newer version because of copyright issues. At this time the club also had problems with counterfeit match shirts, which the board hoped to solve with the aid of a new emblem.

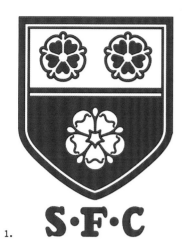

1. **S·F·C**

2.

3.

Nicknamed by 'Le God' by Saints fans, Matthew Le Tissier was an exceptional '90s player and the first midfielder to score 100 goals in the Premier League. He had a career penalty kick record of 47 conversions from 48 attempts.

4.

SUNDERLAND

THE BLACK CATS OF THE NORTH-EAST

The Latin motto *Consectatio Excellentiae* graces Sunderland's emblem, meaning 'Striving for perfection'. If we look at the modern history of Sunderland FC, it seems appropriate . . . up to a point. This north eastern club, with its proud and successful tradition, has not quite managed to live up its own motto in recent years. Although Sunderland can boast six league titles and two FA Cup victories, you have to go back to 1973 for their most recent triumph. Since then, the club has floundered blindly, acquiring the reputation of a yo-yo team that swings between the Premier League, Championship and League One.

Founded in 1879, Sunderland had already won four league titles by time the they adopted the black cat crest in 1905. The original black cat was an 1800s artillery gun sited on the bank of the River Wear, but it was the feline symbol that would inspire fans' badges, giant cardboard cut-outs and 1980s inflatables. However, in Sunderland's greatest moments, this good luck omen has been shunned. The 1937 FA Cup victory saw them wear town crest badges and in the legendary 1973 Cup Final, when they slew the giant Leeds United, they sported a then-fashionable monogrammed logo.

A new crest introduced in the late 20th century referenced the area's shipbuilding links – only for the club to mirror that industry's struggle and decline rather too often. Then in 1997 an impressive new arena, the Stadium of Light, brought fresh optimism. Along with it came a new crest: an emblem celebrating the heritage of the local area and accompanied by a *Latin motto Consectatio Excellentiae*. Maybe it's time to focus on striving for perfection again.

1. 1905–1977. In Sunderland's first emblem, their nickname, the Black Cats, was given prominence by the black cat at its centre. One hundred years after the artillery the black cat was created the then chairman FW Taylor was photographed with a black cat. Since then the cat has symbolised the club on match programmes, team shirts and even as a mascot.

2. 1977–1997. At the end of the 1970s, an updated emblem appeared – from which the cat had vanished. Instead the crest reinforced the identity of Sunderland as a port, thanks to the image of a boat on the Wear. The background to the boat was initially blue but was changed to black in 1991.

3. 1997–present. Along with the move from Roker Park to the newly built Stadium of Light in 1997, the emblem was brought up to date. The boat went, but other local elements were included. The black lions, taken from Sunderland's city crest, flank the shield, on which there are two local sights. Down on the right is the Wearmouth Bridge and up on the left the Penshaw monument. At the top of the crest is the Latin motto *Consectatio Excellentiae* and a wheel symbolising coalmines – a reminder of the industry that was of vital importance to the city for so long. In fact, the Stadium of Light was built on the site of an old coalmine.

CLUB: Sunderland AFC
NICKNAME: The Black Cats
FOUNDED: 1879
STADIUM: Stadium of Light, Sunderland (49,000 capacity)
HISTORIC PLAYERS: Jimmy Montgomery, Bobby Gurney, Charlie Buchan, Kevin Phillips and Niall Quinn

1.

3.

2.

While wearing the red stripes of Sunderland, Kevin Phillips was the Premier League top scorer in the 1999/2000 season with 30 goals. This secured him the Golden Boot, a prize awarded each season to the leading goalscorer in league matches from Europe's top divisions.

SWANSEA CITY

WALES'S BLACK SWANS

The journey from football's darkest abyss to the Premier League is a long and arduous one. It is also quite remarkable. Just ask Swansea City AFC.

Saturday, 3 May, 2003, is an historic date for the Welsh city. That was the day when the home team beat visitors Hull City 4–2. The victory came courtesy of a hat-trick by James Thomas, in front of a crowd of 9,585 watching a match in the fourth flight of English football. Coming on the last day of the season, it meant that the club escaped relegation to the Football Conference by the skin of their teeth.

Just eight years later, in 2011, the club reached the Premier League, the first Welsh club ever to do so. They won the Championship Play-Offs final, this time over Reading, again with a 4–2 victory and again with a hat-trick, from Scott Sinclair.

Leon Britton, a player who joined in 2003 and has played for the club in every division, epitomises the rise up the leagues. Alongside Ashley Williams and Àngel Rangel, he was a key figure in establishing Wales's second city in the top flight of football. Their peak achievement – thus far – came in the spring of 2013, when the club won their first ever trophy in the shape of the League Cup.

The club was originally founded in 1908 as Swansea Town, and early versions of the club crest depicted the city's castle, a rampant lion, an osprey and Welsh dragon. The iconic swan was adopted in 1970 and has been interpreted in a number of different styles and forms, before today's striking, pared-back design was settled on.

1. 1992–1995 and 1995–1998. Like many other football clubs, Swansea was originally represented by the city crest, but in 1970 a black swan was introduced as the club emblem. This happened in conjunction with the club changing its suffix from 'Town' to 'City' after the town of Swansea was granted city status. Six black swans and a Welsh dragon had time to appear on the town crest before this white version was introduced in 1992. The bird is, of course, taken from the name of the city. The castle, on which it perches, was founded in 1107 by the Norman nobleman Henry de Beaumont, and the town was subsequently built around it. The stripes behind the castle are taken from the city crest and illustrate Swansea's significance as a city port. This emblem was updated after three years.

2. 1998–2004 and 2014–present. Towards the end of the 1990s, a crest was introduced which has been the most enduring in Swansea's modern history. Inspired by the club's historic models, a simplified black swan was introduced as an homage to the successes of the late 1970s, led by the player-manager John Toshack. This crest also existed in red for a couple of seasons – much to the displeasure of the fans.

3. 2005–2007. In a further celebration of the relatively successful '70s, the swan was framed by a circle. Just as it was back then.

4. 2012–2013. The club's centenary was celebrated with a specially designed emblem and the season couldn't have ended better: in the spring of 2013 came victory in the League Cup.

CLUB: Swansea City AFC
NICKNAME: The Swans
FOUNDED: 1912
STADIUM: Liberty Stadium, Swansea (21,088 capacity)
HISTORIC PLAYERS: Ivor Allchurch, Alan Curtis, Scott Sinclair, Leon Britton, Ashley Williams and Gylfı Sigurðsson

1.

2.

3.

4.

The distinctive black swan, as introduced in 1970. Len Allchurch, brother of fellow Welsh international Ivor, may have been born in Swansea but this was his last club in a long career. He signed in 1969 and made 71 appearances.

TOTTENHAM HOTSPUR

HARRY HOTSPUR'S FIGHTING COCKEREL

The Latin motto *Audere est facere*, which translates as 'To dare is to do', is a phrase that has long characterised Tottenham Hotspur. Even if it took until 1983 before this exhortation reached the club's emblem, the motto has made its mark on the North London team.

The Spurs have certainly dared when it came to their crest, having changed and modernised it five times in almost a century. Formed in 1882, Tottenham played with an insignificant red H on the left breast of players' shirts until 1921, when a blue cockerel in a shield was adopted. The club stretched back to the 14th century for its inspiration, to the name and crest of Sir Henry Percy, a knight who caught the public imagination of his time. His habit of driving his spurs into his horses' flanks in the charge gave way to the nickname Hotspur – and earned him a place in Shakespeare's *Henry IV, Part 1*.

The spurred cockerel appeared on the club crest after the team's second FA Cup win in 1921, and the bird has been synonymous with the club since. The club's 1951 First Division championship saw it change to a slimline cockerel, which has remained a constant even while the crest itself has varied.

Even though the club is known for good football and for having footballing superstars like Jürgen Klinsmann, Gareth Bale, Luka Modric, David Ginola and Gary Lineker represent it, the big titles have eluded them in modern times. Instead the supporters have had to identify themselves with one of the league's most attacking and crowd-pleasing teams, whose tactics have largely been about scoring goals.

CLUB: Tottenham Hotspur FC
NICKNAMES: Spurs, The Lilywhites
FOUNDED: 1882
STADIUM: Tottenham Hotspur Stadium, London (62,062 capacity)
HISTORIC PLAYERS: Jimmy Greaves, Steve Perryman, Osvaldo Ardiles, Glenn Hoddle, Gary Lineker, Paul Gascoigne, Gareth Bale and Luka Modric

1. 1921–1930. In 1921 when Tottenham won their second FA Cup title, it was the first time they had worn an emblem with a cockerel on their jerseys. The bird has its origins in Sir Henry Percy (1364–1403), better known as Sir Harry Hotspur, after whom the club was named. He was a nobleman, notorious for his bad temper, and often wore spurs. He was also interested in cockfighting. In 1909, a bronze statue of a cockerel was erected above White Hart Lane's west stand. Since then the cockerel and Tottenham have been inseparable.

2. 1951–1966. After the club's first league title in 1951 the club crest was given a facelift which saw the cockerel becoming considerably thinner. This slimline cockerel appeared in several different variations, among them this one.

3. 1983–1995 and 1999–2006. Tottenham's cockerel was altered many times over the last century. To make the crest harder to pirate, the motto *Audere est Facere* was included and the club's initials were flanked by two lions.

4. 1997–1999. Before the new millennium Tottenham chose a more heraldic crest with many different elements. The cockerel, the initials, the lions and the motto were joined by the nearby Bruce Castle and by seven trees representing the Seven Sisters, a famous, perhaps mythical copse, in North London.

5. 2006–present. To help modernise the club, another emblem was introduced. This version was modelled on the crest used between 1967 and 1982 when the cockerel stood on a leather ball. The club name was spelled out below the bird. Before the 2017/18 season, the cockerel was once more framed by the classic shield on the match jerseys to honour the league title of 1961.

Club motto *Audere est facere*, or 'To dare is to do', is a phrase that encapulates the striking talents of Harry Kane, a prolific goalscorer who plays for a club famous for great strikers, incuding Jimmy Greaves, Clive Allen, Jürgen Klinnsman and Gary Lineker.

1.

2.

3.

4.

5.

WEST BROMWICH ALBION

THE SONGBIRD OF THE MIDLANDS

As one of the 12 original members of the Football League, West Bromwich Albion are one of the oldest clubs in the United Kingdom. Founded in 1878, the WBA club badge dates back to the late 1880s and depicts a throstle, or song thrush, sitting on a crossbar. The bird has mostly been used ever since, usually on a blue and white striped shield. The crossbar was changed to a hawthorn branch when the club moved to their new ground, the Hawthorns, in 1900.

It is impossible to talk about the history of West Bromwich Albion without mentioning three great black players of the late 1970s: Cyrille Regis, Laurie Cunningham and Brendon Batson. Cyrille Regis was a classic centre forward with a striker's instinct for goal, Laurie Cunningham was the eccentric attacking genius on the left, and Batson an accomplished fullback. Together they mesmerised the crowd, while lifting West Brom to previously unknown heights: the club finished in the top half of the League throughout the 1970s. The high point came on 30 December, 1978, at Old Trafford, when West Brom, led by Regis, Cunningham and Batson, beat the mighty Man Utd 5-3 in what came to be known as 'the best match ever played'.

CLUB: West Bromwich Albion FC

NICKNAMES: The Baggies, The Throstles and Albion

FOUNDED: 1878

STADIUM: The Hawthorns, West Bromwich (26,688 capacity)

HISTORIC PLAYERS: Ronnie Allen, Tony Brown, Bryan Robson, Cyrille Regis, Brendon Batson and Laurie Cunningham

1. 1968–1972 and 1986–1994. It was in the late 1880s that the then club secretary Tom Smith suggested a thrush as the club's official emblem, the reason being that just such a songbird had made its home in the players' changing room. But it wasn't until the FA Cup final of 1968 that the thrush was seen on the players' jerseys for the first time, replacing the city crest which had appeared in previous finals. In the early 1970s, the club crest was redesigned to represent a caged songbird. The emblem had a double meaning, the bird's cage also representing an A for Albion.

2. 1975–1986. After three years with the caged bird as their symbol, a simplified logo was introduced, consisting only of the club's initials – a fashion that was prevalent at the time. This emblem lasted for 11 years until the thrush made an enthusiastically received comeback on the team jerseys.

3. 2000–2006. Between 1994 and 2000, the WBA players were once more wearing the city crest on their shirts, but this was changed at the turn of the millennium when this emblem was introduced. Again the bird was perched on its hawthorn branch, but this time against the blue and white shield. The stripes of the shield represent the team's kit, while the branch has its origin in the home stadium, The Hawthorns, where the club had moved in 1900.

4. 2006–present. An updated version of the club crest began to be used in 2006, when the club were playing in the Championship. The branch has been replaced by a few leaves and berries and the club's full name was spelled out for the first time ever.

W.B.A.

1.

2.

3.

4.

The shortlived but modern-looking club crest from 1975 as worn by Geoff Hurst. The bird's cage was styled to represent the *a* of Albion. The emblem appeared most often in navy blue as shown here.

WEST HAM UNITED

HAMMERS AND HERITAGE

For more than 100 years, West Ham United has been represented by two riveting hammers, which is not strange considering the history of the club and the area. West Ham were originally founded in 1895 as Thames Ironworks, as a football club for the area's iron and dock workers and those in the heavy industry associated with shipbuilding. At the end of the 1800s, industry was thriving in London, not least in the East End district of Newham where West Ham United have their roots.

During the latter part of the 20th century, West Ham established themselves as one of England's iconic clubs. They lacked title success, but became popular, particularly in the 1960s, thanks to their attacking, entertaining brand of football. This established their reputation as the Academy of Football, and during this period they won the FA Cup in 1964 and the European Cup Winners' Cup the following year.

The crest has always reflected the soul of the area, but has also developed over time. For instance, the local Boleyn Castle was incorporated in the 1960s.

Like so many other clubs, even the legendary West Ham has been subject to the forces of modernity, and in 2016 they moved from the Boleyn Ground (aka Upton Park) to the London Olympic Arena. The Boleyn Castle was removed from the crest – partly to illustrate the move and partly to clarify the connection to the club's roots, by leaving only the two hammers as their symbol.

CLUB: West Ham United FC
NICKNAMES: The Irons and The Hammers
FOUNDED: 1895
STADIUM: London Stadium, London (57,000 capacity)
HISTORIC PLAYERS: Bobby Moore, Geoff Hurst, Trevor Brooking, Tony Cottee, Julian Dicks, Joe Cole, Michael Carrick and Paolo Di Canio

1. 1958–1997. It is unclear precisely when the two hammers became symbols for West Ham United. The earliest known image of them comes from a match programme from the 1910/11 season. When the club was promoted to the top division in 1958, the castle and the two hammers were shown together for the first time. It would take until the mid-1960s before the castle was officially included in the emblem though. The castle is said to have been the home of Anne Bolyen, the second wife of Henry VIII. This particular logo is from 1987.

2. 1997–2016. In 1997, the designers Springett Associates were given the task of updating the crest. The castle was widened, there were fewer windows, and the peaks of the towers disappeared. (The earlier castle was thought to look like something from a Disney film.)

3. 2016–present. In July 2014 the club's members were given the opportunity to vote on a new emblem that would be introduced to coincide with the move to the new stadium in the autumn of 2016. In this new design the castle is gone, and the name of the city has appeared, which suggests that the club wants to establish itself on the wider international scene. The form of the emblem was inspired by the British navy frigate *HMS Warrior*, which was built in 1860 by Thames Ironworks.

1.

2.

3.

Hammers legend Bobby Moore takes flight in 1962 with the famous irons resplendent on his chest. The 2016 crest is a clear return to these design origins.

WOLVERHAMPTON WANDERERS

THE WOLVES WHO INSPIRED THE EUROPEAN CUP

Wolverhampton lies in the West Midlands, in the very heart of England. Seen from a British perspective it is not a particularly big town, but regardless of its modest size it has played a crucial role in both English and European football.

Wolverhampton Wanderers was founded in 1877 and soon became a force to be reckoned with. In 1888 the club was one of the first 12 to play in the Football League, the world's first. Wolves took part in the league's premier match against Aston Villa and finished third that year while also playing in that year's FA Cup final. Their successes continued and in 1893 they won the cup.

But Wolverhampton's golden era did not come until the 1950s, when the club won three league titles while also, albeit unknowingly, laying the foundations for today's Champions League. After an impressive 3-2 victory in a friendly against the Hungarian team Budapest Honvéd in 1954, Wolves' coach Stan Cullis declared that the team were 'world champions', a statement which gave the French journalist Gabriel Hanot the idea for a European club tournament. A year later the European Cup for league champions was born.

Even if Wolves didn't take part in the first tournament the club do not lack in continental success. They came second in the UEFA Cup in 1972, losing 3-2 to Tottenham. Since then the club have gone through economic hardships and several changes of owners which has led to them playing in League One as recently as 2014.

CLUB: Wolverhampton Wanderers FC
NICKNAMES: Wolves and The Wanderers
FOUNDED: 1877
STADIUM: Molineux, Wolverhampton (31,700 capacity)
HISTORIC PLAYERS: Steve Bull, Billy Wright, Derek Parkin, Kenny Hibbit and Jimmy Mullen

1. 1921–1939, 1947–1948 and 1993–1996. During the first half of the 20th century Wolverhampton's town crest was used as the club's emblem on special occasions such as cup finals. The 1947/48 season was the only one in which this crest was seen continuously on match jerseys. Within the shield there are four symbols with a local connection: the book represents the city's famous grammar school; the pillar is a well-known graveyard monument; the bale of wool refers to the trade carried out in the area in the middle ages; and the padlock suggests the lock industry that has long thrived in Wolverhampton. The motto 'Out of darkness cometh light' inspired the club in its choice of colours: black for darkness and gold for light. The town crest returned in 1993 under the legendary owner Sir Jack Hayward.

2. 1970–1974 and 1974–1979. Before the 1970/71 season Wolves introduced the first emblems of their own. Naturally enough wolves became symbols of the team, here seen jumping over the club's initials. This logo brought good luck, as the team reached the UEFA Cup final in 1972 and won the League Cup in 1974. Between 1974 and 1979 the initials were replaced by two more jumping wolves.

3. 1996–2002. The wolf's head had already been introduced in 1979 and has since appeared in various versions. This logo is from 1996, when Jack Hayward wanted to see a change in the club. During the whole of this period Wolves were however playing in Division One (now the Championship).

4. 2002–present. For the third time during his years in charge, Jack Hayward introduced a new club crest. The logo was cleaned up and the wolf became more aggressive. This design is one of the most enduring in the club's history and has even experienced a couple of seasons in the Premier League.

1.

2.

3.

Wolverhampton Wanderers' Derek Dougan (right) embraces
Manchester City striker Denis Law after the 1974 League
Cup final. The Midlanders won 2-1.

4.

SPAIN

ATHLETIC BILBAO

REGIONAL PRIDE ABOVE ALL

Athletic Bilbao is an unique football club. The Basque giant is one of Spain's most successful clubs and has won eight league titles – the fourth best tally after Real Madrid, FC Barcelona and Atlético Madrid. Bilbao is also one of only three clubs who have played every season in La Liga since it began in 1928; the other two are Real Madrid and Barcelona. What makes the club even more special is that they have used only Basque players.

The Basque Country is a region covering parts of northern Spain and southern France. Today it has three million inhabitants and is, of course, Athletic Bilbao's catchment area. The policy of only allowing Basque players has limited the club in today's world, where money has an increasing influence over football. As a result, their most recent title dates to 1984, when Bilbao won the Double (La Liga and the Copa del Rey). Since then they have made it to the final of both the Spanish Cup and the Europa League, but that is nothing compared to the successes of their former rivals Real Madrid and Barcelona. Even so, most Bilbao fans are happy. They are proud of their team and their region, which is also reflected in the club's motto: *Con cantera y afición, no hace falta importación* ('With our own talents and passion, we don't need any imports'). To understand this motto, we need to turn to the history books.

The Basque Country has never allowed itself to be absorbed into Spanish culture. Basque is a separate language, and as late as 2010 the terrorist organisation ETA was fighting for Basque independence, a fight borne out of resistance to the dictator Franco's regime (1939–1975). Under Franco's reign the Basques were oppressed; among other restrictions, the Basque language itself was forbidden. This was a dark era that strengthened the Basque people's pride in their origins – a self-respect manifested in the crest for Athletic Bilbao.

CLUB: Athletic Club
NICKNAME: Los Leones (the Lions) and Lehoiak (the Lions)
FOUNDED: 1898
STADIUM: San Mamés, Bilbao (53,289 capacity)
HISTORIC PLAYERS: Pichichi, Telmo Zarra and Joseba Etxeberria

1. 1902–1910. Athletic Bilbao's first emblem is markedly different from today's. The initials AC are framed by a football, which in turn is surrounded by a blue and white belt. As the club was founded by Englishmen, the team played in a kit that had been bought from Blackburn Rovers, hence the colours.

2. 1910–1917. On a journey through England, the trainer Juan Elorduy was inspired by Southampton's red and white jerseys, which came to be reflected in the club's crest. The red and white colours of the pennant are to be found in the Basque flag. This emblem came in two versions, of which this is the latter.

3. 1917–1922. Athletic Bilbao and Atlético Madrid were both founded by Basque students, a fact that is reflected in this crest. The similarity between this emblem and that of today's Atlético Madrid is striking. Apart from the emblem that was carried on 21 August, 1913 at the opening match for San Mamés, Athletic Bilbao's home stadium, this was the first emblem in the history of the club to include regional symbols.

4. 1922–1941. The start of the 1920s saw the first appearance of the emblem that we still associate with Athletic Bilbao today. The Basque symbols seen in the crest are the San Antón cathedral (on the left), the San Anton bridge (in the middle) and the Guernica oak (on the right). The oak represents Basque independence while the two other symbols are well known landmarks in Bilbao. Over the trunk of the oak you can see two wolves that have their origins in the Bilbao city crest. The two crosses flanking the shield come from the equivalent crest of Biscay, the province of which Bilbao is the capital.

5. 1941–1972. Under Franco's regime foreign club names were outlawed which forced Bilbao to change its name from 'Athletic' to 'Atlético'.

6. 1972–present. At the end of Franco's dictatorship, foreign club names were allowed again and Athletic Bilbao were quick to reclaim their old one. Since then, the crest has looked the same apart from the choice of colour. This one is from 1995.

1.

2.

3.

4.

5.

6.

Athletic Bilbao celebrate a win over Newcastle United in the 1994 UEFA Cup. The Basque country team has recorded eight La Liga titles – only Real Madrid, Barcelona and Atlético Madrid have won more.

ATLÉTICO MADRID

THE LITTLE BROTHER IN THE SPANISH CAPITAL

Of late the Atlético Madrid philosophy has been to acquire and improve world-class attackers and then sell them on to Europe's greatest clubs. Sergio Agüero, Diego Fórlan and Radamel Falcao are just some of the star strikers who have reperesented the red and whites from Madrid over the past few seasons. But it was through another striker, Diego Costa, that Atlético created a stir across Europe by breaking the dominance of Real Madrid and Barcelona in La Liga. In the 2013/14 season Atlético won the Spanish league for the first time since 1996 and also reached the Champions League final. And that has so often been the picture with Atlético Madrid: periods of greatness alternating with deep troughs.

In 2012, Diego Simeone's second season as manager, Atlético reached the top three in La Liga – the first time in 17 years. The period after the league win in 1996 was marked by mid-table mediocrity and also, around the turn of the millennium, by two seasons in the second tier of Spanish football.

In spite of their relatively good successes, Atlético Madrid has nurtured something of a Little Brother complex vis-à-vis their arch-rival Real Madrid. This is a role that the club could be said to have been born to play because it was founded in 1903 by three Basque students who regarded the newly launched Madrid outfit as a branch of their mother club in the Basque Country, Athletic Bilbao. That is also the reason for Atlético Madrid's colours, emblem and original name. It was not until 1921 that the team became independent from big brother Bilbao.

CLUB: Club Atlético de Madrid

NICKNAMES: Colchoneros (the Mattress-Makers), Rojiblancos (the Red and Whites), Los Indios (the Indians) and Atléti

FOUNDED: 1903

STADIUM: Wanda Metropolitano, Madrid (67,703 capacity)

HISTORIC PLAYERS: Adelardo, Adrián Escudero, Luis Aragonés, Sergio Agüero, Diego Fórlan, Radamel Falcao and Fernando Torres

1. 1903–1911. Atlético Madrid was founded in the image of Athletic Bilbao, so they shared the same emblem in the beginning. The initials stand for Athletic Club and the blue and white colours were inspired by Blackburn Rovers from whom both clubs bought their kit.

2. 1911–1917. During the period that Athletic Club de Madrid and Athletic Bilbao were linked, they changed their emblem at the same time. So when the Basque club changed the colours of their kit and their emblem to a red and white flag, the Madrid club followed suit, even if they chose to keep their blue shorts.

3. 1917–1939. A further change of emblem was carried out in 1917. For the first time in the club's history, symbols from the Madrid area appeared. The bear and the wild strawberry tree (*arbutus unedo* in Latin) are taken from the Madrid city crest; these figures had represented the city as early as the 13th century.

4. 1939–1947. After the Spanish Civil War, the team merged with the club of the Spanish air force, forming the Athletic Aviación de Madrid. Wings were added to the crest to symbolise the air force, and a royal crown placed on top. This was the logo with which the club won its first league title in 1940 and a second in 1941, the year they adopted the name Atlético (rather than Athletic) after foreign names were forbidden.

5. 1947–2017. When the air force separated from Atlético Madrid, their flying symbols also disappeared from the crest. Over the years the contours of the emblem have been both yellow and blue. The seven stars are taken from the constellation Ursa Major. The five points of the stars symbolise provinces around Madrid: Segovia, Ávila, Guadalajara, Cuenca and Toledo.

6. 2017–present. Atlético Madrid's effort to expand as a club prompted the move to the newly built, ultra-modern stadium Wanda Metropolitano, in time for the 2017/18 season. At the same time as the stadium's name was announced in December 2016, the club's new emblem was revealed: the colours were changed and the shield rounded in memory of the original emblem, while the bear and the tree were inverted, taking up more space than before. This was all designed to signal a new era in the history of the club. Although the new emblem respects the regional symbols, there has been a lot of criticism from fans, who have even formed protest groups. The emblem was created by the Barcelona-based design group Vasava.

1.　　　2.　　　3.

4.　　　5.

Diego Simeone was an industrious midfielder for Atlético and has since gone on to become a highly influential manager for the club, leading them to a La Liga win in 2014, two Champions League finals and a Europa League victory in 2018.

6.

BARCELONA

JOAN GAMPER'S HERITAGE

Barcelona – and the footballing world – are indebted to Swiss footballer, economist and journalist Joan Gamper, the man who founded the now world-famous club and established its enduring links to Catalan nationalism.

In 1899, Gamper, working as an accountant and sports journalist in the Catalan capital, advertised for players for a new football team. FC Barcelona was founded soon after and Gamper took a seat on the board. He also became team captain, playing 50 matches and scoring 121 goals between 1899 and 1903. However, by 1908 the club was in financial trouble, so Gamper took over as chairman. He steadied the ship and just a year later the club was able to move to a new stadium. To celebrate, they held a competition to design a new badge. This was won by Carles Comamala, a medical student and cartoonist – and Barça top striker.

Comamala drew on the club's original crest, which had in turn drawn on the city's crest. In the upper half of the emblem, he retained the yellow and red stripes of the Senyera, the flag of Catalonia, and the George Cross, the symbol of Barcelona's patron saint. The club's identification with its fiercely proud region could not have been stated more strongly.

By the 1920s, Gamper had established FC Barcelona as a symbol for the independently minded region of Catalonia. The politicisation of his club strained relations with the Spanish government and in July 1925, after the Catalan supporters booed the Spanish national anthem before a match, Gamper and his whole board were fired by order of the Spanish Prime Minister, Miguel Primo de Rivera.

This, combined with economic crisis, led to Gamper's suicide in 1930, but Gamper had created more than a club. He had built an institution that would become one of the most celebrated names in football, and which would also set itself against the authority of the Spanish government.

CLUB: FC Barcelona

NICKNAMES: Barça, Blaugrana (the Red and Blues) and Culés (it derives from the Catalan word cul, or 'backside')

FOUNDED: 1899

STADIUM: Camp Nou, Barcelona (99,354 capacity)

HISTORIC PLAYERS: László Kubala, Johan Cruyff, Diego Maradona, Michael Laudrup, Carles Puyol, Andrés Iniesta, Xavi and Lionel Messi

---

1. 1899–1910. Barcelona's first emblem was taken from the city crest. The square and crown are still symbols of the Catalan metropolis. The red and white parts represent the George Cross, which is associated with Jordi, Barcelona's patron saint. The yellow and red stripes come from Senyera, the Catalan flag. Even the bat is an important heraldic symbol in the city. The shield is flanked by two branches, which are symbolic of mastery.

2. 1910–1920. After Joan Gamper had saved the club from going under in 1908, it was decided that the club crest should be changed. A competition was organised and in 1910 Carles Comamala was announced as the winner. Comamala had created a crest that would become known around the world. Both the George Cross and the Senyera were retained, but there were changes. The club's initials were incorporated, and a football was placed in front of the team's colours. Legend has it that the blue and red stripes have their origin in FC Basel, the club for which Joan Gamper once played. The story has been rejected by FC Barcelona.

3. 1941–1974. Barcelona's emblem continued to develop with small alterations up to 1941, when the club was forced to change its name to the Spanish Club de Fútbol Barcelona because of the dictator Franco. Two of the stripes from the Catalan flag were taken out in order to sever the links to the region. At the club's 50th anniversary, the use of the Senyera in the crest was once more approved, but the change of name stayed until 1974, the year before Franco's death.

4. 1975–2002. After Franco's death a new emblem was introduced, which was like the one from 1910. The following year it was upgraded to this one, which was the club's crest throughout the great era when Johan Cruyff was the manager of players such as Hristo Stoichkov, Ronald Koeman and Romário.

5. 2002–present. At the start of the new millennium, the designer Claret Serrahima was given the task of modernising the club crest. The shape was simplified and the full stops between the initials were removed. The similarities to the earliest crests remain striking.

1.

3.

2.

4.

5.

With its roll call of global superstars and millions of supporters, FC Barcelona may seem worlds away from the club Gamper founded in 1899, but the club's traditions are retained in the club crest designed more than 100 years ago by Carles Comamala.

DEPORTIVO LA CORUÑA

THE UNTOUCHED EMBLEM

At the start of the new millennium, the impossible happened: this little Galician club landed its first – and so far only – title, finishing ahead of such giants as FC Barcelona and Real Madrid. A few years earlier, in 1996, the league win of Atlético Madrid had also been unexpected – but that was nothing compared to this extraordinary turn of events. Apart from the year of Atlético's triumph, Barcelona and Real Madrid had monopolised the league title since 1985. Deportivo's glorious achievement didn't simply reverberate across European football, it actually cracked open the Spanish league, albeit temporarily: two of the upcoming possible four titles were won by teams other than Barcelona and Real Madrid. For Deportivo the victory of 2000 ushered in a golden age that brought two second places in the league, two triumphs in the Copa del Rey and two titles in the Supercopa de España.

While Barcelona and Real Madrid could buy global stars for millions, Deportivo started by buying cheaply. They built a squad around such players as Roy Makaay, Djalminha and Nourredine Naybet, a team that nevertheless got to the Champions League semi-final in 2004. But every season the transfer fees paid by the club grew larger. Then, like most Spanish clubs, Deportivo was hit by the global financial crisis. With that, the golden era was over and the club dropped out of La Liga in 2011. Since then Deportivo has been performing some kind of precarious balancing act and has been playing in the Primera and Segunda División, far removed from the glories of their recent past.

1. 1912–present. Deportivo La Coruña's crest has been relatively unchanged since the first in 1912, six years after the club's founding. By itself, that is very unusual, as is the fact that the emblem featured on the players' kit even in those early years. A knight's belt frames the pennant of the Sala Calvet gymnasium, where the club was founded. The diagonal blue stripe comes from the flag of the Spanish region of Galicia and, as with many Spanish clubs, the crown symbolises royal support and recognition. Even if this has been Deportivo's official badge for over 100 years, it has not appeared continuously on the kit. Furthermore it appeared all in red during the 1980s.

2. One of the earlier versions, the intertwined letters C and D featuring neither pennant nor crown, can be glimpsed in this team photo from 1908.

CLUB: RC Deportivo de La Coruña

NICKNAMES: Super Depor, Los Branquiazuis (the Blue and Whites) and Turcos (the Turks)

FOUNDED: 1906

STADIUM: Estadio Riazor, La Coruña (32,912 capacity)

HISTORIC PLAYERS: Fran, Mauro Silva, Manuel Pablo, Rivaldo, Roy Makaay, Diego Tristán and Bebeto

---

1.

2.

Roy Makaay made 133 appearances
for Super Depor and scored 79 times
wearing the famous blue and white. His
29 goals in the 2002–03 season made
him the top scorer in Europe.

RAYO VALLECANO

THE BOHEMIAN LIGHTNING FLASH FROM MADRID

The outskirts of Madrid, more precisely the working class area of Vallecas, is home to Rayo Vallecano. In the shadow of local rivals – the noble Real and its antithesis Atlético – Rayo has become the club of rebels, Bohemians and exiles. This is a club with a strong connection to the area and has become a meeting place for leftist activists and anarchists.

Founded in 1924, Rayo Vallecano made its debut in the top flight only in 1977, but the club have never really managed to establish themselves at the top of Spanish football, and have yo-yoed between divisions.

Their greatest successes came in 2001, when they reached the quarter-finals of the UEFA Cup, and in 2013, when they came eighth in the Primera División. But the club have become more famous for their progressive attitudes.

When Teresa Rivero took over as chairman in 1994, Rayo became the first club in Spain's top division to have a female president. Since then the club have made an impresssion on various levels: the players have done voluntary work on the Madrid Underground to support environmental causes, and in 2012 they took part in anti-corruption demonstrations to promote democracy and economic reforms. In 2014 they offered to pay the rent for the 85-year-old Vallecas resident Carmen Martínez Ayuso, who had been evicted from her flat.

In the 2015/16 season, the club attracted huge headlines for their match kit. Instead of the classic red stripe, the away jersey was given a diagonal rainbow. This symbolised, among other things, the club's attitude to the LGBT community. Their third kit had a pink stripe, standing for the fight against breast cancer.

1. 1924–1947. Rayo Vallecano's emblem has remained relatively unchanged through the years. The alterations to the crest have been made because of three name changes in the 20th century. Rayo's first crest featured the initials ADR because the club was originally called Agrupación Deportiva El Rayo.

2. 1947–1970. In 1947 the name of the club was changed to Agrupación Deportiva Rayo Vallecano in order to strengthen their ties to the area where the club was born. In this emblem you can also see for the first time, on the left, the town crest of Valleca.

3. 1995–present. This emblem has been used since 1995 when the club was given its present name, Rayo Vallecano de Madrid. Between 2009 and 2012 the letter "V" was red. Rayo means lightning in Spanish which explains the central symbol and the stripe on the jerseys.

CLUB: Rayo Vallecano de Madrid
NICKNAMES: Los Franjirrojos (the Red Stripes) and Los Vallecanos (the Vallecans)
FOUNDED: 1924
STADIUM: Campo de Fútbol de Vallecas, Madrid (14,708 capacity)
HISTORIC PLAYERS: Hugo Sánchez, Kasey Keller, Míchel and Diego Costa

---

1.

2.

3.

Jordi Ferrón made his debut for Rayo Vallecano in the 1999–2000 season. Impressively for a right-back, he scored seven league goals in 35 appearances to help Rayo Vallecano complete a top half La Liga finish.

REAL BETIS

SUPPORTED DESPITE THE 13 STRIPES IN THE CREST

Viva el Betis manque pierda – 'Long live Betis even when they lose'. Thus goes the motto of Real Betis, and it says a lot about the club. In 1943, a couple of years after the end of the Spanish Civil War, Real Betis crashed out of the top division, not to return for another 15 years. In between, the club spent eight seasons in the Segunda División (the Spanish second division) and seven seasons in the third. The motto comes from this period which, though tough from a footballing point of view, saw Betis become one of Spain's most popular clubs. Even in the third division their home matches were often sold out and the club's travelling fans, the *marchas verdes* ('green marchers'), were becoming well known.

The club retains loyal support today and Real Betis are always one of the teams with the highest average attendances in Spain. The 2017/17 season was no exception: the club drew average crowds of 46,387, a figure surpassed only by the giants Barcelona, Real Madrid and Atlético Madrid.

It is lucky for the green and white club from Seville that the fans keep the faith. How many other supporters would have stuck with a club through all that Real Betis has suffered? Having played nearly half of its total number of seasons outside La Liga, the club has been close to bankruptcy several times. Deals like the acquisition of the dribbling phenomenon Denílson haven't helped. The Brazilian midfielder was bought in 1998 for around £21.5 million, which made him the world's most expensive player at the time. Two years later both he and Betis went out of La Liga. To add insult to injury, their local rivals Sevilla have surpassed them since the turn of the millennium. But what does all this matter when supporters turn up anyway?

CLUB: Real Betis Balompié

NICKNAMES: Béticos, Los Verdiblancos (the Green and Whites), El Glorioso (the Glorious), Los Verderones (the Great Green Ones) and Heliopolitanos

FOUNDED: 1907

STADIUM: Benito Villamarín, Seville (60,720 capacity)

HISTORIC PLAYERS: Julio Cardeñosa Rodríguez, Hipólito Rincón, Antonio Prats, Alfonso, Denilson and Joaquín

1. 1907–1914. Real Betis was founded as Sevilla Balompié. Although Balompié means 'football', this was an unusual name compared to the word borrowed from English: fútbol. One of the first emblems shows the name of the club inside a belt. Another early variant has the initials painted within a blue circle.

2. 1915–1922 and 1922–1925. After the merger with Betis FC, new crests were designed and the reference to *real* ('royal') meant the inclusion of a crown. After a couple of years the shape of the emblem was changed.

3. 1932–1941. After the Spanish king had been forced to flee in 1931, sports associations were forbidden from using royal symbols, and Real Betis reshaped its emblem. The shield became triangular and the club's initials were placed in a square at the top. Although the club won their first and so far only league title in 1935 with this crest, it was regarded with widespread scepticism because of the 13 stripes. The number 13 symbolises life, death and change which may be the reason why the club has adopted a number which is otherwise seen as bringing bad luck.

4. 2012–present. In 1941, when football resumed after the Spanish Civil War (1936–1939), the crown returned to the club crest. Since then it has been made smaller and the initials have been placed in a circle as a kind of fusion of the earlier emblems. The name Betis comes from *Baetis*, the Latin name for the river Guadalquivir, which flows through Seville.

1.

2.

3.

4.

Real Betis broke the world-record transfer fee when they paid £21.5 million for Denilson. Despite the significant investment, Betis were relegated a couple of years later.

REAL MADRID

THE ROYAL CLUB

They may be the kings of Europe, but Real Madrid boasted a crown on its crest many years before its continental exploits began. The Madrid Football Club had been in existence for 18 years and had established itself as one of the nation's top teams when King Alfonso XIII gave it his royal approval in 1920. To celebrate the royal patronage, the club added Real (royal) to its name and a crown to its simple M, C and F monogram.

Of course, what ultimately sealed the team's reputation is their success in the European Cup/Champions League; they were the first team to count their victories in double figures, *La Decima* (the tenth) coming in 2014 in a victory orchestrated by Cristiano Ronaldo and Gareth Bale. And *La Decima* was just the beginning of a new era for the club, one which saw Real win the Champions League four times in five years. In the spring of 2018 they beat Liverpool 3-1 at the Olympic Stadium in Kiev to seal their 13th title. But this is just the modern Real Madrid – the foundations of the club's greatness were laid further back in time.

During the 1950s the club established itself as a footballing superpower with successes in both Spain and Europe. With Alfredo Di Stéfano, Ferenc Puskás and Raymond Kopa, regarded as some of the greatest players of all time, Real Madrid won five consecutive European Cup titles. Success seems to be written into the club's DNA, reflected in the simplicity of its confident crest.

CLUB: Real Madrid Club de Fútbol
NICKNAMES: Los Blancos (the Whites), Los Merengues (the Meringues) and Los Vikingos (the Vikings)
FOUNDED: 1902
STADIUM: Santiago Bernabéu, Madrid (81,044 capacity)
HISTORIC PLAYERS: Alfredo Di Stéfano, Ferenc Puskas, Santillana, Raúl, Iker Casillas, Gareth Bale and Cristiano Ronaldo

1. 1902–1908. On 6 March 1902, a group of supporters founded Madrid Foot-Ball Club. The first crest was a mix of the club's three initials – M, C and F – in navy blue. It had to be replaced, however, by the Madrid City Hall crest for matches against other teams due to a local ruling.

2. 1908–1920. In 1908, the club's initials on the crest, which had survived despite the ruling, took on a more stylised form. The M for Madrid stood out from the rest and the design was fitted into a circle.

3. 1920–1931. On 29 June 1920, King Alfonso XIII bestowed the title of 'Real' upon the club, which from that point onwards would be known as Real Madrid Football Club. The position and shape of the initials were adjusted slightly.

4. 1931–1941. The crown was removed from the crest after the abolition of the Spanish monarchy. The circle stayed in place and the initials were centred once again, with a more stylised design. A diagonal purple stripe, which represents Castile, was added to the emblem.

5. The crest had a similar appearance after the Spanish Civil War, apart from the crown. In many instances, the navy blue on the circle was replaced by gold. The team's name became Real Madrid Club de Fútbol. This crest would remain in use until the start of the 1990s.

6. 2002–present. The more stylised current crest has a narrower blue stripe. The letters are wider and have a navy blue border, with a bigger M. The emblem is used as a logo to promote the 'Real Madrid' brand around the world

1.

2.

3.

4.

5.

6.

REAL OVIEDO

THE CLUB SAVED BY SUPPORTERS

In the autumn of 2000 the future was looking bright for Real Oviedo. The Asturian club had established themselves in the Primera División and had just inaugurated their publicly owned stadium, the Carlos Tartiere, with its capacity of 30,500 spectators. But the season did not work out as planned and on the very last day Real Oviedo were relegated, after 13 years in the top flight.

With relegation came financial problems that threatened the club's very existence. Their spell in the Segunda División lasted only two years, because in the 2002/03 season they were demoted still further, to the Spanish fourth division, after failing to pay their players. At this point, politicians in Oviedo chose to support local rivals Astur CF instead, which appeared to spell disaster for Real Oviedo. But the supporters mobilised, there were protest marches and they managed to raise enough money to save their club, if only temporarily.

After a number of years in the lower divisions, there was still more trouble in the 2012/13 season. Real Oviedo, at that point in the third division, were once again in acute need of funds to stave off bankruptcy. At that point three global stars who had been nurtured by the club stepped up to the plate: Santi Cazorla, Juan Mata and Michu (Miguel Pérez Cuesta) joined up with the fans and contributed money for shares in the club. Real Madrid and Carlos Slim, one of the world's richest men, also bought into the club. Word spread and within two weeks more than 20,000 people in more than 60 countries had bought shares in Real Oviedo. The club was saved.

Since relegation from La Liga in 2001, the club have never sold less than 10,000 season tickets, which bears witness to their popularity, status and potential.

1. 1926-1931. Real Oviedo's emblem has gone through a number of minor changes over the years. There have been 11 different versions and this one originates from the year that the club was founded. The first version was simpler, in black and white, and was quickly replaced by the colour version pictured.

2. 1931-1934. The biggest change in the club crest came in 1931, when the crown had to go because of the political unrest throughout the country. But by 1934 the crown was back, if somewhat toned down.

3. 2013-present. The majority of symbols, such as the crown, the cross and the ball, have generally been retained since the club was founded in 1926. The crown above the shield refers to Oviedo's prefix, 'Real', a tradition which the club shares with many Spanish teams. The initials have varied over the years but today's 'RO' are the ones that have appeared most regularly. The cross comes from Oviedo's town crest and has always been part of the emblem.

CLUB: Real Oviedo

NICKNAMES: Carbayones (a reference to an oak tree which was an important symbol of the city's identity), Los Azules (the Blues), Los Godos (the Goths) and Oviedistas

FOUNDED: 1926

STADIUM: Carlos Tartiere, Oviedo (30,500 capacity)

HISTORIC PLAYERS: Abel Xavier, Paulo Bento, Berto, Viktor Onopko and Michu

1.

2.

3.

Real Oviedo winger Néstor Susaeta played for the club for four years from 2013, scoring 27 times in 150 apprearances.

REAL SOCIEDAD

ROYAL FOOTBALL SOCIETY

Founded in 1908 and one of the founding members of La Liga, the San Sebastián club received royal patronage in 1910 because the city was the monarch's summer residence. This meant they could now be known as Real Sociedad, or 'Royal Society of Football', a connection that is revealed through the club crest. The team's colours stem from the city's flag: a blue canton on a white field.

The most successful years for La Real came in 1980 and 1981, when the club managed to win two consecutive league titles. Then, in the spring of 2003, Real Sociedad were agonisingly close to staging one of the greatest shocks in modern Spanish football. In an era dominated by the giants Real Madrid and Barcelona, Real Sociedad nearly won the Primera División. With two remaining fixtures, they were on top of the league, but a 3-2 defeat to Celta Vigo meant that the title once more ended up in Madrid.

Like Bilbao, Real Sociedad used only Basque players until 1989, when the Irish striker John Aldridge was bought from Liverpool. The decision to abandon the policy was taken the previous year. Foreign players were now welcome in Real Sociedad, but not until 2001 would Spanish players from outside the Basque region be allowed to represent the club. The transition was not painless. For instance, Aldridge's arrival was criticised for not recognising local traditions. Today the situation is rather different: Aldridge spent only two seasons in San Sebastián, but is nowadays seen as a club legend, celebrated by fans for having broken down barriers.

1. 1910–1931 Real Sociedad was founded in 1909 in the Basque town of San Sebastián, a holiday resort often visited by King Alfonso XIII, who granted the town his royal warrant. In the club's first emblem, this was reflected via the crown above the football. The third part of the emblem consists of a blue and white flag with the city's initials. The colours were taken from the town crest of San Sebastián.

2. 1931–1940. King Alfonso XIII was forced to leave the country in 1931 after political unrest, which led to the crown being removed from the emblem. The club changed its name to Donostia Club de Fútbol, Donostia being the Basque name for San Sebastián.

3. 1997–present. The year after the end of the Spanish Civil War (1936–1939) the crown was back in the emblem and the name had changed to Real Sociedad, or the Royal Society. The emblem has changed very little since then, even if details like the stitching of the football, the initals and the crown were updated in 1997.

CLUB: Real Sociedad de Fútbol

NICKNAMES: Txuri-urdin (the White and Blues), Erreala and La Real

FOUNDED: 1909

STADIUM: Anoeta, San Sebastián 25,000 capacity)

HISTORIC PLAYERS: Jesús Maria Zamora, Alberto Górriz, John Aldridge, Valery Karpin, Darko Kovacevic, Nihat and Xabi Alonso

1.

2.

3.

In January 2001, Real Sociedad were bottom of the league when in a surprise move 20-year-old Xabi Alonso was made team captain. Despite his youth and relative inexperience, Alonso guided the team to 14th place and safety by the end of the season.

SEVILLA

WHERE FOOTBALL AND RELIGION MEET

Seville, Spain's fourth largest city, is a place rich in mythology, filled with places of historic and religious significance. Up to the 13th century, the Muslim Moors ruled this part of Spain, but they were defeated by Ferdinand III of Castille when the town was converted to Christianity. In the 16th century, the world's largest Gothic cathedral was built in Seville, with a bell tower that started out as a minaret. The cathedral provides the last resting place for the remains of Christopher Columbus.

During the 2000s, Sevilla FC conquered Europe. The Andalusian club may have had limited success at home, but it holds the record for the number of Europa League titles. This was achieved in 2015, when they beat the Ukrainian club Dnipro 3-2 in the final, securing their fourth title in the competition. This was just nine years after they first wrote their name into the European footballing annals, beating Middlesbrough 4-0 in the final. This was a golden age during which players like Dani Alves, Luís Fabiano and Jesús Navas represented the club.

The foundations for these successes were laid when José María del Nido was elected president in 2002. Under his guidance, the finances of the club were straightened out and Sevilla established themselves as a top team in Spain. Since 2013, del Nido has been serving a prison sentence for corruption. In his absence, the sports supremo Ramón Rodríguez Verdejo, better known as Monchi, just carried on this tradition of success, securing another Europa League triumph, this time against Liverpool in the spring of 2016.

CLUB: Sevilla FC
NICKNAMES: Sevillistas, Los Rojiblancos (the Red and Whites), Los Nervionenses (the People of Nervión, a district of Seville) and El Grande de Andalucía (the Pride of Andalusia)
FOUNDED: 1890
STADIUM: Ramón Sánchez Pizjuán, Seville (42,500 capacity)
HISTORIC PLAYERS: Biri Biri, Manolo Jiménez, Antonio Puerta, Sergio Ramos and José Antonio Reyes

1. 1905–1921 and 2013–2014. Seville may have been founded as early as 1890 as Spain's first football club, but it took another 15 years before the club was registered and an official emblem introduced. The first crest represented the club's initials in the team's colours — red and white. Between 1905 and 1921, this emblem appeared in different versions. In 2013, the same year that José María del Nido went to jail, this emblem was again to be seen on the Sevilla shirts.

2. 1909–1921. This emblem was used in parallel with the first one but only in administrative contexts, never in any match. Even so, it is a more developed emblem, since the name is spelled out.

3. 1921–present. When the time came for Sevilla to update their emblem in 1921, a Barcelona-inspired version was rejectedin favour of this one. The initials were still there, while the historic inheritance of the town was reflected in the inclusion of three saints. Saint Isidore (here, on the left) was a bishop in the town in the seventh century and was canonised in 1598. On the throne in the centre is Ferdinand III of Castille, who was canonised in 1671. On the right is St Leander of Seville, who was Isidore's brother and precursor. At the centre of the crest is an old-fashioned football, under which are 11 red and white stripes. The colour's are said to originate from the standard of Ferdinand III. Since 1921, changes have been made and today's crest was unveiled in 1982.

4. 2006–present. In 2006 the club's second team, Sevilla Atlético, was given its own club crest, which portrays one of the town's most famous sites, the Giralda — the cathedral whose bell tower started out as a minaret.

1.

2.

3.

4.

VALENCIA

IN A FIGHT AGAINST A SUPERHERO

In May 2013, Valencia's club crest attracted a great deal of international attention as the American comic book publisher DC Comics protested against an alternative version of the emblem. Valencia were going to introduce a new clothes label with a modified version of the bat which can be found in the club's badge. DC Comics, who own the rights to Batman, thought that this logo was too like the image of their winged superhero and lodged a protest with the EU Commission on the grounds of copyright infringement. The case went no further, as the Spanish club chose to back down.

In sporting terms Valencia is one of Spain's greatest clubs, and they were also the team that challenged Real Madrid and Barcelona in the early years of the new millennium. During their golden era between 2000 and 2004, the club secured two league titles, one UEFA Cup win, and two consecutive Champions League finals. But Valencia was no newcomer on the international scene; they had won European as well as domestic titles.

After some years of financial problems, Valencia are once again aiming for the top with the acquisition of expensive players, a much longed-for stadium and a world class youth academy. There is a lot to suggest that the bat may be watching over a glorious future for the club. As it happens, the bat was first incorporated into Valencia's emblem back in 1919, a full 20 years before DC Comics' guardian of Gotham City first saw the light of day.

1. 1919. The football club Valencia was founded in 1919 and was for a short while represented by this emblem. The square, the crown and the bat are taken from the town's heraldic shield. The club added the intials and the football on which the emblem rests.

2. 1919–1920. This emblem was produced in the club's first year and has been associated with the club ever since. The crest in the picture is the first of six similar versions used over the years. The changes made in this time have involved the look of the bat, the shape of the shield and also the initials – at the time of its founding the name of the club was Valencia Football Club.

3. 2009–present. This latest club crest is from 2009 and contains all the well known elements. The yellow and red stripes look like those on the Catalan flag Senyera, but in this case they come from the flag and city crest of Valencia. The bat is an important regional symbol: it is said to have brought James I of Aragon luck when he conquered Valencia in 1238 and liberated the town from the Moors. The bat can also be seen in the emblem of the neighbouring club, Levantes.

CLUB: Valencia CF

NICKNAMES: Los Che (the Pals), Els Taronges (the Oranges), Valencianistes and Los Murciélagos (the Bats)

FOUNDED: 1919

STADIUM: Mestalla, Valencia (49,500 capacity), pending the completion of Nou Mestalla

HISTORIC PLAYERS: Edmundo Suárez, Fernando Gómez Colomer, Mario Kempes, Gaizka Mendieta and Santiago Cañizares

1.

2.

3.

Valencia's team goalkeeper Pereira claims the ball in the 1980 European Cup Winners' Cup. His side, with their iconic bat motif, overcame Arsenal 5–4 on penalties.

VILLARREAL

THE YELLOW SUBMARINE

In April 2006, Villarreal were just one penalty kick away from making football history. The Champions League debutants had surprised everyone by getting to the semi-final, where Arsenal were awaiting them. After Arsenal won the first leg in London 1-0, Villarreal had the chance to level the tie from the penalty spot in the return fixture at El Madrigal. The 22,000 home supporters held their breath as the playmaker and fan-favourite Juan Román Riquelme stepped up to take the spot kick. But the Arsenal goalkeeper Jens Lehmann saved the penalty and torpedoed the Champions League dreams of the Yellow Submarine. At that point, it seemed like a heavy defeat, but with a little distance from that historic miss, Villareal's European adventure must be seen as some kind of heroic achievement.

The town Villarreal has just over 50,000 inhabitants, making it the second smallest ever to play a semi-final in the Champions League. (Monaco, who reached the final in 2004, had a population of 35,000 at the time). Villarreal's fight against the European giants looks even more impressive considering that the club entered La Liga as late as 1998. Although their rival, Valencia, are the big team in the region, Villarreal quickly established themselves in the top division and in the course of just 13 seasons qualified for both the Champions League and the Europa League. During this period the team built its successes on young Spanish talent and the financially sound purchases of players who had not been successful at bigger clubs – players such as Riquelme, but also Diego Forlán and Giuseppe Rossi. And it is by following this same model that Villareal continue their hunt for new successes.

1. 1923-1936. Club Deportivo Villarreal was founded in 1923, when they played in white jerseys and black shorts, which is reflected in the emblem. It was used for 13 years and disappeared, along with the club, when the Spanish Civil War broke out in 1936.

2. 1942-1954. Three years after the end of the Civil War, the club was recreated, this time under the name Club Atlético Foghetecaz Villarreal. The name was a construction from the surnames of some of the founders: Font, Gil, Herrero, Teuler, Catalá and Zaragoza. The idea was that the newly formed team would play in black and white as CD Villareal had done, but there were no white jerseys available, so they chose yellow ones. And so the emblem changed colour as well. The two full stops symbolise Manuel Vilanova and Manuel de Jeroni, another two of the founding fathers.

3. 1954-1966. In 1954 the board voted through a change of name to Villareal CF, and with this a new club crest was unveiled. The square, the crown and the colours were taken from the town crest of Villarreal.

4. 1966–present. To coincide with the club's return to the Spanish third division in 1966, after a five-year absence, this emblem was introduced. This modernised version with a different choice of colours, a simpler crown and no full stops, has represented the club ever since.

CLUB: Villarreal CF
NICKNAME: El Submarino Amarillo (the Yellow Submarine)
FOUNDED: 1923
STADIUM: Estadio de la Cerámical, Vila-real (24,890 capacity)
HISTORIC PLAYERS: Marcos Senna, Juan Román Riquelme, Diego Forlán, Giuseppe Rossi and Bruno Soriano

1.

2.

3.

4.

Argentian playmaker Juan Román Riquelme represented Villarreal from 2003–2007. In 2005 Spanish sports newspaper *Marca* awarded Riquelme the title of 'Most Artistic Player'.

ITALY

AC MILAN

FOOTBALL ARISTOCRACY

Founded in 1899 as a football and cricket club by two expatriate Englishmen, AC Milan is one of the foremost aristocratic families of world football. Here such gentlemen as Franco Baresi, Alessandro Nesta and Carlo Ancelotti have plied their trade. Here you also find such artists from the upper footballing echelons as Roberto Baggio, Zvonimir Boban and Andrea Pirlo. AC Milan is an institution partly held together by family ties, passed from father to son, as in the case of Cesare and Paolo Maldini. But AC Milan also has a strong connection to Italy's former prime minister, Silvio Berlusconi. Partly loved, partly hated by the Italian people, Berlusconi still has an important place in the history of this great European club because he is the man who saved it.

In the spring of 1986, things were looking grim for AC Milan; the club found itself far from the top and the threat of bankruptcy was hanging over it. Then Silvio Berlusconi bought the club. With Berlusconi as president, the club launched a major gamble by acquiring the promising Arrigo Sacchi as manager and that trio of Dutch masters: Ruud Gullit, Frank Rijkaard and Marco van Basten. Two years later, in 1988, Milan won Serie A for the first time in nine years, and the following year the club won its first European Cup title in two decades.

Their successes continued into the early '90s, when Milan won the league in three successive seasons and played in three Champions League finals. The club was living up to the great days of the '50s, when they were led by the Swedish trio Gre-No-Li" Gunnar Gren, Gunnar Nordahl and Nils Liedholm. They were as popular as they were successful; Nordahl is actually Serie A's third best goalscorer of all time with 225 strikes.

1. 1986–1998 and 1998–present. It is not, as many believe – not least the Englishmen who helped to found the club – the cross of St George that adorns AC Milan's crest, but in fact the regional St Ambrose cross, which is also to be found on the flag of the city. Between 1900 and 1940 the badge consisted solely of the St Ambrose cross, which would later be incorporated into the club crest. The version on the left was created after Berlusconi took over the club, building on earlier designs. It was updated in 1998 (right) and is in use today. At the outset the colour red was chosen to represent the players' sense of will and eagerness, and the black was meant to engender fear in the opposition.

2. 1980–1986. The colours inspired the club's nickname *Il Diavolo* (The Devil), a name coined by one of the founders, the Englishman Herbert Kilpin. The nickname became so popular that a devil has often come to accompany the crest or, in this case, form the actual emblem itself.

3. 2014–2015. When St Ambrose's cross made a comeback on the club shirts a couple of years ago, this symbol was used as well. It never became the club's official emblem, but it was used on their away kit to celebrate the newly built headquarters Casa Milan, where it stands as a symbol to this day.

CLUB: AC Milan
NICKNAME: I Rossoneri (the Red and Blacks), Il Diavolo (the Devil) and Casciavit (the Screwdriver)
FOUNDED: 1899
STADIUM: San Siro, Milan (80,018 capacity)
HISTORIC PLAYERS: Gunnar Nordahl, Franco Baresi, Marco van Basten, Andriy Schevchenko and Paolo Maldini

1.

2.

3.

Milan legend Paolo Maldini playing in 1999. That season's shirt, in celebration of the club's centenary, depicted the St Ambrose as well as a gold star. The latter represents more than 10 Serie A titles.

BARI

THE COCKERELS FROM PUGLIA

Because of bribery scandals and match-fixing, Italy is sometimes known as the country where football clubs can buy referees. In FC Bari's case, the opposite is true. Here it was the referee who bought the football club. In May 2014 the ex-UEFA Cup referee Gianluca Paparesta took over AS Bari, a club that had gone bankrupt a couple of months earlier. This was an eye-catching purchase because Paparesta's career as a referee had come to a sudden end after he had been mixed up in Calciopoli, the Italian bribery scandal of 2006.

Founded in 1908, Bari is a club with a great tradition and is recognised as one of Italian football's most successful clubs. Its 33 years in the top division is impressive by Southern Italian standards. International stars like David Platt have played in Bari, and future national players such as Antonio Cassano, Leonardo Bonucci and Gianluca Zambrotta all broke through here.

In recent years, the club has struggled to return to the Italian top flight. Although being close to promotion back to the Serie A in 2018 the season ended in horror. The once proud Puglian side went bankrupt and restarted their quest for Serie A in Serie D, Italy's fourth division.

CLUB: SCC Bari
NICKNAME: I Galletti (the Cockerels) and I Biancorossi (the Red and Whites)
FOUNDED: 1908
STADIUM: San Nicola, Bari (58,270 capacity)
HISTORIC PLAYERS: Luigi Bretti, Igor Protti, Klas Ingesson, Antonio Cassano and Jean-François Gillet

1. 1979–2014. Since Bari Football Club and Ideale were forced by the fascist regime to merge in 1928, the cockerel has represented the club. It was first chosen as the mascot and was later included in the club crest. The club used several emblems up to 1979, when this one was created by the designer Piero Gratton, who was also responsible for one of Roma's badges, the logo for Euro '80 (held in Italy), and the UEFA emblem. The cockerel was easily identifiable and was immediately popular with Bari fans. It was originally chosen because it stands for vitality and the fighting spirit.

2. 2014–2016. In the summer of 2014, Paparesta and his consortium introduced a new club logo, a design full of regional symbolism. The club's colours are still red and white, originating from Bari's town crest. The gold-coloured halo symbolises San Nicola (St Nicholas), who is Bari's patron saint and has also given his name to the home stadium. All that remains of the cockerel is the red coxcomb above the new club name. The 11 black lines stand for the team's 11 players, the leaning lines suggest players getting up and moving off. The uneven length represents speed, dynamism and action. This is a crest charged with symbolism, but it was coolly received by the fans, who missed their old cockerel.

3. 2016–2018. In June 2016, Bari changed owners when the former minority owner Cosmo Giancaspro took over the club. He immediately introduced a new emblem that restored the cockerel in a more precise design and spelled out the club's full name. All against a red and white background, of course.

4. 2018–present. After the rebirth of the club it took a while for the new owner Aurelio de Laurentiis (the owner of Napoli as well) to summon a new identity. By the end of 2018 a new badge was in place. The new crest depicted a cockerel's head resembling the original version much to the joy of the supporters.

1.

4.

2.

3.

Bari-born Antonio Cassano was raised in poverty in the city's San Nicola district and made his Serie A debut for the club in 1999. Highly skilled and a precocious talent, 'Fantantonio' played for *I Galletti* for two seasons.

CAGLIARI CALCIO

THE MOORS FROM SARDINIA

Although Cagliari made its debut in Serie A as late as 1964, the Sardinian club were still the first team south of Rome to win the domestic league. In 1970, six years after promotion, the team secured the title, finishing four points ahead of Juventus – after only two defeats in 30 matches and conceding only 11 goals, a record that stands to this day. They were almost as strong in attack as defence. Their offensive line was led by Luigi 'Gigi' Riva, who scored 21 goals to become *Capocannoniere* (top goalscorer). Riva was picked for the Italian World Cup squad alongside five teammates. He was just as successful in the national team and remains Italy's leading international goalscorer, with 35 goals.

But things didn't work out quite so well for Cagliari. In 1976 they were relegated to the second division, a demotion that was followed by a long downturn. They spent only four seasons in Serie A until 1989, when the team was promoted under the new coach Claudio Ranieri. The *Isolani* (Islanders), with their eye-catching crest depicting Moors and the team's Sardinian heritage, have since returned to Serie A.

In recent times the club has been marked by the chairmanship of Massimo Cellino, a controversial businessman who led Cagliari between 1992 and 2014. Cellino's reign saw both promotions and relegations and matches being moved to stadiums other than their usual Sant'Elia because of its poor condition and building work. In the course of his 22 years at the club he went through no fewer than 36 coaches. Since 2014 the club has been owned by Tommaso Giulini.

CLUB: Cagliari Calcio
NICKNAMES: I Rossoblu (the Red and Blues), Gli Isolani (the Islanders), I Sardi (the Sardinians) and Castéddu (Cagliari in the Sardinian dialect)
FOUNDED: 1920
STADIUM: Sardegna Arena, Cagliari (16,233 capacity)
HISTORICAL PLAYERS: Gigi Riva, David Suazo, Gianfranco Zola and Daniele Conti

1. 1931–1990. While most Italian clubs waited until the 1970s to put emblems on their shirts, Cagliari was an early adopter and introduced this shield in 1931, 11 years after the founding of the club. It is taken from the Sardinian flag and depicts four Moors; Sardinia was for a while ruled by the Moors, and the symbol has its origins in the 13th century. Over the years, the shape of the crest has been modified and the red lips have disappeared.

2. 1996–2015. The emblem was changed pretty soon after the arrival of Massimo Cellino in 1992. Shortly thereafter it would be updated and for the following 20 years it consisted of a two-tone oval-shaped shield: the red stands for the royal house of Savoy, which ruled Sardinia; the blue represents the sky and the water.

3. 2015–present. In the summer of 2015, before the start of the season in Serie B, the relatively new owner Tommaso Giulini unveiled a new club crest. The Moors were again the dominant symbol but now, and for the first time, they were facing to the right. This was meant to symbolise belief and hope in the future, an alteration that had already been made in the Sardinian flag in 1999. The Corsican clubs SC Bastia, AC Ajaccio and Gazélec Ajaccio also feature Moors in their club crests.

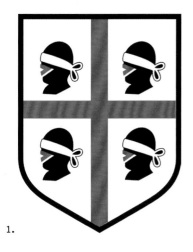

1.

2.

2.

Nicolò Barella was born in Cagliari and made his Serie A debut for the club in 2015. Given its clear links Sardinian heritage, Barella will understand more than most the significance of the Moors depicted in the *Isolani* (Islanders') crest.

2.

3.

FIORENTINA

THE LILAC LILIES

Florence is a city of great historic and cultural significance, reaching way back through the centuries. Long ago it was the capital of Italy and was also the seat of the Renaissance. The poet Dante and the artists Leonardo da Vinci, Michelangelo and Donatello all worked here. In a different sphere and perhaps never quite at this level, Florence has also played a significant role in the history of Italian football.

In the 15th century, the city was the birthplace of il *calcio Fiorentino* (also known as *calcio storico*), a late-medieval version of football. The popularity of this historic game was a prerequisite for the smooth introduction by some Englishmen at the end of the 19th century of the sort of football we know today. The sport quickly became popular, though it wasn't until 1926 that Fiorentina was founded. The club chose to reference the history of the sport by taking as its own emblem the city crest, the fleur-de-lis (the French lily).

The fleur-de-lis has always been part of Fiorentina's emblem, albeit in many different forms. The latest big change came in 2003; the club had gone bankrupt the year before and then re-formed as Florentia Viola. In 2003 the owner Diego Della Valle bought back the name Fiorentina and the old emblem. With that Fiorentina's crest became the most expensive in the country: Della Valle had to pay £2.5 million.

1. This is the city crest that the club once used. The fleur-de-lis has long been a symbol for Florence. Of course, it isn't really a lily at all. The origin is the iris, which was initially presented as white against a red background. In the 13th century, the colours were inverted and since then the flower has been strongly linked to Florence as the city crest.

2. 1980–1992. In 1980, after several variations on the original emblem, the then owner Flavio Pontello decided to modernise the crest by combining the fleur-de-lis with the letter F. The new emblem met with criticism from fans, who were not pleased that the badge looked like a halberd. In spite of the criticism, this remained Fiorentina's emblem for 12 seasons.

3. 2003–present. This is Italy's most expensive emblem, the one for which Diego Della Valle paid £2.5 million to buy back the club's name, Fiorentina, following bankruptcy. This emblem was actually introduced in 1992 by the earlier owners, the Cecchi Gori family, but with yellow contours and a more rounded fleur-de-lis.

CLUB: ACF Fiorentina

NICKNAME: Viola & Gigliati (the Lilies)

FOUNDED: 1926

STADIUM: Stadio Artemio Franchi, Florence (47,282 capacity)

HISTORIC PLAYERS: Gabriel Batistuta, Kurt Hamrin, Giancarlo Antognoni, Angelo Di Livio and Luca Toni

1.

2.

Fiorentina legend Gabriel Batistuta scored 168 goals in 269 games while wearing the fleur-de-lis club crest. He also won the *Capocannoniere* (Serie A top goalscorer award) in 1994/95 season, scoring 26 goals, playing for Fiorentina.

3.

INTER

THE CHERISHED CLUB

On 22 May, 2010, Inter had done it again. Under José Mourinho, they had won the Champions League final 2-0 against Bayern Munich at Madrid's Bernabéu stadium. After selling Zlatan Ibrahimovic to Barcelona the previous summer, the club had bought world class players in the form of Samuel Eto'o, Diego Milito, Wesley Sneijder, Lúcio and Thiago Motta – players who were good enough to win the triple in the 2009/10 season, in a team that was good enough to bear comparison with the team managed by Helenio Herrera in the 1960s.

Over the years, Inter has enjoyed great success. Helenio Herrera was the coach who led Inter to consecutive finals in the European Cup in 1964 and 1965. The blue and black Milan club became champions on both occasions, beating Real Madrid and Benfica in the respective finals. The strategy they employed was the defensive *catenaccio* and among the players were legends like Giacinto Facchetti and Sandro Mazzola. Then Inter were, as they would be again in 2010, the best in Europe.

It is enormous successes such as these, combined with occasional moments of disappointment, that have given the club its nickname, *Pazza Inter* (Crazy Inter). On the one hand Inter is the only Italian club to have played every season in Serie A. On the other, the team is seen by some as underachieving and for failing to manage and build on their great players and previous successes.

CLUB: FC Internazionale Milano

NICKNAME: I Nerazzurri (the Dark Blues), La Beneamata (the Beloved), Il Biscione (the Big Grass Snake) and Pazza Inter (Crazy Inter)

FOUNDED: 1908

STADIUM: Giuseppe Meazza, Milan (80,018 capacity)

HISTORIC PLAYERS: Giuseppe Meazza, Lennart 'Nacka' Skoglund, Giacinto Facchetti, Javier Zanetti, Ronaldo and Christian Vieri

---

1. 1908–1928. After a schism in the Milan Football and Cricket Club (as AC Milan was then known) in 1908, when the club had forbidden any more foreign players from joining the team, an irritated group left to create Football Club Internazionale, a club where all foreigners would be welcome. Inter's first emblem was created by Giorgio Muggiani, one of the founders, and represented the club's initials. Blue is said to have been chosen as a counter to the red of AC Milan.

2. 1932–1945. With its generous attitude towards foreigners, Inter was not tolerated by Italy's fascist rulers and was forced into a merger and a change of name. The new name, Società Sportiva Ambrosiana, was adopted in 1928. The club crest was changed in the same year; this emblem, though, is from 1932, when Inter had re-assumed their original name after pressure from fans. At the end of the Second World War, both the old name and emblem were taken up again.

3. 1979–1988. In the 30 years that followed the Second World War, Inter switched between different crests, most of which were reminiscent of the earliest version. The grass snake appeared in an emblem from the 1960s, but it wasn't until 1979 that it was seriously included in the design. The snake, *Il Biscione*, came from the crest of the Visconti family who controlled Milan in the 13th century. Since then this animal has represented the dukedom of Milano, the aristocratic family Sforza, the car manufacturer Alfa Romeo, and Inter. The star has its origin in the club's 10th league title, won in 1966.

4. 1998–2007. Il Biscione had been gone for 10 years when the emblem was once more modified, after Inter's UEFA Cup triumph of 1998. The colours were radically changed, and for the first time the year of the club's founding was included.

5. 2007–2014 and 2014–present.
In 2007 Inter reverted to a
variation of the emblem that had
represented the club for much of
the '90s. Seven years later it was
updated again when the number of
circles was reduced, the colours
changed, and the letters modified.
The star was taken out, though it
still appears on match shirts.

Dennis Bergkamp signed for Internazionale in 1993. He stated that the club 'met
all my demands... the stadium, the people at the club and their style of play.'

1.

2.

3.

4.

5.

JUVENTUS

THE OLD LADY OF TURIN

Like a phoenix, Juventus rose out of the ashes of Calciopoli, the bribery scandal of 2006 that shook Italian football to its very foundations. Clubs such as Milan, Lazio, Fiorentina and Reggina were mixed up in it. Juventus as well. Italy's biggest and most loved club was vilified, even hated. Juventus's managing director Luciano Moggi was the spider in the criminal web and the club was punished with relegation to Serie B. Huge stars left the team double quick. By contrast, others stayed. Gianluigi Buffon, Pavel Nedved and Alessandro Del Piero chose to play on and help raise the 'Old Lady' back to the top flight, proof of the enduring attraction of the club.

Today, Juventus has reclaimed its throne. After the return to Serie A in 2007, the black and white Turin team showed that they were far from beaten by securing a third-place finish in the top flight. But it would take another four seasons before the club would again be crowned as League Champions, a 2012 title that was followed by several successive *Scudetti* (Serie A shields).

Juventus's popularity doesn't rest only on its success. Although the club was formed in 1897, the foundations for modern success were laid when Edoardo Agnelli, owner of the Fiat car company, bought the club in 1923. With the Agnelli family in charge, Juventus became Italy's first professional club, and strong bonds developed between the team and the workers at the car factory Mirafiori, built in 1939. As many southern Italians migrated north to Turin to work in the car factory, so the club's fame spread throughout the land. The esteem gained lives on and Juventus remains the best-supported club in the country. The black and white stripes of 'Juve' are recognisable globally.

The club's stability was reflected in the fact that the club crest changed little for seven decades. The one radical exception was from 1929 to 1931, when the bull of Turin was replaced by a zebra to reflect the team's nickname. The zebra returned for the 1980s before a revamp brought back the eliptical shape with the bull and the crown.

CLUB: Juventus FC

NICKNAMES: La Vecchia Signora (the Old Lady), La Fidanzata d'Italia (the girlfriend of Italy), I Bianconeri (the White and Blacks) and Le Zebre (the Zebras)

FOUNDED: 1897

STADIUM: Juventus Stadium,Turin (41,507 capacity)

HISTORIC PLAYERS: Giampiero Boniperti, Michel Platini and Zinedine Zidane

1. 1905–1979. Juventus's first emblem set the tone for future generations. Between 1905 and 1979 the club used several variations of the same logo. The crown and the rampant bull are taken from Turin's city crest, in which the bull has been a feature since the 14th century. The blue colour also has historic significance because this, too, can be seen in the city crest.

2. 1929–1931. For 70 years, with one exception, Turin's bull was the main element in Juventus's emblem. That exception came in 1929, at the suggestion of the journalist Carlo Bergoglio: in reference to the club's nickname, Le Zebre (the Zebras), a zebra took the place of the bull. The number of stripes was also increased, from seven to nine. In the beginning Juventus played, like today's Palermo, in pink and black, but in 1903 when the club needed a new kit, they ordered them from Notts County, where one member of the team, John Savage, had played.

3. 1979–1990. The zebra returned at the end of the '70s, and subsequently appeared in three different versions. The two stars were introduced in 1982, when Juventus won its 20th league title. Juventus was the first club in the world to use stars to symbolise the number of league titles, a practice they began in 1958.

4. 1990–2004. When the emblem was modernised in 1990, it returned to its roots. The bull and the crown were back, but now they were golden to symbolise glory.

5. 2004–2017. In 2004 Juventus employed the agency Interbrand to update the club crest. The result was in tune with the times: a highly stylised emblem, with the historic symbols toned down. Oddly the club name comes from the Latin word *iuventus*, meaning 'youth', which stands in stark contrast with the club's nickname: *La Vecchia Signora*, or the 'Old Lady'. The latter nickname originates from the early 1900s, when the supporters referred to the club as their 'lady'.

6. 2017–present. On 16 January, 2017, the Agnelli family shocked the whole world of football when they unveiled the new club crest. The bull and the crown were discarded and replaced with a stylised J. The logo met with a certain amount of scepticism. Supporters raged at not having been consulted and took to Twitter to say so. Criticism was also directed at the club's declared intention to establish the emblem outside football. The crest was adopted in July 2017, and came in two versions (black on white, and white on black). Like its predecessor, it was designed by the agency Interbrand.

1.

2.

3.

4.

5.

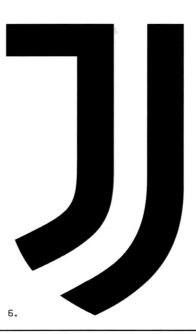

Alessandro del Piero in 1997 in Juventus' famous black and white stripes. Serie A *Scudetto* winners are permitted to use the tricolore or 'little shield' as a club crest to mark the previous season's championship win.

6.

LAZIO

THE TALE OF THE MISUNDERSTOOD EAGLE

Founded in 1900, SS Lazio has been criticised for its crest because the eagle in the emblem can be seen as a fascist symbol. It's an unfair accusation because the club was founded in 1900 and the bird was incorporated into its emblem 12 years later – almost a decade before Benito Mussolini founded the National Fascist Party, in 1921. The eagle, which stands for power, victory and success, was an important symbol in the Roman Empire, and this is what had influenced the club's choice.

Furthermore, the club demonstrated its rejection of fascism in 1927, when the fascist regime merged a number of the capital's teams to create AS Roma. Lazio was the only club to oppose the suggestion.

The club is famed for their light blue strip, colours that nod to the Hellenic inheritance that shaped ancient Rome. The club's most successful era's came with the appointment of Sven-Göran Eriksson in 1997. Under the ownership of Sergio Cragnotti, Lazio invested heavily in their playing squad and paid out large sums of cash in pursuit of success. Juan Sebastián Verón, Christian Vieri and Hernán Crespo were brought in within a few years and, helped by the inflow of global talent, the titles began to arrive. Between 1997 and 2001, Sven-Göran Eriksson led the team to seven trophies, a notable highpoint being the year 2000, when they won the double: *Lo Scudetto* (the Serie A title) and the Italian cup.

CLUB: S.S. Lazio

NICKNAMES: I Biancocelesti (the White and Sky Blues), Le Aquile (the Eagles) and Gli Aquilotti (the Little Eagles)

FOUNDED: 1900

STADIUM: Stadio Olimpico, Rome (70,634 capacity)

HISTORIC PLAYERS: Silvio Piola, Giorgio Chinaglia, Alessandro Nesta, Pavel Nedved and Giuseppe Favalli

1. 1912–1914. An early crest depicting the misunderstood eagle. Far from being a symbol of fascism, the crest is inspired by the Roman empire. The bird is also strongly associated with the Greek god Zeus, a fact that suited Lazio as the club's founders wanted to honour the legacy of ancient Greece. This also explains the derivation of the club's colours, white and blue.

2. 1914–1921. After a few years, 'Roma' was incorporated into the crest to clarify the team's origins.

3. 1927–1940. Although Lazio refused to become a part of the club created by the fascist regime in 1927, the club was forced to change their emblem that same year. At the centre of the crest, the eagle was replaced with the fasces, wooden sticks bundled together with an axe – the fascist symbol. Two years earlier, the club had changed their name to Società Sportiva Lazio from Società Podistica Lazio.

4. 1982–1987. From 1940 onwards a number of versions of the eagle appeared on the club crest. Perhaps the most popular emblem among supporters was the one introduced in 1982. Although this was during one of the club's dark periods, it was popular enough to make a comeback on match shirts in 2015, and would feature once more on the home kit in the 2017/18 season.

5. 1993–present. Today's emblem is a modernised version of the original club crest. The eagle rests once more on the blue and white shield, and it was under its sharp-eyed gaze that Sven-Göran Eriksson guided the club to their second ever league title, in the year 2000.

1.

2.

3.

4.

5.

Giuseppe Signori scored 107 goals in 152 games for *Le Aquile* (the Eagles). He was also the Serie A top goalscorer three times (1993, 1994 and 1996) while playing for the Rome club.

PALERMO

ITALY'S SOUTHERN EAGLES

Maurizio Zamparini, the former owner who led Palermo back to Serie A, was not a patient man. On the contrary, he was known for his explosive temper, his controversial statements and his ability to work his way through managers as if they were on a conveyor belt. From the time he bought the Sicilian club in 2002 to the summer of 2018, Zamparini changed managers more than 40 times, something reminiscent of his days as the owner of Venezia between 1987 and 2002. Among his questionable claims to fame, Zamparini can boast of being the only owner in the history of Serie A to have changed his head coach eight times during one season.

Palermo's fans and the club's eccentric owner had a love-hate relationship. On the one hand, the fans have suffered through Zamparini's destructive capriciousness. On the other hand, the club would not have made it to Serie A without him. Until then, the great Sicilian club Palermo had spent 31 years languishing in the lower divisions, most often in Serie B and occasionally even the third division. With the arrival of the businessman Zamparini came money and a vision that the club was good enough for Serie A. Players of the calibre of Luca Toni and Fabio Grosso were acquired, and it would take only two years under the new owner for Palermo to return to Serie A.

Thereafter the club experienced a roller coaster of seasons. Success, including European campaigns, alternated with major downturns and fights for survival in Serie A. In the end Zamparini would be the death of the club since it folded in 2019, after his departure due to lack of interest. They were made to restart in the lower tiers of Italian football.

CLUB: SSD Palermo
NICKNAMES: Rosanero (the Pink and Blacks) and Le Aquile (the Eagles)
FOUNDED: 1900
STADIUM: Stadio Renzo Barbera, Palermo (36,349 capacity)
HISTORIC PLAYERS: Santiago Vernazza, Roberto Biffi, Luca Toni, Andrea Barzagli, Edinson Cavani and Fabrizio Miccoli

1. 1920–1929. Despite the club officially beginning in 1900 under the name Anglo-Palermitan Athletic and Football Club, the first emblem announces that the team was in fact founded in 1898. In the beginning they used red and blue match jerseys. It wasn't until 1907 that they began to play in pink and black, inspired by the journalist Giuseppe Airoldi, who argued that the colours suited the uneven performances of the team, symbolising 'sorrow and sweetness'. Palermo's first emblem was blue and white because the club was inspired by the Argentine side Racing. Only in 1926 was it changed to pink and black.

2. 1982–1987. The eagle took its place in the club crest in 1947 and comes from Palermo's city crest. The bird was then modernised in 1982, by the owner Roberto Parisi, who wanted to put his mark on the club from the outset. This emblem was dropped when Palermo went bankrupt in 1986, in order to be re-formed the following year.

3. 1987–1991. Even after the bankruptcy the eagle came to play a central role in Palermo's emblem. This time it was white to symbolise purity and a new beginning. The emblem was the first to include the club's new name.

4. 1991–1995. In 1991 the owner Giovanni Ferrara presented this crest. The posture of the eagle is meant to symbolise Palermo striving upwards through the leagues.

5. 2000–2019. Two years before Zamparini's arrival, this emblem was introduced by then owner Franco Sensi, who also owned Roma. It was with this crest that Palermo lived up to the image of the eagle's upward thrust, with their promotion to Serie A in 2004.

6. 2019–present. When Palermo restarted in Serie D a new crest was designed with the famous eagle now integrated with the letter P. With the wings heightened as in flight, the eagle is no doubt a symbol of the club's upward ambitions.

1.

2.

3.

4.

5.

6.

PARMA

FROM SERIE A TO A VILLAGE LEAGUE – AND BACK AGAIN

Rarely is the essential transience of football so evident as when the fates of teams like Parma are discussed. This little North Italian club from the Emilia-Romagna region managed, during a 25-year period, to make their debut in Serie A, become Italian Cup holders, win four European titles, own some of the world's best players – and go bankrupt twice.

It took the club 77 years before they got to Serie A for the first time in 1990. Led by the coach Nevio Scala, and assisted by funds from the dairy giant Parmalat, the team were a surprise package with their sixth-place finish in the league. With that the club began a run of success, which culminated in European Cup finals and a runners-up place in Serie A. In April 2004, the story of this upstart team suffered a proper setback when the club went bankrupt.

The club was re-formed, and although they were without an owner for almost three years they managed, with relatively modest means, to retain a place in Serie A until the spring of 2008. Their subsequent stay in Serie B lasted only one year, and having re-established themselves in Serie A, Parma spent the five following seasons fighting for a place in the top half of the league. But instead of playing in Europe after securing their sixth place in 2014, Parma faced another financial crisis. Unpaid taxes triggered the collapse. Within the space of a couple of months, the club was banned from Europe, had points deducted in the league and changed owner twice. Nothing helped, the debts grew and in March 2015 Parma declared bankruptcy for the second time in 11 years.

That summer, Parma made a fresh start in Serie D, the Italian fourth division, with fixtures against village clubs like Clodiense instead of their old rivals Juventus. After a number of seasons of hard battling, they were promoted in 2017/18 to Serie A, ready to take on the best in Italian football once again.

CLUB: Parma Calcio 1913
NICKNAMES: I Crociati (the Crusaders), I Gialloblù (the Yellow and Blues), I Ducali (the Dukes) and Gli Emiliani (the Emilians)
FOUNDED: 1913
STADIUM: Stadio Ennio Tardini, Parma (22,352 capacity)
HISTORIC PLAYERS: Luigi Apolloni, Tomas Brolin, Gianfranco Zola, Hernán Crespo and Alessandro Lucarelli

1. 1970–2000 and 2001–2004. Believe it or not, Parma has been re-formed more than twice, including in 1970, when the Serie D club AC Parmense took over the bankrupt club Parma FC's licence in the Italian league. With this, Parma AC saw the light of day along with this new club crest. The blue and yellow stripes were taken from Parma's town crest, which features a blue cross against a yellow background.

2. 2000–2001. As a stage in a PR plan, Parma introduced a new emblem in 2000. They borrowed and modified the cross from the town crest, and the bull is an homage to Torello de Strada, a mayor of Parma in the 13th century. The supporters criticised this new logo and it was changed after one season.

3. 2004–2013. After Parmalat's crash and the club's bankruptcy, the team was reshaped as Parma FC. This crest, virtually identical to the earlier one apart from the initials, would represent the club for nine years.

4. 2013–2014. In spite of a turbulent history, Parma managed to celebrate their centenary with this anniversary emblem and by achieving a sixth-place finish in Serie A in the spring of 2014. But their joy was short-lived: the day after securing this place, the club was banned from Europe.

5. 2014–2015. This emblem was designed during the wait for a new owner. The crest would accompany the team to the grave with their bankruptcy of 2015.

6. 2015–2016. When the classic Parma began again in Serie D, it was with a new name and a new emblem, which had been chosen after a poll among the fans. The traditional symbols – the cross, the colours and the year of the club's founding – were retained.

7. 2016–present. One year after the bankruptcy, the club paid a little over £200,000 for the right to use this crest again, plus their old homepage and earlier social media accounts. Even if the shield is the same as before, the name at the top is different.

1.

2.

3.

4.

5.

6.

I *Crociati* (the Crusaders) have endured some seasons in recent years. In happier times, Gianfranco Zola lifts the UEFA Cup in triumph in 1995.

7.

ROMA

THE INHERITANCE FROM ROMULUS AND REMUS

They say that all roads lead to Rome. Unfortunately, this doesn't apply to football. The domestic titles have not ended up in the Eternal City but rather with the great northern clubs: Juventus, Milan and Inter. This was already true in the 1920s, when AS Roma was founded by the Italian fascist politician Italo Foschi to challenge their power. In 1927 he initiated a merger of three clubs in the capital: Roman FC, SS Alba-Audace and Fortitudo-Pro Roma SGS. The idea was to create a team strong enough to take on the northern football elite.

Initially the merger seemed effective. The newly born AS Roma came second in Serie A in 1931 and won its first league title in 1942. However, the club didn't manage to build the footballing empire that people had hoped for, one that would match the city's great past. Indeed, the club had to wait until 1983 before lifting the prize of the *Scudetto* again. This they did under the leadership of Nils Liedholm, who also led the club to three cup victories and the final of the European Cup.

Beyond the golden era of the '80s, Roma did not establish itself as a continuously successful top team in Serie A until more recent times. After the club's third *Scudetto* in 2001, they have often been fighting at the top of the table and have also picked up a couple of cup titles. All this with icons like Francesco Totti and Daniele De Rossi. But even so the clubs in the north are still not fearful.

1. 1934–1936 and 1936–1938. The first emblem that appeared on the kit was introduced in 1934. The crest featured the club's initials in the team's now classic colours. The image was modernised after two seasons, both the circle and the letters becoming broader.

2. 1937–1943. At the end of the '30s, a logo was designed that was used only for away games and up to 1943. Then followed 30 years when Roma did not continuously sport any emblem on their kit. The crest from 1934 turned up sporadically, and during some seasons there was a variant with 'AS Roma' spelled out.

3. 1978–1997. In order to bolster the sale of souvenirs and market themselves more efficiently, Roma introduced this club crest in 1978. The image represents the head of a wolf and is a gesture towards the city's history. According to myth, the brothers Romulus and Remus were saved and nurtured by a she-wolf. Romulus, of course, went on to found Rome.

4. 1997–2013. At the end of the last millennium, AS Roma returned to its roots when this crest was introduced, an emblem which the club had already used in 1928 – including on the season tickets. Then, as distinct from now, the club did not receive permission from the city to use the historic sculpture in the emblem. But in 1997 the parties came to an agreement and the club was able to use the image that they had wanted for decades. There are many copies of the statue of the she-wolf that nursed Romulus and Remus; the original is in the Capitoline Museums.

CLUB: AS Roma

NICKNAME: I Giallorossi (the Yellow and Reds), La Maggica (the Magical One), I Lupi (the Wolves) and La Lupa (the She-wolf)

FOUNDED: 1927

STADIUM: Stadio Olimpico, Rome (70,634 capacity)

HISTORIC PLAYERS: Roberto Pruzzo, Bruno Conti, Aldair, Francesco Totti and Daniele De Rossi

5. 2013–present. On 16 April, 2011 Roma acquired new proprietors from the United States. One of their departures was to give the emblem a makeover, which was carried out in 2013. Apart from the different look of the image, the initials were changed to 'Roma' and the foundation year was shown. The new crest met with an enormous amount of criticism from fans, who felt that the sculpture had been vandalised and was no longer faithfully copied.

1.

2.

3.

4.

5.

Starting in the early '90s, Francesco Totti played 619 games for the *I Lupi*, scoring 250 goals.

SAMPDORIA

THE SMOKING SAILOR OF GENOA

Sampdoria is one of Italy's more mythical football clubs although it was formed as late as 1946 through a merger of the Genoa clubs Sampierdarenese and Andrea Doria. The purpose was to create a counterbalance to the town's historically dominant team, Genoa CFC. As both Sampierdarenese and Andrea Doria played in Serie A, the new club UC Sampdoria could continue in the top flight. Out of respect for both clubs, Sampdoria was thus a fusion of their respective names, and Andrea Doria's blue and white colours were used as the base for the match shirts while the red and black stripes of Sampierdarenese adorned the chest. Sampdoria's emblem bore the image of Genoa's city crest, the cross of St George.

Sampdoria began with an impressive, if brief, period in Serie A, but the greatest successes were not achieved until the oil magnate Paolo Mantovani took over the club in 1979. In the era of Mantovani, Sampdoria were promoted to Serie A in 1982, the start of a golden age that would last just over 10 years. Sampdoria won the Italian Cup in 1985, 1988, 1989 and 1994 and managed the impressive feat of winning Serie A in 1991. The team also won the Cup Winners Cup in 1990 and played in the 1992 European Cup Final against the mighty Barcelona.

In 1980, Sampdoria adopted a new club crest featuring a pipe-smoking sailor called Baciccia – the dialect name for Giovanni Battista (John the Baptist), who happens to be Genoa's patron saint. This is one of world football's most striking crest designs.

1. 1946–present. The city of Genoa is represented by the cross of St George. Andrea Doria, one half of the club that became Sampdoria, wore both the shield and the cross from Genoa's city crest, a tradition that continued after the merger. The cross of St George has appeared on Sampdoria's match jerseys since the club was founded.

2. 1980–present. This may be one of the world's best known emblems, but few know what it actually portrays. The silhouette shows a bearded sailor in profile with a pipe in his mouth and a hat on his head – not illogical because Genoa is Italy's greatest port. The sailor is called Baciccia after the dialect name for Giovanni Battista (John the Baptist), Genoa's patron saint. Baciccia was an early symbol for Sampdoria but didn't appear on match shirts until the 1980/81 season. Since then, the smoking sailor has represented the club, though the placing of the emblem has alternated between the chest and the left arm. In 2009 the emblem was reported to an anti-smoking group in Italy, which felt that the pipe set a bad example for young people – a criticism that the then owner Riccardo Garrone dismissed. The pipe was allowed to stay.

CLUB: UC Sampdoria
NICKNAMES: I Blucerchiati (the Blue Hooped Ones), La Samp and Il Doria
FOUNDED: 1946
STADIUM: Stadio Luigi Ferraris, Genoa (36,536 capacity)
HISTORIC PLAYERS: Roberto Mancini, Attilio Lombardo, Sinisa Mihajlovic, Gianluca Vialli and Angelo Palombo

1.

2.

Roberto Mancini (left) and
Gianluca Vialli in Sampdoria's
colours in 1989. Note the
additional 'tricolore' cockade
or roundel on their shirts.
The current holders of the
Italian Cup are permitted to
wear this motif.

TORINO

THE BULL OF TURIN

Torino FC could have been a much bigger club than they are today. In the 1940s, 'Grande Torino' were considered one of the world's best teams. With players like Valentino Mazzola, Mario Rigamonti and Guglielmo Gabetto, they won five consecutive League titles between 1943 and 1949. (In the two seasons spanning 1944 and 1945, the league was suspended because of the Second World War). 'Grande Torino' were also the first to win the Italian double when they secured the league and cup in 1943. During this period, the core of the Italian national side was made up of Torino players. Indeed on one occasion the Italian national team took to the field with 10 Torino players.

But just as the team looked set to continue on their successful path, tragedy intervened. On 4 May, 1949, on the way back from a friendly in Lisbon, the team's plane crashed. Flying blind due to a heavy fog, the plane crashed straight into La Superga, a church in Turin. No one in the plane survived. Not only the entire squad, but both coaches, the team masseur, three journalists and two other passengers died. In all, 31 people lost their lives in the disaster.

Torino were forced to start from scratch, a laborious task that also entailed the club's first demotion to Serie B in 1959. Since then Torino have experienced both triumphs and misfortunes. The league title in 1976 and cup successes in 1968, 1971 and 1993 proved that the club was back in business. But on 9 August, 2005, Torino Calcio declared bankruptcy after years of financial mismanagement. Thanks to the new owner, Urbano Cairo, the club was able to start up again in Serie B and regain their old titles and thereby their history. In recent years, Torino have bounced back and forth between Italy's top two divisions, seemingly far removed from the club's erstwhile greatness.

1. 1983–1990. Torino's emblem has always incorporated a rampant bull, a symbol for the city of Turin. This crest is one of the most popular in the club's history and in 2013 was voted the world's most beautiful of all time by readers of *Guerin Sportivo*, the world's oldest sports magazine, whose headquarters just happen to be in Turin.

2. 1990–2005. Between 1990 and the bankruptcy in 2005, the club adopted this emblem as a tribute to 'Grande Torino', and this was the crest that the club had used during their golden age in the 1940s. The letters here stand for Torino Calcio, and this was the only difference between it and the original version, where the initials A, C and T stood for Associazione Calcio Torino.

3. 2005–present. When Torino Calcio went bankrupt, they created in its stead Torino FC, and in conjunction with this a new club crest was introduced. The rearing bull was kept, of course. A year later, just in time for the centennial, the year 1906 was added to mark the founding of the club.

CLUB: Torino FC
NICKNAMES: Il Toro (the Bull) and I Granata (the Clarets)
FOUNDED: 1906
STADIUM: Stadio Olimpico, Turin (28,140 capacity)
HISTORIC PLAYERS: Julio Libonatti, Lido Vieri, Giorgio Ferrini, Paolo Pulici and Marco Ferrante

1.

2.

3.

As Torino were reigning Serie A champions, this 1976 club crest combines the iconic raging bull and the Scudetto winners' 'tricolore' shield.

GERMANY

BAYER 04 LEVERKUSEN

THE PHARMACEUTICAL COMPANY'S PLAYTHING

It can't be easy to be known as the eternal runners-up. Just ask Bayer Leverkusen. The club bears the nickname *Neverkusen* because of their inability to win any titles. They have, in fact, won both the UEFA Cup and the German Cup, but it's the losses, the near misses for which the club is remembered. Bayer Leverkusen have finished in second place in the Bundesliga on a handful of occasions. Worst of all must be the 2001/2 season. Then, with players like Michael Ballack, Lúcio and Zé Roberto, the team finished second in the league, the cup and the Champions League. To rub salt in the wound, some of the club's German players also played in the team that lost the World Cup Final that summer.

Bayer Leverkusen's stamp as eternal losers is somewhat unfair if you consider the club's geographical conditions. With its 161,000 inhabitants, Leverkusen sits squeezed into the centre of North Rhine-Westphalia. The area borders Cologne with its million-plus inhabitants, and shouldn't really be able to measure up against the other clubs in the area, such as Borussia Dortmund, Schalke 04 and Fortuna Düsseldorf. The reason that little Leverkusen does have a top team in the Bundesliga is money. In Germany it's forbidden for any individual person or company to own 50 per cent or more of a club. This is in order to promote the influence of members over the sport. There are, however, exceptions and one of them is Bayer Leverkusen. The sports club was founded by workers at the pharmaceutical enterprise Bayer AG, so the company has been given special dispensation for their ownership, a fact which means that the club can be where it is today in spite of tough demographic conditions.

CLUB: Bayer 04 Leverkusen
NICKNAME: Werkself (the Company Eleven), Pillendreher (the Pill-Makers) and Neverkusen
FOUNDED: 1904
STADIUM: BayArena, Leverkusen (30,210 capacity)
HISTORIC PLAYERS: Thomas Hörster, Ulf Kirsten, Lúcio, Michael Ballack and Stefan Kießling

1. 1904–1907. As Bayer Leverkusen was formed by the workers at Bayer AG, it was self-evident that the emblem would refer to the company. Hence the globe, Bayer AG's traditional lion and the staff in its paw. The staff is called Kaducé and symbolises peace, trade and economy. It can be found in Greek and Roman mythology and is carried by both Hermes and Mercury (the same god in the respective mythologies). Not until 1907 was football incorporated into the club, and on Christmas Day in the same year the team played their first match with this crest.

2. 1950–1969 and 1969–1975. In 1923 the football section parted company with the club and was named Sportvereinigung Bayer 04 Leverkusen. Thirteen years later, in 1936, the players wore the Bayer cross for the first time, and this is now a well-known symbol for the club, the company and the town. The cross stands in the centre of Leverkusen and is hard to miss. The club crest was created years before it came to be used on the kit. It has appeared in a number of variations over the years, two of them shown here.

3. 1975–1996. In the middle of the '70s the club was represented by an unusual divided emblem. On the left is the Bayer cross and to the right the name of the club. Both the colour and text of the crest would be changed four times; this version represented the club between 1988 and 1996.

4. 1996–present. The lion from Bayer Leverkusen's first crest made a comeback at the end of the last millennium. But instead of one lion there were now two flanking the Bayer cross. The year of the club's birth is also shown. Soon after the presentation of this emblem the club experienced its golden era, securing four runners-up places in the Bundesliga in five years (1997–2002).

1.

2.

3.

4.

Michael Ballack was a driving force in taking
Bayer Leverkusen to the Champions League final
in 2002, where they were defeated 2–1 by Spanish
giants Real Madrid.

BAYERN MUNICH

PRIDE AND DOMINANCE

Bayern Munich's Bavarian motto *Mia San Mia* means 'We are who we are', which says a lot about the great German club. With a straight back and chest puffed out, Bayern has long nourished the myth about itself: the self-satisfied South German giant who knows what is best and acts accordingly.

Founded in 1900, the club has always represented the region of Bavaria rather than the city of Munich. The evolution of the crest reflects this: the lozenges are the blue and white of the Bavarian flag and prominent alongside the club colours of red and white. The four stars above the badge represent their 20 Bundesliga titles (they won their 28th in 2018). It is a crest that has become familiar across Europe thanks to their three successive European Cup triumphs from 1974 to 1976, and their two Champions League trophies.

The club actively fosters a sense of 'us against them': the Bavarian family against the rest of Germany. Bayern Munich has never been ashamed of being number one and has never been shy of buying the best players of their nearest rivals. Fewer people are aware of Bayern's more humble history. Before the Second World War, Bayern was a Jewish club, which made it a target for the Nazis. Bayern resisted and in 1934 a number of players were involved in confrontations with the Nazis. In the following years players and officials displayed acts of civil courage that were forgotten during the post-war era, but which have now been incorporated into its proud history.

CLUB: FC Bayern München

NICKNAMES: Der FCB, Die Bayern (the Bavarians), Stern des Südens (the Stars of the South), Die Roten (the Reds) and FC Hollywood

FOUNDED: 1900

STADIUM: Allianz Arena, Munich (75,000 capacity)

HISTORIC PLAYERS: Sepp Maier, Franz Beckenbauer, Gerd Müller, Karl-Heinz Rummenigge, Jürgen Klinsmann and Oliver Kahn

1. Bayern Munich was founded by members of the sports association MTV München. The club's first emblem was a blue and white flag — the colours of Bavaria — with their initials in the centre.

2. At the start of the 1920s, after a number of reorganisations, the club began to use their initials as an emblem. Unfortunately, there is some uncertainty about the exact year for this particular crest. In 1939, Bayern's legendary chairman Kurt Landauer, a German-Jewish veteran of the First World War, was forced to flee to Switzerland. He returned to the club after the Second World War.

3. 1961–1965, 1965–1970 and 1970–1979. The early '60s saw the design of the crest that came to be synonymous with Bayern Munich. Initially it was oval with the whole name written out, but the most important change was the blue and white geometric pattern in the centre. This was taken from the area's flag and crest, forming part of an emblem that would gradually change with the club's successes during the '70s.

4. 2002–2017. In the year the club secured the historic double (Bundesliga and Champions League), the emblem was modified again. The club crest is the result of a number of new departures, and this emblem was the first since 1970 not to include E.V. in the design. E.V. stands for *Eingetragener Verein*, which translates as 'registered association'.

5. 2017–present. In the summer of 2017, the world saw evidence of the meticulous German attitude to design and form, because that is when Bayern Munich changed the details of their crest. In an attempt to make it clearer, the font was renewed, the red colour became warmer, the blue darker, and the white Bavarian pattern now reached all the way to the edge of the circle.

Jürgen Klinsmann finished club top scorer in the two seasons he played for *Der FCB*. His goals secured the UEFA Cup (1996) and yet another Bundesliga title for the Bavarians.

1.

2.

3.

4.

5.

BORUSSIA DORTMUND

THE YELLOW WALL OF THE RUHR

Attacking football and low ticket prices create one of the highest average attendances in Europe – this is a popular team. Jürgen Klopp's arrival at Borussia Dortmund in the summer of 2008 heralded an upswing for the great German club. A Champions League final in 2013 and two Bundesliga titles under the charismatic Klopp made the world pay attention once more to Dortmund, a club that had been in the doldrums for a while.

Dortmund's earlier golden era reached its peak with victory in the 1997 Champions League sinal, with a lob from Lars Ricken over the head of the Juventus goalkeeper Angelo Peruzzi. This glorious period was followed by economic crisis, and despite winning the Bundesliga shield of 2002 the club suffered financial hardships. They were eventually saved by, among other measures, a loan from their rivals Bayern Munich. To survive in the long term, Dortmund needed to rethink and they now started to take a chance on homegrown talents. This policy led to the production of talented players such as Mario Götze, Marcel Schmelzer and Nuri Sahin, which led to Champions League success in 2013.

The club's simple yellow-and-black roundel badge carries the year the club was founded and the legend BVB – by which the team are commonly known in Germany). BVB stands for *Ballspielverein Borussia* (literally 'Ball games club Borussia'), although some fans insist it stands for *Borussen vom Borsigplatz*, or 'Borussia fans from Borsigplatz', after the city square where the club's founders drank the local Borussia beer at the restaurant Zum Wildschütz.

CLUB: Ballspielverein Borussia 09 Dortmund
NICKNAMES: Die Borussen, Die Schwarzgelben (the Black and Yellows) & Der BVB
FOUNDED: 1909
STADIUM: Westfalenstadion (Signal Iduna Park), (81,359 capacity)
HISTORIC PLAYERS: Michael Zorc, Karl-Heinz Riedle, Matthias Sammer, Mario Götze and Marco Reus

1. 1945–1964. On 19 December, 1909, Ballspielverein Borussia was founded by a group of young men who were dissatisfied with the management of the church team for which they all played. Although Borussia means 'Prussia' in Latin, the name was in fact taken from a nearby brewery. The club's first emblem was not adopted until after the end of the Second World War.

2. 1964–1974. After the league title in 1973, the club's badge was changed and the background rendered in black, a colour that suggested power, authority and strength. Whether the new design succeeded in frightening the opposition is debatable: the team won only one title in this period.

3. 1976–1978. In the wake of Eintracht Braunschweig's successful Jägermeister coup, which meant that the German rules for sponsorship agreements on the strip were relaxed, Dortmund decided to experiment with their badge. The club entered into an agreement with the tobacco company Samson which meant not only that the brand name would appear on the shirts but also that the emblem would change to the company logo. This was not a very popular deal with the fans. The fact that the team registered its greatest ever loss – 12-0 against Borussia Mönchengladbach – hardly helped.

4. 1974–1976 and 1978–1993. Two years after the lion's appearance, Dortmund reverted to using gold as the background colour in their emblem – a change that was implemented to the joy of their fans after the agreement with Sansom had run its course. This crest was the first in the club's history not to include the name Dortmund.

5. 1993–present. Today's emblem is near enough the same as the one from 1945, and differs only in the colour and in leaving out the name of the town. A simple badge with the club's initials and the year it was founded – it doesn't have to be any more complicated than that.

1.

2.

3.

4.

5.

Dortmund's Klaus Ackermann wearing the unpopular Samson tobacco-influenced club crest in 1976.

BORUSSIA MÖNCHENGLADBACH

THE GREAT PRUSSIAN CLUB

Although Borussia Mönchengladbach won the German Cup in 1960, that wasn't enough for them to gain a place in the first line-up of the Bundesliga in 1963. The club had to wait until the 1965/66 season, when they were promoted alongside Bayern Munich. Thus began a rivalry that defined German football for a decade. Bayern were the first of the two to win the league in 1969, but Mönchengladbach were quick to respond. In 1970 the club won their first league title and the following year they were the first to defend the Bundesliga shield. Led by the legendary coach Udo Lattek, Gladbach went on to lift the shield a further three times in the 1970s, a decade which also brought a runner-up place in the European Cup and four UEFA Cup final appearances, of which two ended in victory.

For a while, Borussia Mönchengladbach were one of the best teams in Europe, but harsh reality caught up with them in the 1980s. Financial problems meant that the club was forced to sell its best players. Bayern Munich took over as the dominant team in the Bundesliga while Gladbach slowly sank downwards in the table. They were gradually overtaken by their rivals, and in 1999 they were relegated. At that point, the iconic centre-back Patrik Andersson left a shattered Mönchengladbach team to move to Bayern Munich.

Founded in 1900 as FC Borussia, Borussia Mönchengladbach has been rejuvenated in recent years. This is thanks to the combination of the Borussia-Park stadium, inaugurated in 2004, wisely chosen coaches and the equally wise purchases of players.

CLUB: Borussia VfL 1900 Mönchengladbach
NICKNAMES: Die Fohlen (the Foals) and Die Borussen (the Prussians)
FOUNDED: 1900
STADIUM: Borussia-Park, Mönchengladbach (54,057 capacity)
HISTORIC PLAYERS: Jupp Heynckes, Berti Vogts, Allan Simonsen, Uwe Kamps and Marco Reus

1. 1900–1904. FC Borussia 1900 was founded in Prussia on 1 August, 1900, Borussia being the Latin name for the former kingdom. At this time the town was called München-Gladbach; the name Mönchengladbach was not adopted until 1960. Eicken is the part of the town where the club was formed and where they eventually played. The club's first emblem, which was also produced in inverted colours, includes an old-fashioned football.

2. 1904–1919. After a couple of years, the club's crest was simplified. The shield became slimmer while the club's initials formed the rest of the emblem. However, this logo didn't last long. Between this one and the classic version introduced in 1961, the question of which emblems Mönchengladbach used and why is not at all clear; the available information is contradictory.

3. 1961–1970. The diamond with the letter B is documented as far back as 1906, but it took some time before it became the club's official emblem. The diamond was originally black and white; the colours of green and white were taken at a later date from the flag and crest of the Rhineland. Mönchengladbach lies in the part of the Rhineland that is in Prussia.

4. 1970–1999. The club chose to go back to the original colour scheme, now placed against a green background. In this way the earlier emblem was combined with the original diamond. It was under this crest that Borussia Mönchengladbach experienced their greatest years in the 1970s.

5. 1999–present. After the relegation at the turn of the millennium, Gladbach underwent a facelift to inspire their fans. The green colour was removed and the emblem reverted to the diamond that has followed the team for about a century. The choice of colours may be inspired by the Prussian flag, which is black and white.

1.

2.

4.

3.

5.

EINTRACHT BRAUNSCHWEIG

THE ALCOHOL GIANT'S ADVERTISERS

Eintracht Braunschweig revolutionised German football in 1973 as the first club to display a sponsor on their shirts. Although it was allowed in France, Denmark and Austria, it was forbidden in the rest of the footballing world. At least until Eintracht Braunschweig cheated the system.

In 1972, five years after the club's surprising league victory, Eintracht were suffering financially because of the previous year's bribery scandal in the Bundesliga. The club needed help and started a collaboration with the alcohol giant Jägermeister: in exchange for sponsorship money, the Braunschweig players would display the company logo. In August 1972, this project was given the thumbs down by the German Football Association, which made Jägermeister's owner Günter Mast and Eintracht's chairman Ernst Fricke think again. Advertising on the kit may have been forbidden, but perhaps they could do something with the club crest?

In January 1973, members of the club voted through a proposal that meant that the club's red lion was exchanged for the stag's head of Jägermeister. Furthermore the emblem was given a central position on match shirts. The German Football Association was bewildered – and could do nothing because there were no rules concerning club crests. The only thing they could oppose was the size of the crest, which was not allowed to be bigger than 14 cm (5½ inches), so the referee Franz Wengenmayer measured Braunschweig's emblem when it was first used, on 24 March, 1973,. When the match kicked off, so began a new era in the history of fooball. Seven months later, approval was given for sponsors' names and logos to appear on match kits in Germany, and clubs including Hamburg, Eintracht Frankfurt, Fortuna Düsseldorf and Duisburg joined Braunschweig. UEFA took another nine years before approving sponsorship on shirts.

CLUB: Braunschweiger Turn- und Sportverein Eintracht von 1895
NICKNAME: Die Löwen (the Lions)
FOUNDED: 1895
STADIUM: Eintracht-Stadion, Braunschweig (23,325 capacity)
HISTORIC PLAYERS: Werner Thamm, Franz Merkhoffer and Paul Breitner

1. 1906–1920. Between 1895 and 1906, the club was represented solely by the city of Braunschweig's red lion, a symbol that harked back to the 14th century and which features in the city crest. In 1906 it was framed by the name of the club with the additional colours blue and yellow. These colours have a historic link to the region, coming from the flag of the province of Braunschweig.

2. 1973–1987. For nearly 50 years the club used four different emblems portraying the lion. But after the advertising coup with Jägermeister, a crest with the company's stag and its adjoining cross, flanked by the club's initials, started to be used. The only element remaining from earlier crests was the blue circle and the name of the club. In 1983 the brewing magnate Günter Mast took over the role of chairman and immediately proposed that the club be renamed Jägermeister Braunschweig. Although the members backed the proposal, it was stopped by the German Football Association, leading to the departure of Günter Mast from both club and football in 1985.

3. 1987–2012. With Jägermeister out of the picture, Eintracht Braunschweig returned to its roots and reintroduced the lion into its crest. The early colours were also brought back, but in place of the circle the heraldic animal was now framed by a square. This particular form was much criticised by fans.

4. 2012–present. At the end of 2011, the members of Eintracht Braunschweig voted through a change of their crest. Therefore, in March 2012, and much to the joy of many of their supporters, the classic emblem returned albeit with a modern twist.

5. 2016/2017. To celebrate the 50th anniversary of the club's only league title, the Braunschweig players wore this badge for the 2016/2017 season.

1.

2.

3.

4.

5.

With the Jägermeister brand embedded in the club badge, Eintracht Braunschweig were trailblazers in terms of using the club crest as a means to generate commercial revenue.

HAMBURG

THE SQUARES

Der Dinosaurier (the dinosaur) of the Bundesliga, Hamburger SV certainly lives up to its nickname. Until its relegation at the end of the 2017/18 season, HSV was the only club to have played every season in Germany's top flight since its founding in 1963. The club, formed in 1919 with the merger of three clubs, is also one of the most successful in the country with six league titles, three cup victories and a win in the European Cup – a trophy cabinet that means Hamburg can claim to be one of Europe's greatest clubs. During HSV's golden age, between 1976 and 1983, world stars like Kevin Keegan and Franz Beckenbauer graced the team.

The club crest in its various forms over the past 99 years has always been a visual representation reflecting the club's history and its host city of Hamburg. The first, following a merger of SC Germania, Hamburger FC and FC Falke Eppendorf, was a combination of the three clubs that became Hamburger SV. Quickly the old heraldic style was scrapped for a modern style of a black diamond inside a white diamond – the colours of SC Germania. The white diamond represented the marine Blue Peter flag, an homage to the port city of Hamburg.

1978 saw the crest modified slightly but still favouring the diamond motif, which means that *Der Dino* was the club in the Bundesliga whose crest has remained the most intact since the league's start in 1963.

Following relegation, it remains to be seen if the club can make a swift return to the top flight and recapture its glory days.

1. Hamburger SV was founded in 1919 through a merger of SC Germania, Hamburger FC and FC Falke Eppendorf. HSV has adopted 1887, the year of SC Germania's founding, as its own. The first crest was a combination of the three merged clubs, a badge that did not last very long.

2. 1919–1978. This emblem was introduced during the club's early days, and in time it became one of the most recognisable in the world. Although the club play in red and white, which are the colours of the city of Hamburg, they chose the white and black of SC Germania for the crest. In reference to Hamburg's seafaring traditions, the white diamond is inspired by the Blue Peter flag which means, 'All persons should report on board, as the vessel is about to proceed to sea.'

3. 1978–present. At the end of the 1970s, Hamburg's emblem was modified, the dimensions and colours changed. Apart from these modifications, not much has been altered since 1919.

CLUB: Hamburger Sport-Verein

NICKNAMES: Die Rothosen (the Red Shorts) and Der Dino (the Dinosaur)

FOUNDED: 1887

STADIUM: Volksparkstadion, Hamburg (57,000 capacity)

HISTORIC PLAYERS: Uwe Seeler, Felix Magath, Kevin Keegan, Sergej Barbarez and Rafael van der Vaart

1.

Kevin Keegan in 1978 showing off the simple yet striking Hamburg club crest, a design that pays tribute to the city's rich nautical heritage.

2.

3.

HERTHA BERLIN

CLEAN FLAG. CLEAN FOOTBALL.

Founded in 1892, Hertha Berlin has been the German capital's only continuous representative in the Bundesliga since its formation in 1963, something that ought to guarantee an influx of sponsorship money and an equal flood of incoming talent. On top of this, Hertha play in the country's second biggest stadium, the Olympiastadion, where an average of 50,000 spectators watch every home match. So why haven't Hertha Berlin – whose name and colours are inspired by a childhood trip on the steamer Hertha by one of the club's founder's – established themselves as a powerhouse in German football?

Hertha's history is marked by several dark periods. During the Hitler years German football was restructured, with the formation of 16 regional top divisions. Hertha achieved success with three league wins (1935, 1937 and 1944) under a Nazi flag; the club chairman, Hans Pfeifer, was a prominent member of the party.

It took until the creation of the Bundesliga in 1963 before German football could seriously pick itself up after the war. Hertha took part in the first Bundesliga season but were forceably relegated in 1965 after a bribery scandal. The club returned to the premier division in 1968, but three years later, in 1971, things took another serious downturn. Once again Hertha was involved in a match-fixing scandal, this time with debts running into the millions.

Thus, Hertha have never given themselves a proper chance to establish themselves as a real force in German football. After the latest bribery scandal, the club has played mainly in the premier division, although since 1980 they have spent a total of 17 seasons outside the top flight.

CLUB: Hertha Berliner SC
NICKNAMES: Die alte Dame (the Old Lady) and Die Blau-Weißen (the Blue and Whites)
FOUNDED: 1892
STADIUM: Olympiastadion, Berlin (74,475 capacity)
HISTORIC PLAYERS: Otto Rehhagel, Gábor Király, Arne Friedrich, Michael Preetz and Marcelinho

1. 1892–1923. Hertha Berlin was founded as BFC Hertha 92. Both the name and colours were inspired by a steamer: one of the club's founders, Fritz Lindner, had made an unforgettable trip as a boy on the steamer Hertha, its own name a variant of Nerthus, the fertility goddess of German mythology. The blue and white colours were taken from the boat's funnel. Hertha's first emblem survived until 1923, when the club merged with Berliner Sport-Club and was given its present name.

2. 1933–1948. The historic first flag was introduced the year that the Nazi Hans Pfeifer took over Hertha. This emblem represented the club until three years after the Second World War.

3. 1960–1968 and 1974–1987. At the start of the '60s this much discussed emblem was introduced, one that was rumoured to mimic the form of a disco ball in order to attract younger supporters. The crest was used for two relatively long spells.

4. 1995–2012. The flag has cropped up in different guises over the years. This emblem has been one of the more unpopular ones among fans because Berlin's name appears twice within the ring, since BSC stands for Berliner Sport-Club. In 2012, pressure from the fans led to its demise.

5. 1987–1995 and 2012–present. Hertha suppporters' dissatisfaction with the emblem that was used between 1995 and 2012 helped ensure the return of the unadorned flag that had previously represented the club. The director of sports Michael Preetz unveiled this emblem on the club's 120-year anniversary with the motto 'Clean flag. Clean football.' Not only did this choice reconnect the club with their history, it also pleased the fans.

1.

2.

3.

4.

5.

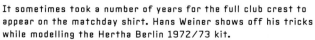

It sometimes took a number of years for the full club crest to appear on the matchday shirt. Hans Weiner shows off his tricks while modelling the Hertha Berlin 1972/73 kit.

1. FC KÖLN

THE CATHEDRAL AND THE GOAT

In the south-west part of the German federal state of North Rhine-Westphalia lies the financial metropolis of Cologne. With over a million inhabitants, Cologne is the cultural and financial centre of the area and this ought to bring the football club advantages over other clubs in the region. Despite initial success, however, FC Köln has fallen behind the local competition. While clubs like Borussia Dortmund, Schalke 04, Borussia Mönchengladbach and Bayer Leverkusen have made their mark in European football in recent years, Köln has swung back and forth between Germany's top two divisions.

Founded in 1948, FC Köln was a force to be reckoned with in the early days of the Bundesliga. They won the League in the first season (1963/640, collected another couple of league titles and four cup titles in the following years, and as recently as 1986 played in the UEFA Cup final against Real Madrid (losing 5-3 on aggregate). Though they haven't experienced recent glory, the club is blessed with one of the most iconic club crests in German football – with elements depicting the city's famous cathedral and the club's goat mascot, Hennes.

1. 1948–1950. FC Köln was founded relatively late. On 13 February, 1948, the clubs Kölner BC 01 and SpVgg Sülz 07 were merged to form 1. FC Köln. The two towers in the emblem depict the Kölnerdom, Cologne's famous cathedral, the 19th biggest in the world. The number 1 in the emblem is a German tradition signifying that the club was the first in the city, a position that is always a matter of pride in this country.

2. 1950–1960. On Köln's two-year anniversary – February 13, 1950 – the club was given a goat as a gift by a circus. The idea was that the goat would bring the team luck. FC Köln received the gift and named the mascot Hennes, after player-coach Hennes Weisweiler. The goat quickly became popular and later that same year was included in the club's emblem. The first time Hennes appeared on the team shirts was in the cup final against Stuttgart in 1954. Sadly, the years for this emblem are a little uncertain.

3. 1970–1980. Since FC Köln lost Hennes, other goats have come and gone – when one dies a new one is chosen. As for Hennes II, it is said that he was poisoned by fans from Borussia Mönchengladbach, Köln's arch-rivals, a rumour that has intensified the rivalry between the two clubs. The truth is that Hennes II was killed by a sheepdog in 1970. Like the previous emblem, it is not clear when exactly this one was used.

CLUB: 1. FC Köln

NICKNAME: Die Geißböcke (the Billy-Goats)

FOUNDED: 1948

STADIUM: RheinEnergie Stadion, Cologne (50,000 capacity)

HISTORIC PLAYERS: Wolfgang Overath, Toni Schumacher, Klaus Allofs, Thomas Häßler and Lukas Podolski

4. 1990–present. Since Hennes was included on the emblem there have been only minor alterations, which testifies to the status the mascot enjoys. Beyond joining the players for the team's home games, Hennes has his own label, his own brand of perfume, and also plays a murder victim in the German TV series *SK Kölsch*. Since the summer of 2014, Hennes VIII has been living in Cologne Zoo. Anyone who's interested can follow Hennes live via webcam on FC Köln's home page. In 2015 Hennes' celebrity status rose to new heights after a German PR agency projected FC Köln's crest onto the Hoover Dam. The image covered an area of 39,000 square metres (420,000 square feet), establishing a new world record.

1.

2.

3.

Thomas Häßler played for Köln for six seasons (1984–1990). He helped the Billy-Goats become Bundesliga runnners-up in 1989 and 1990.

4.

SCHALKE 04

THE MINERS

Schalke 04 is one of Germany's most popular football teams. Formed in 1904 as a result of the coming together of a number of sports clubs, the club drew many players and supporters from the coalmine workers of Gelsenkirchen, hence their nickname The Miners. Their greatest successes came in the 1930s and 1940s, but nearly 70 years later they were on the cusp of a momentous triumph.

On 19 May, 2001, the Parkstadion in Gelsenkirchen erupted. Ebbe Sand had just slid in his 22nd goal of the season, deciding the home fixture against the League's bottom team Unterhaching in the 89th minute. The league title was now almost theirs, the first since 1958. Schalke 04 just needed Hamburg to triumph over Bayern Munich, and with the northern Germany club leading 1-0 in the 90th minute, Schalke's players and some of the officials began to celebrate while several fans ran on to the pitch. But the match in Hamburg wasn't quite finished and just as those in the Parkstadion were celebrating Schalke's first title for 43 years, Bayern Munich were awarded an indirect free kick 8 metres (26 feet) from goal. Patrik Andersson scored with the last kick of the game. The score was 1-1 in Hamburg, and the Bundesliga shield ended up with Bayern Munich instead. The joy of the Schalke fans dissolved into sadness and tears. Their much longed-for League triumph had been cruelly snatched from them.

The hunt for a league title has continued and since 2001 Schalke have four times finished runners-up in the Bundesliga. In recent years, the club has become known for its youth academy, which has produced world class talents like Manuel Neuer, Mesut Özil, Benedikt Höwedes and Julian Draxler. Such a production line of talent would suggest that the long-sought league title may well be achieved one day.

CLUB: FC Gelsenkirchen-Schalke 04
NICKNAMES: Die Königsblauen (the Royal Blues) and Die Knappen (the Miners)
FOUNDED: 1904
STADIUM: Veltins-Arena, Gelsenkirchen (62,271 capacity)
HISTORIC PLAYERS: Klaus Fichtel, Norbert Nigbur, Klaus Fischer, Gerald Asamoah and Klaas-Jan Huntelaar

1. 1924–1929. Schalke 04 was formed in 1904 through a merger of Schalke Turnverein 1877 and Westfalia Schalke, but it was not until 1924 that football got its own section within the club. To mark the event, this emblem was created, which simply features the letter S and the numbers 04.

2. 1929–1945. Only a couple of years before Hitler came to power, Schalke unveiled this emblem. It was also during the Hitler years that Schalke 04 came to achieve their greatest successes. Six league titles and one cup triumph are just some of the trophies won by the club in this period, successes which led to the belief that Hitler was a Schalke fan – a suggestion that has been investigated and rejected by the club.

3. 1945–1958. Like many German clubs, Schalke was affected by the war even if the Gelsenkirchen team didn't have to change their name. The emblem was changed to revert to the club's classic blue and white colours, and a G for Gelsenkirchen was introduced into the crest.

4. 1995–present. In 1958 Schalke unveiled an emblem that celebrated Gelsenkirchen's coalmines and the miners who worked them. Hence the blue mining hammer, which serves as the background to the club's initials. This emblem has been updated three times. Today's logo was first used in 1995.

1.

2.

3.

4.

Ilyas Tüfekçi action for *Die Knappen* (the miners) in 1982/83. The blue mining hammer design is the same as today's crest but note that the badge carries an extra blue outline.

FC ST. PAULI

AMID CASTLES, SKULLS AND WHOREHOUSES

At one end of the Reeperbahn, Hamburg's red light district, and among the punks, prostitutes and bohemians, you will find FC St. Pauli, the German middle finger raised at the whole football establishment. Although the club lacks any titles, they have a massive fanbase stretching far beyond the country's borders. This is where, at the Millerntor-Stadion, the pirate flag the Jolly Roger sways next to the rainbow flag, an important symbol for the LGBT movement. Odd and different, they have been exiled and spat on. Transvestite, extremist or drug addict? It doesn't matter who or what you are, you are always welcome at FC St. Pauli. That is the message from St. Pauli, and it's one that is in tune with the area from which the club emerged.

That great trading metropolis Hamburg has a long history of economic prosperity. There, in the 17th century, poorhouses and hospitals were huddled together in an area called Hamburger Berg, a place for society's outcasts which would later be called St. Pauli. This came to be a haunt for dockers, ropemakers and sailors who came looking for a variety of pleasures, and it was here that the football club St. Pauli was founded on 15 May, 1910.

For a long time St. Pauli was a club like so many others, but in the early '80s they achieved cult status. At the time people would congregate around Reeperbahn and FC St. Pauli as a reaction against the fascist, extreme right-wing fans of HSV (Hamburger Sport Verein). Awareness of the club's anti-fascism and social activism spread, and in the space of only a couple of years the stands that had previously held perhaps a thousand fans were now packed. In footballing terms, St. Pauli are finding it incredibly difficult to establish themselves in the Bundesliga, but that leads to the obvious question: Is success really what they're all about?

CLUB: FC St. Pauli von 1910

NICKNAME: Freibeuter der Liga (the League's Freebooters)

FOUNDED: 1910

STADIUM: Millerntor-Stadion, Hamburg (29,546 capacity)

HISTORIC PLAYERS: Peter Osterhoff, Franz Gerber, Klaus Thomforde, Thomas Meggle and Gerald Asamoah

1. The sports club Hamburg St. Pauli Turnverein was founded in 1862, and the football section was formed in 1910. The club was named after the area, and the emblem portrayed the castle Hammaburg, borrowed from the city crest.

2. 1924–1947. The football section broke out in 1924 and formed FC. St. Pauli, which was reflected in the respective club logos. FC was spelled out in the emblem of the football team while the original read TV.

3. 1947–1998. Soon after the end of the Second World War, St. Pauli became Hamburg champions and so the club crest was updated. The castle looked the way it did in the original emblem, with the club's name and the year of its founding spelled out in a circle around it. This emblem existed in a number of variations throughout the second half of the '90s.

4. 1998–present. Two years before the new millennium, the logo was updated. A darker shade of brown and a lighter red were used. The emblem remains current and has been seen alongside the motto 'non established since 1910'.

5. The skull and crossbones, the Jolly Roger, has been seen at Millerntor since the '80s, when the club's supporters adopted it as a protest against the establishment. Since then the Jolly Roger has been an unofficial symbol for St. Pauli, and in the 2000/01 season it even appeared on the match shirts.

1.

2.

3.

4.

5.

Castles to skull-and-crossbones –
St Pauli fans with flags displaying
their team's various emblems.

VfB STUTTGART

THE PRIDE OF SWABIA

In just a few years VfB Stuttgart has gone from pole position – regular Champions League appearances and a Bundesliga title – to fighting for survival and bouncing between the two top tiers of German football.

In the spring of 2007, things were looking good: 250,000 people gathered in Stuttgart to celebrate a most unexpected league title. In a dramatic final game, the team had turned from being underdogs to victors and defeated Energie Cottbus 2-1, a win that gave Stuttgart their fifth league title and their first in 15 years. The team certainly relied on such key players as Pável Pardo and Thomas Hitzlsperger, but the outstanding fact was that 10 of the players in the squad had been brought on by their own academy. Among them were stars of the German national side, including Timo Hildebrand, Sami Khedira and Mario Gómez.

Since the Bundesliga shield was won, the club have been mired in chaos. Between 2007 and 2016 they went through 10 coaches, three managers and three presidents, a lack of continuity that threatens Stuttgart's position as Swabia's leading club. Here VfB has traditionally been the dominant force, even if Stuttgarter Kickers made a brave attempt to assert themselves around 1910. Now the map is being seriously redrawn. In recent years clubs like FC Augsburg, Hoffenheim and Karlsruher have challenged, and in some cases nearly overtaken, the old pride of Swabia. A shame, considering the club's promise.

1. 1912–1949. VfB Stuttgart was born through the merger of the clubs FV Stuttgart and Kronen-Klub Cannstatt. The emblem chosen was taken from the royal house of Württemberg and its crest. The shield, whose three black symbols represent antlers, has been documented as far back as the 13th century. They also appear in the logo of Porsche, the famous car company founded in Stuttgart.

2. 1993–1998 and 1998–2014. After the 1992 Bundesliga title, the crest was updated. The antlers were straightened and the background was given a different shade of yellow. The contours of the shield were changed from red to black and the style of the initials was clarified. In 1998, the same year that Stuttgart took part in the last ever Cup Winners Cup final at Råsunda in Stockholm, the emblem was changed again. The letter V was opened up and the year was replaced with 'Stuttgart'. The antlers were also further simplified.

3. 1949–1993 and 2014–present. After the end of the Second World War, when the German football league had been restarted, the club emblem was reworked. The former crest was incorporated in the larger shield, which also featured the initials alongside the year of the founding of FV Stuttgart, the forerunner of VfB. The emblem returned later, after 21 years' absence, thanks to its popularity among fans – a smart move from the newly elected club president Bernd Wahler.

CLUB: VfB Stuttgart 1893
NICKNAMES: Die Roten (the Reds) and Die Schwaben (the Swabians)
FOUNDED: 1893
STADIUM: Mercedes-Benz Arena, Stuttgart (60,441 capacity)
HISTORIC PLAYERS: Karlheinz Förster, Guido Buchwald, Jürgen Klinsmann and Krasimir Balakov

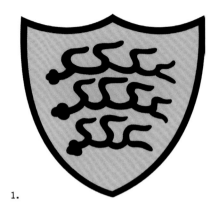

1.

2.

2.

A dejected Hans Mueller after VfB Stuttgart lose 3–2 to Schalke 04 in a German Cup match in 1978/79.

3.

VfL WOLFSBURG

THE WOLVES FROM VOLKSWAGEN

VfL Wolfsburg is a relatively young football club from a town that is not much older. The club was founded as the team of the Volkswagen factory, on September 12, 1945, just four months after the German surrender.

On 1 July, 1938, the Nazis founded the Stadt des KdF-Wagens bei Fallersleben, a purpose-built town to house the workers employed in the area's Volkswagen factories. This is where the Volkswagen Beetle was created, but during the Second World War, the factories produced military vehicles, both cars and planes, as well as other materiel for the German forces. To separate the young town from its history, the British decided after the end of the war to rename it Wolfsburg, a name taken from a local castle. The work in the factories changed direction and the town, the workers and the football team became inseparable. As the town grew, so did the club.

For a long time, VfL Wolfsburg played in Germany's lower divisions, making their debut in the Bundesliga only in the autumn of 1997. The team were tipped for failure but quickly established themselves in the top flight with the help of support from their owners Volkswagen. This facilitated the club's unexpected league triumph in 2009, helped by stars Edin Džeko, Grafite and Diego Benaglio. Today the town has over 122,000 inhabitants: 72,000 work for Volkswagen, and the team's home games attract an average attendance of 28,199.

1. 1950–1951. The club's first emblem was taken from Wolfsburg's town crest, which depicts a wolf and a castle. Castle Wolfsburg is close to the Volkswagen factory and is mentioned as early as 1302. Since then the castle has been rebuilt numerous times, but it remains one of the town's great sights.

2. 1951–1956. Between 1951 and 1956 a similar emblem was used along with the letters VfL, which stand for *Verein für Leibesübungen* (sports association).

3. 1956–1998. In the mid-1950s, the club created a completely new crest, a W in which the castle is suggested by the three towers. Between 1998 and 2002 a further two similar emblems were used, both with the castle represented.

4. 2002–present. On 16 July, 2002, Wolfsburg introduced an updated emblem, in which the circle framing the W is open at the top to symbolise the club's striving towards the pinnacle of German football. However, the emblem was much criticised by the fans, who objected to the removal of the castle.

CLUBS: VfL Wolfsburg

NICKNAME: Die Wölfe (the Wolves)

FOUNDED: 1945

STADIUM: Volkswagen Arena, Wolfsburg (30,000 capacity)

HISTORIC PLAYERS: Martin Petrov, Edin Džeko, Grafite, Zvjezdan Misimovic and Diego Benaglio

1.

2.

3.

4.

VfL Wolfsburg captain Waldemar Gust retrieves the ball from his own team's goal as they lose 4-0 to VfL Bochum in a 1970/1971 Bundesliga promotion match.

FRANCE

FC GIRONDINS DE BORDEAUX

THE CHEVRON-WEARING TRENDSETTERS

It is no secret that Paris Saint-Germain has dominated French football over recent seasons, thanks to the club's finances. It's a state of affairs that has attracted criticism in France, but nouveau riche clubs buying themselves titles is not news in the football world, and FC des Girondins de Bordeaux offers the proof.

In 1979, when Claude Bez, the property magnate and former club treasurer, took over the presidency of the club, Bordeaux had long been away from the spotlight. Les Girondins hadn't won the title for 30 years, and had even spent a couple of seasons in the second division – something that the visionary Claude Bez was determined to put right. Money was pumped into the club and suddenly Bordeaux were a team to be reckoned with. Between 1984 and 1987 they won the league three times and the French Cup twice, a feat which also meant that for a while Bordeaux would provide the backbone of the French national team. The success came at a cost, however, and in 1991 they were forcibly demoted because of their enormous budget deficit (around £45 million).

After the scandal, the club returned straight to the top tier in 1992. Since then players like Zinedine Zidane, Christophe Dugarry and Yoann Gourcuff have taken the team to further successes, albeit not quite as dramatic as those of the mid 1980s.

CLUB: FC des Girondins de Bordeaux

NICKNAME: FCGB, Les Girondins, Le Club au Scapulaire (the Club with the Chevron) and Les Marine et Blanc (the Navy and Whites)

FOUNDED: 1881

STADIUM: Matmut Atlantique, Bordeaux (41,458 capacity)

HISTORIC PLAYERS: Alain Giresse, Jean Tigana, Bixente Lizarazu, Zinedine Zidane, Ulrich Ramé and Christophe Dugarry

1. 1936–1955. The emblem of FC Girondins de Bordeaux has undergone several changes through the years. The first version was inspired by the rugby tradition, according to which several early teams wore a V on the front of their shirts. The symbol is now strongly associated with Bordeaux. The V-shape detail on the shirts is called le *scapulaire* after the sacred dress item that hangs around the neck, suggesting a V-shape, hence the nickname *Le Club au Scapulaire* (the Club with the Chevron). This shape has also been copied by several other football teams.

2. 1955–1971. Bordeaux is a port, so maritime symbols were included in the emblem in the mid 1950s. The anchor stands for the lively port and its importance for the city that lies on the river Garonne.

3. 1981–1993. In 1981, under Claude Bez, the football section was separated from the other sports in the club. They would now manage their own legal and economic affairs. At the same time, the club reverted to the original badge although it was now modified just for football.

4. 1993–2002. After their forced demotion in 1991, the club opted for a fresh start. They took the opportunity to update the design of the club badge, removing several elements, though le scapulaire remained. There was also a version of this badge in red.

5. 2002–present. In the beginning of the new millennium, another emblem was introduced. The colours were inverted from the previous ones and, possibly most importantly, the symbol from the city of Bordeaux was reinstated. The three interlaced crescent moons come from the city crest and have appeared in all emblems except one. The local association is clearly important for the club. The name Les Girondins refers to the department in which Bordeaux is situated: Gironde.

1.

2.

3.

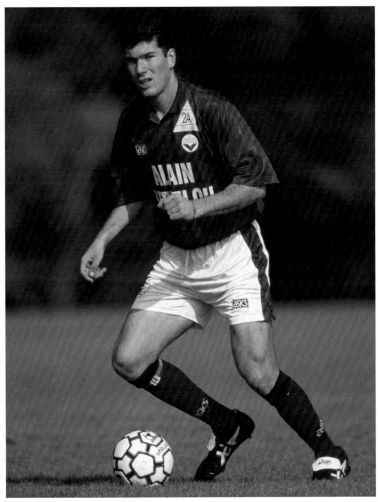

4.

5.

Zinedine Zidane wearing the famous chevron crest of Bordeaux. In his four years with the club the France midfielder made 139 apprereances and scored 28 goals. In 1996 Zidane received the award for Ligue 1 Player of the Year.

FC LORIENT

FISH AND FOOTBALL

In Northwest France lies Britanny, a region with its own history and language. It is also recognised for its football: Stade Rennais, Stade Brestois, En Avant de Guingamp and FC Lorient are teams that have each, in their own way, made an impression on French football. For Lorient, this includes a cup win in 2002, a triumph that would have been impossible a couple of years earlier.

FC Lorient was founded in 1926, but it wasn't until 1998 that the club made its debut in Ligue 1. Up to that point the team had led a rather anonymous life in the country's lower divisions. The journey upwards through the divisions began in 1991, when Christian Gourcuff began his second spell as coach at the club. The team won the third division title and reached Ligue 1 within six years.

The club's greatest success came, however, in the first year without Gourcuff at the helm. The 2001/02 season did end with relegation, but also with two cup finals. In the less prestigious league Cup, Lorient scrambled through to the final, where Bordeaux were too strong (Lorient lost 3-0). In the French Cup, however, the team were immortalised by beating Bastia in the final at the Stade de France – a title that wasn't just the club's first but would also take them into Europe for the first time.

Since then there have been no more titles, but the club managed to get themselves back into Ligue 1 in 2006, again thanks to Christian Gourcuff. They stayed there for 11 years before being relegated again in the spring of 2017.

1. 1994–2002. The fishing industry is important for Lorient, and since they were founded in 1926 their famous emblem has incorporated a fish. Up to 1994 the crest was diamond-shaped, but in the club's quest for Ligue 1 status, they reshaped the emblem in the mid-'90s. The number 56 refers to the département of Morbihan (département 56) where Lorient is located. The fish is a hake, *merlu* in French – hence the nickname *Les Merlus.*

2. 2002–2010. After the cup win in 2002, the club crest was updated. Several elements disappeared, the number 56 was removed and the club name FC Lorient Bretagne Sud was moved up, above the shield. The design of the circle, fish and ball was also updated.

3. 2010–present. In May 2010, the club introduced their third shield in the space of 16 years, because it had acquired a new owner, Loïc Féry. The hake looked quite different as did the shape of the crest. Féry explained that the new shape, which resembles a V (for victory), represents the history and ambition of the club. For the first time it showed the year the club was founded, and at the top the Breton flag, the Gwenn-ha-du. Other Breton clubs have also indicated their origins with similar symbols in their crests, including Stade Brestois, Stade Rennais and En Avant de Guingamp.

CLUB: FC Lorient-Bretagne Sud
NICKNAME: Les Merlus (the Hakes) and Le FCL
FOUNDED: 1926
STADIUM: Stade du Moustoir, Lorient (18,500 capacity)
HISTORIC PLAYERS: Christian Gourcuff, Jean-Claude Darcheville, Fabien Audard, Laurent Koscielny and Kévin Gameiro

1.

2.

Lorient midfielder Tchiressoua Guel in action in the French Cup in 2002. Against the odds, Lorient reached the final and triumphed 4–1 over Bastia in front of a 60,000 Stade de France crowd.

3.

AS MONACO

FRENCH FOOTBALLING ROYALTY

In the summer of 2013, after spending two dark years in the second division, Monaco returned to Ligue 1. Funded by the investment of owner Dmitry Rybolovlev, one star after another joined this well-heeled newcomer to the top flight, including James Rodríguez, João Moutinho, Ricardo Carvalho and Anthony Martial. The gamble aimed to make Monaco the leading club in France and take it back into Europe.

Historically speaking, AS Monaco, with a strong connection to the principality's royal family, are one of France's leading club's, as their eight league titles bear witness. The club takes the colours of the principality's crest, and the crown has adorned the club badge since 1949. One of their greatest successes came in 2004 when the club surprised the world of football by finishing Champions League runners-up behind Porto. With players like Fernando Morientes, Ludovic Giuly and Patrice Evra, Monaco had knocked out both Chelsea and Real Madrid on their way to the final.

The foundations of these successes were laid under Arsène Wenger's reign between 1987 and 1994. That was when Monaco became a great name in Europe. Led by top players like George Weah, Jürgen Klinsmann and Lilian Thuram, they won domestic titles and enjoyed success in the Cup Winners' Cup.

1. Today AS Monaco is closely linked to the principality and its rulers (the Grimaldi family), but this wasn't always the case. The club was founded without any official support from the ruling family, which is the reason why the first emblem did not include the now well-known crown. The colours – red and white – are taken from Monaco's crest. Unfortunately it is unclear when this emblem was first used.

2. 1949–2013. In 1949, when Prince Rainier III took over the crown of the principality from his grandfather Prince Louis II, much would change for AS Monaco. Prince Rainier III offered the club his family's support, and thus the crown was introduced into the emblem. The club's crest has changed through the years as both initials and colours have been altered.

3. 2013–present. The emblem was updated in time for the return to Ligue 1. For the first time ever, the name of Monaco was spelled out in full. 'The new logo shows our intention to lead Monaco into a new era, while the club will still be connected to its culture, its history and its roots,' said the club's executive director Konstantin Zyryanov when the crest was unveiled.

CLUB: AS Monaco FC

NICKNAME: Les Rouges et Blancs (the Red and Whites)

FOUNDED: 1924

STADIUM: Stade Louis II, Monaco (18,523 capacity)

HISTORIC PLAYERS: Jean-Luc Ettori, Claude Puel, Delio Onnis, George Weah, Lilian Thuram, Youri Djorkaeff and Thierry Henry

1.

2.

3.

Kylian Mbappe celebrates scoring for Monaco in 2016. The crown has adorned the club crest since 1949 when Prince Rainier III offered his family suppport for the club.

FC NANTES

PASSING SHIPS

FC Nantes have earned their place in French football history. The club was founded in 1943 in the middle of the Second World War, and it wasn't long before they were successful. Just 22 years after the foundation of the club they won their first league title, a triumph achieved under the guidance of coach José Arribas. With Arribas in charge, Nantes won two further league titles (1966 and 1973) and the League Cup (1965). They also developed a crowd-pleasing game that would become known as *le jeu à la nantaise* (the Nantes style of play). This club from the Atlantic coast charmed French football with their attacking strategy built on a quick, short-passing game and great mobility. During the 1980s and '90s the coaches Jean-Claude Suaudeau and Raynald Denoueix further developed this playing style, which was reminiscent of Barcelona's 'tiki-taka'.

In spite of the flattering comparisons with Barcelona, FC Nantes' story is not always a happy one. In 1992 the club was forced into a restructuring process because of its financial problems. They managed to get over this quite quickly, going on to win the league title in 1995. They secured another league title in 2001 (their eighth), but Nantes did not manage to build on their successes. Instead, they collapsed, and in 2007 they dropped out of Ligue 1 for the first time. While struggling with poor finances and shrinking attendances, Nantes, with their iconic crest, have managed to re-establish themselves in the top tier.

In the summer of 2019, the owner of FC Nantes, businessman Waldemar Kita, drew attention to himself by presenting future plans of a move into a new stadium as well as the introduction a new club crest. The news was met with huge criticism from the supporters and there were even demonstrations on the streets of Nantes.

CLUB: FC Nantes
NICKNAME: Les Canaris (the Canaries) and La Maison jaune (the Yellow House)
FOUNDED: 1943
STADIUM: La Beaujoire - Louis Fonteneau, Nantes (37,473 capacity)
HISTORIC PLAYERS: Henri Michel, Vahid Halilhodžić, Didier Deschamps, Claude Makélélé, Mickaël Landreau and Emiliano Sala

1. 1960–1970. The club's first emblem never appeared on the team kit, but it was used in other official capacities like the match programme. A sailing boat – a schooner, to be precise – was chosen as a symbol for the club since Nantes is a port.

2. 1977–1987. A simplified variation of the original crest was the first to be seen on team jerseys. The schooner is now turned the other way and the cross on the top of the mast has been removed. This emblem appeared in several versions between 1982 and 1986 with the colours inverted.

3. 1987–1997. At the end of the '80s a radically different emblem was introduced featuring a green wave taken from Nantes' town crest. The wave was initially decorated with six stars representing the club's six League titles. This particular version is from the years after the seventh league victory in 1995. The change of initials is due to the club adopting the new name FC Nantes Atlantique at the same time as the reorganisation of 1992.

4. 1997–2003 and 2003–2008. After 10 years with the green wave, the popular schooner returned. In 2003, several elements were removed when the emblem was updated.

5. 2008–2019. In August 2007, FC Nantes was bought by the Polish-French businessman Waldemar Kita. He immediately put his mark on the club by taking back the old name and also changing the crest. Kita organised a poll in the newspaper *Ouest France* in which supporters were asked to choose between three different crests. Of the 4,089 voters, 57 per cent chose this Barcelona-inspired version. The emblem includes important symbols like the ship and the number of league titles (represented by the stars). In the top right-hand corner there are five heraldic symbols: called *hermine* in French (ermine), they have their origin in Britanny. The yellow and green stripes represent the match jerseys that the successful team wore in 1995.

1.

2.

3.

4.

6. 2019-present. A total renovation of the crest which meant that popular symbols such as the ship and the colour green were removed. Instead the club were inspired by the city coat of arms which is seen in the new shape of the badge. The letter N, for Nantes, takes center stage, in a badge that is similar to the one of Juventus. Luckily the breton hermine is still there.

5.

6.

OLYMPIQUE LYONNAIS

THE LIONS FROM LYON

Olympique Lyonnais was founded in 1950 when a splinter group left Lyon Olympique Universitaire, the sports club of which the city's rugby team is a part of today. The newly formed football club, which adopted the rampant lion from the Lyon city crest, started out in the second division and success was a long time coming. The club did win the French Cup three times between 1964 and 1973, but it wasn't until the end of the '80s that they achieved serious success.

In 1987 the businessman Jean-Michel Aulas bought the club, which was then in the second division, with a view to taking it into Europe. He was as good as his word and two years later Lyon were playing in the UEFA Cup. Aulas invested huge sums in OL, but it was thanks to their own talents that the club came to dominate French football. Between 2002 and 2008, Lyon set a new French record by winning seven consecutive League titles, a feat achieved with the help of homegrown players Karim Benzema and Sidney Govou alongside inexpensive finds like Juninho Pernambucano and Michael Essien. Along with the burgeoning success, the club began to abandon their philosophy of nurturing talent and instead began to buy players for vast sums – a fatal decision that led to the club's fall from the pinnacle of French football.

Today Lyon is again recruiting domestic talent, and is well rewarded for it. The club have certainly found it hard to shift PSG, but with the help of their own gifted players they have managed to establish themselves once more as one of France's top teams. In 2014 the number of players nurtured by Lyon who were then playing in the five top European Leagues was surpassed only by Barcelona – testament to the fact that their philosophy works.

CLUB: Olympique Lyonnais

NICKNAMES: OL, Les Gones (the Children) and Les Rhodaniens (People of the Rhône)

FOUNDED: 1950

STADIUM: Parc Olympique Lyonnais, Lyon (59,186 capacity)

HISTORIC PLAYERS: Serge Chiesa, Grégory Coupet, Karim Benzema, Juninho Pernambucano, Samuel Umtiti and Alexandre Lacazette

1. 1950–1972. The club's first emblem borrowed the lion and colours from the Lyon city crest, both of these having great importance for the city. The lion has its origin in the 14th century, and in the crest it represents the city of Lyon itself. The club crest was created in the year that OL was founded and was barely modified over the subsequent 20 years.

2. 1972–1989. During the '70s, Lyon's mythical lion appeared in various versions, and here we see two of them. The lion, the football and the club's initials appeared in every emblem.

3. 1989–1996. Two years after his purchase of the club, Jean-Michel Aulas changed the Olympique Lyonnais emblem. The initials appeared in what was, for the time, a modern font and they were covered by the colours blue and red in the shape of a V, a pattern that the club had used on its match shirts.

4. 1996–2006. In the mid-'90s the lion made a welcome return although in a new colour. The football was now gone, but the name of the club was spelled out for the first time. This emblem was to signal Lyon's nascent dominance in French football.

5. 2006–present. After a decade the emblem was modernised: the colours were given a new tone while 'Olympique Lyonnais' was widened at the top of the shield.

1.

2.

3.

3.

4.

5.

Karim Benzema playing for Olympique Lyonnais in 2007 in a shirt carrying the latest club crest. Benzema made 112 club appearances for Les Gones between 2004–2009 and scored 43 goals.

OLYMPIQUE DE MARSEILLE

A CLUB THAT HAS LEFT THEIR MARK

The Southern French port of Marseille is a melting pot where fishermen, immigrants and refugees come together, a meeting place that is as beautiful as it is rough. But it is also a Mediterranean metropolis where OM, Olympique de Marseille, rule.

As unpredictable as they are successful and with a more impressive fanbase than that of PSG, OM are a mighty club whose presence and importance are evident wherever you are in the town. In cafés, shops and restaurants, on cars, buses and boats you can see the club's iconic crest, itself inspired by the personal seal of the original club founder. OM have marked their territory throughout Marseille and the people love the club.

Olympique de Marseille has become a sanctuary for supporters, and that is largely thanks to the club's former owner Bernard Tapie. Like the town, Tapie was himself multi-faceted: singer, businessman, actor and politician. In 1986 he bought OM, which only five years earlier had gone bankrupt, and in the space of just a few years turned them into one of Europe's top teams. Soon Jean-Pierre Papin, Eric Cantona, Rudi Völler, Chris Waddle, Abedi Pele and Didier Deschamps were playing in the team, a world class investment that led to the Champions League title in 1993.

The following year, the club were relegated and Tapie was jailed for corruption, but they bounced back and secured the Ligue 1 victory in 2009/10.

CLUB: Olympique de Marseille
NICKNAMES: OM, Les Olympiens (the Olympians) & Les Phocéens (the Phoenicians)
FOUNDED: 1899
STADIUM: Stade Vélodrome, Marseille (67,394 capacity)
HISTORIC PLAYERS: Gunnar Andersson, Josip Skoblar, Steve Mandanda, Chris Waddle, Jean-Pierre Papin and Didier Drogba

1. 1899. Olympique de Marseille was established at the end of the 19th century by René Dufaure de Montmirail as a club for fencing, billiards and rugby. The name Olympique was chosen to honour the town's history: the city of Marseille was founded by the Greeks around 600 BC. The emblem was taken from Montmirail's own seal, hence the letters D and M.

2. 1899–1910 and 1910–1930. The logo was changed during the first years of the club in order to reflect the club's initials and not the founder's. The motto *Droit au but* means 'Straight on goal' and is taken from rugby. In the emblem from 1910 the colours were changed and the letters intertwined.

3. 1930–1970. The crest was simplified through an Art Deco design and the removal of the motto. During this period Marseille won their first title in 1937, and this was also the era of the club's best-ever goalscorer, the Swede Gunnar Andersson.

4. 1970–1980. In the '70s, the tricky winger Roger Magnusson and the striker Josip Skoblar mesmerised French fans. Together they helped the team to three titles under this Art Nouveau-style crest.

5. 1980–1993. After 50 years the club motto came back, although it had appeared on match jerseys from time to time over the years.

6. 2004–present. Since 1993, and apart from today's crest which was introduced in 2004, five different emblems have been used. Now, for the first time, the motto appears below the club initials, and the letters are no longer intertwined. The star was introduced in the '90s and celebrates the Champions League title.

1.

2.

3.

4.

5.

DROIT AU BUT

6.

PARIS SAINT-GERMAIN

IN THE KING'S CRADLE

Zlatan Ibrahimovic, Ángel Di María, Thiago Silva and Neymar. Paris Saint-Germain have become synonymous with global stars and success, and the club have been the dominant force in Ligue 1 since Qatar Sports Investments bought the club in 2011.

During the 2011/12 season, Montpellier surprised everybody by winning the league, but it was only a matter of time before the capital's nouveau riche club would take over the driving seat of French football. With seemingly inexhaustible funds, great players were acquired, one after the other.

But Paris Saint-Germain have not always been such a powerhouse in Ligue 1. The capital fought for a long time over its footballing identity, and the birth of the club in 1970 did not mean that the romantic city was at once and miraculously transformed into a football-loving city. Eventually the club attracted legends such as Safet Sušic, George Weah and Jay-Jay Okocha, but the fact is that PSG was long known as the underperformer among the great clubs.

The Qatari billionaires recognised an opportunity when they saw that one of the world's most popular tourist destinations lacked a football club worth the name. Since the takeover, PSG has been rejuvenated, off the field as well as on. An early crest depicted a football and a ship, the latter taken from the city crest. In recent years, the crest has included respresentations of the Eiffel Tower and the fleur-de-lis.

CLUB: Paris Saint-Germain FC
NICKNAMES: PSG, Les Rouge-et-Bleu (the Red and Blues) and Les Parisiens
FOUNDED: 1970
STADIUM: Parc des Princes, Paris (47,929 capacity)
HISTORIC PLAYERS: Mustapha Dahleb, Dominique Rocheteau, George Weah, Ronaldinho, Pauleta and Zlatan Ibrahimovic

1. 1970–1972. No Paris club had won the league since 1936 when RCF Paris were crowned champions. Therefore a project was begun to relaunch top football in the French capital. Thus Paris Saint-Germain was founded in 1970 through a merger of Paris FC and Stade Saint-Germain. The club started out in Ligue 2, which they won in their first season. The emblem incorporates a football and a ship taken from Paris's city crest.

2. 1986–1987. The Eiffel Tower was introduced into the emblem in 1972 after Paris FC had broken away from the club. It would be interpreted quite differently during a season when PSG carried a logo referring to the city's candidature for the 1992 Olympic Games, an event that Paris sought but which would be awarded to Barcelona. The crest represents the Eiffel Tower in the French national colours.

3. 1992–1996. The French TV company Canal+ bought the club in 1991 and invested large sums in the team. Stars like Raí and David Ginola were bought, just as PSG and Marseille emerged as the country's greatest rivals on the football pitch. The new crest was received with horror by supporters who missed the previous symbols of local significance.

4. 1996–2002 and 2002–2013. In the mid-'90s, the old emblem made a comeback because of protests from fans. The crest was updated once more in 2002, when the colours were modified. Apart from the Eiffel Tower, the fleur-de-lis and the cradle of King Louis XIV were important symbols. The cradle was chosen because Louis XIV was born in St-Germain-en-Laye in 1638 while the lily is deeply rooted in French history. The colours red, white and blue have their origins in the French Revolution of 1789–99.

5. 2013–present. In order to improve the club's draw as a global brand, the new owners from Qatar separated the words 'Paris' and 'Saint-Germain', so that the former could be made more visible thanks to a larger font. At the same time the year of the club's founding disappeared as did Louis XIV's cradle, while the fleur-de-lis was given more space.

1.

2.

3.

4.

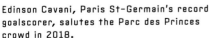

Edinson Cavani, Paris St-Germain's record goalscorer, salutes the Parc des Princes crowd in 2018.

5.

AS SAINT-ÉTIENNE

SLEEPING GIANTS

The world of football is full of sleeping giants and Saint-Étienne is one of them. A working-class club founded in 1919 by workers at the department store Casino, Saint-Étienne is one of the biggest and most successful clubs in France. This is the club where icons such as Michel Platini and Laurent Blanc have played, and the club dominated French football in the 1960s and '70s. In 1981 they hauled in their 10th title, an astonishing record that still stands. But then things started to unravel. In 1982, in the wake of the previous year's league title, Saint-Étienne was dragged into a financial scandal which ended with the imprisonment of the club's chairman Roger Rocher. Thereafter a team that six years earlier had come runners-up in the European Cup were now in freefall. Thus Saint-Étienne departed Ligue 1 in the spring of 1984. Over the following 17 years the team swung between the top two divisions, and chaos reigned. Another crisis erupted in 2001, when the club was again demoted in sensational circumstances: points were deducted for employing players with false passports.

In the autumn of 2004, Saint-Étienne made a much celebrated comeback to the top flight of French football and have since climbed up the table. With players like Blaise Matuidi, Dimitri Payet and Pierre-Emerick Aubameyang, the club succeeded in winning the League Cup in 2013, which suggested they were on their way back.

CLUB: AS Saint-Étienne
NICKNAMES: Les Verts (the Greens), Sainté & l'ASSE
FOUNDED: 1919
STADIUM: Stade Geoffroy-Guichard, Saint-Étienne (42,000 capacity)
HISTORIC PLAYERS: René Domingo, Hervé Rivelli, Salif Keïta, Michel Platini and Laurent Blanc

1. 1933–1940. Loyal to their home city, AS Saint-Étienne grew out of the workers' movement. Saint-Étienne is the region's working class town, while arch rival Lyon is associated with the upper classes. Fittingly enough the club was founded in 1919 by the department store chain Casino, which is based in Saint-Étienne. The first emblem was introduced in 1933, when football was professionalised in France. It's a simple logo with the club's initials printed in green against a white background, the colours of Casino.

2. 1940–1960. After seven years the colours were inverted when a new logo was introduced. However, the initials remained.

3. 1960–1970. Three years after the club's first league title, the emblem was changed once more. Instead of simply relying on the initials, they created a more traditional crest in the form of a shield. It was with this badge that Saint-Étienne began to dominate French football, securing four league titles during the 1960s.

4. 1970–1977 and 1988–1989. Between 1967 and 1972 a Malian striker called Salif Keïta played for the club. His nickname was *La panthère noire* (the black panther) and his popularity was such that the club included a panther in their emblem. Twice actually. Between the two panther logos, the club used two modern variations of the emblem from the '60s. Although these crests are dated, Keïta's heritage lives on in the club: the team's mascot is a panther.

5. 1989–present. After just one year with the second panther logo, Saint-Étienne launched this emblem. The club now made a connection to the earlier crests through the central placement of the initials and the green and white stripes. In 1994 the star on top was added to symbolise the team's 10 Ligue 1 titles.

1.

2.

3.

4.

4.

5.

STADE DE REIMS

CHAMPAGNE FOOTBALL

When we talk of France's greatest and most successful clubs, the names that spring first to mind are giants like Marseille and PSG, historic champions like Saint-Étienne and Nantes and today's high-fliers like Lyon, Bordeaux and AS Monaco. But the name Stade de Reims does also crop up: this is a club that deserve their place at football's top table, a club that has much to toast.

There aren't many French clubs that can boast two appearances in the final of the European Cup, as the Champions League was previously known. Between 1949 and 1962, the club dominated French football and won six league titles, two cups and was the first French team to get to the European Cup final. Once there, Reims lost against Real Madrid, in 1956 and 1959. During this period the team could boast some of the world's top players such as Just Fontaine and Raymond Kopa. But history tells us that all dynasties must eventually fall, and so it was for Stade de Reims.

In 1979 the club crashed out of the top league after a number of seasons of poor results, and the club needed a long time to recover. Instead of a quick comeback to the top flight, the club faced serious financial problems, declaring bankruptcy in 1991. Thereafter, Stade de Reims, this formerly great club, played football in the country's lower echelons, even for a time dropping into amateur leagues and playing at grounds more reminiscent of courtyards than the mighty arenas to which the club had long been accustomed.

Reims has a population of just over 200,000, a relatively small town in a footballing context, but was rehabilitated in football terms when the club re-entered Ligue 1 in 2013.

1. 1931–1991. Reims lies in the northern region of Champagne-Ardenne, the area that produces the world-famous wine, which is reflected in the club's first crest. The Stade de Reims predecessors, Société sportive du parc Pommery, played in yellow and green to resemble bottles of champagne, something that Stade de Reims never did; they favoured the red and white colour combination. This emblem was abandoned when the club went bankrupt in 1991. The club was subsequently re-formed under the name Stade de Reims Champagne, and a new logo was introduced – one that quickly disappeared, however, because a new French law restricted advertising possibilities for both alcohol and tobacco. This meant that Stade de Reims would be without an official crest between 1992 and 1999.

2. 1999–present. At the end of the last century, the club were promoted to the third division and they brought back the original name. This was celebrated with a new emblem, which connected to the club's glorious history by including the year of their founding. The letters S and R are simply the club's initials while the symbol between them refers to a famous sculpture in the town: *Le Sourire de Reims* (the Smiling Angel), on the external wall of Reims Cathedral.

CLUB: Stade de Reims
NICKNAME: Les Rouges et Blancs (the Red and Whites)
FOUNDED: 1931
STADIUM: Stade Auguste-Delaune, Reims (21,628 capacity)
HISTORIC PLAYERS: Robert Jonquet, Just Fontaine, Raymond Kopa, Dominique Colonna and Carlos Bianchi

1.

2.

Frederic Bulot in action for Stade de Reims against Monaco in 2015. The latest club crest depicts *Le Sourire de Reims* (the Smiling Angel), a famous sculpture found on Reims Cathedral.

REST OF
EUROPE

AIK

THE WORLD'S SMARTEST CREST?

'This is the f**king Champions League, not amateur football. Please take your responsibility seriously!' screamed the manager Stuart Baxter to the referee Alain Sars during AIK's Champions League match against Barcelona in the autumn of 1999. The reason for the coach's outburst was that the Spanish giants had just drawn level at 1-1 despite the home team carrying out a double substitution. With two fewer players in the penalty box, and taken unawares by the situation, it proved impossible to resist the mighty Catalans. Abelardo headed in Figo's corner, Baxter was sent up to the stands and moments later Barcelona had won the match 2-1. Even if the loss was scandalous, Stuart Baxter would forever be remembered by his supporters for his contribution to the proceedings, partly because his was a comment that echoed the AIK mentality.

AIK is one of Sweden's biggest clubs, in terms of successs and fan base. The Stockholm club's fans have long nurtured an 'us against the world' philosophy, which partly manifests itself in mottos like 'AIK against not-AIK' and 'We are not you.' These slogans reflect the club's self-image, but contrast with how they actually behave. In fact in recent years AIK has worked for integration through football and has thereby provided opportunities for players such as Alexander Milosevic, Robin Quaison and Nabil Bahoui. These were players who went on to represent the Swedish national team as well as to play abroad.

Today, with its highly complex crest depicting tradition (the towers), strength (the central beam) and the future (the sun), AIK is a club that stands for openness and togetherness – something seemingly at odds with their long-established claims to stand alone.

CLUB: Allmänna Idrottsklubben
NICKNAME: Gnaget (the Rodent)
FOUNDED: 1891
STADIUM: Friends Arena, Solna (50,653 capacity)
HISTORIC PLAYERS: Kurt Hamrin, Sven "Dala" Dahlkivst, Johan Mjällby, Daniel Tjernström and Ivan Turina

1. 1891–1898. Allmänna Idrottsklubben was founded in the Norrmalm area of central Stockholm on 15 Februrary, 1891. The football section was added five years later. The club's first emblem was a crest showing the full range of the association: the sports of fencing, rowing, fishing, shooting and cycling are all represented in the image.

2. 1898–present. At the end of the 19th century, AIK member Fritz Carlsson-Carling was given the task of redesigning the emblem. He set out to capture the three particular qualities of the club: tradition (the towers), strength (the central beam) and the future (the sun). The emblem is often misunderstood. For instance, the towers are asumed to be a crown, even though they are taken from the crest of Stockholm's patron saint, St Erik. Nor does the sun represent Solna (Solna is a name that gives appreciation to the sun in Swedish), where the team play, because this did not become a town until 1943, some 45 years after the emblem was created. Instead it references Sol Invictus (the Invincible Sun), a sun-god in ancient Rome. Finally the colours of the emblem are yellow and blue, not yellow and black as some people seem to think. The club crest was internationally recognised when it was proclaimed, albeit with little competition, as the world's most beautiful by Mr. John Bowmans sport's shop in London in 1934. Sadly history does not tell us whether this publicity led to the crest inspiring foreign clubs like the Italian Real Piedimonte or the English Chiswick Homefields FC.

3. The club crests of Real Piedimonte and Chiswick Homefield FC.

1.

2.

AIK's Eero Markkanen celebrates after scoring a hat trick in a 5–0 victory over KI Klaksvi in a 2017 UEFA Europa League qualifying match.

3.

AJAX

THE MYTHOLOGICAL HERO

When Ajax Amsterdam was created on 18 March, 1900, its founders were inspired by Greek mythology. Ajax fought in the Trojan War alongside Achilles and Odysseus, and is a hero of Homer's Iliad, one of the great literary works of Ancient Greece. He is described as physically imposing, a virtually invincible warrior, stronger than anyone else. The founders of the club may not have known it at the time, but the description undeniably fits the football club Ajax.

Yet it took 28 years after the club's foundation, in 1900, for the hero Ajax to be adopted on the club crest. Initially the emblem was an Ajax player in the club colours of red and white stripes. The player crest was slightly altered following the club's promotion to the top division in 1911 to match the club's new outfits, and it was only in 1928 that the helmeted head of Ajax was introduced. That remained until 1990, when a new abstract of the head of Ajax, drawn with just 11 lines to symbolise the number of players in a team, was launched.

Ajax is not just the Netherland's foremost football club, with an overwhelming number of league championships (more than 30). This club, the pride of the Dutch capital, is also one of Europe's greatest. It's true that today's team is not close to securing any cup successes on the Continent, but the club was once an outstanding presence in Europe. Led by that footballing artist and global star Johan Cruyff, Ajax won the European Cup three years running between 1971 and 1973. The club also won the Champions League as recently as 1995.

The success of the national team on the world stage has been disproportionate to the country's modest size, and Ajax has played a big part in this. With one of the world's leading youth academies, the club has fostered many Dutch internationals and world-class players. Such icons as Marco van Basten, Dennis Bergkamp and Christian Eriksen were forged by the club. The question is: which players of the future will live up to the name of Ajax?

1. 1900–1911. Unlike many other clubs, Ajax Amsterdam already had an emblem in the early years of the club, which simply showed a player. The club's colours – red, white and black – are taken from Amsterdam's flag, a flag that the Ajax captain traditionally wears as the captain's armband.

2. 1911–1928. The club crest changed when Ajax stepped up to the top division in 1911, and the player was given a new style of kit. Ajax was forced to make the change because the previous kit clashed with that of Sparta Rotterdam. The away kit didn't exist at the time – hence the birth of Ajax's classic home kit with a broad red stripe against a white background.

3. 1928–1990. In 1928, the mythological hero Ajax arrived on the crest. In its shape and colouring, the image represents a china plate, which was created for the club's 25th anniversary three years before.

4. 1990–present. After 62 years the club crest was modernised; the earlier one had proved difficult to exploit commercially. The portrait of Ajax was simplified and made more abstract. The gold stars represent Ajax's tens of Dutch Eredivisie league titles.

CLUB: AFC Ajax

NICKNAMES: de Godenzonen (God's Sons), de Joden (the Jews), I Lancieri (the Lancers) and Lucky Ajax

FOUNDED: 1900

STADIUM: Johan Cruyff Arena, Amsterdam (54,033)

HISTORIC PLAYERS: Sjaak Swart, Johan Cruyff and Marco van Basten

1.

2.

3.

4.

Marco van Basten in 1985 in the famous red stripe of Ajax, the dinstictive shirt design came about as as result of a kit clash with Sparta Rotterdam.

FC BASEL

BARCELONA'S SWISS COUNTERPART

That a Swiss club would inspire FC Barcelona sounds impossible today, but such was the case 100 years ago. In 1899 the former FC Basel player Hans Gamper (better known as Joan Gamper) founded FC Barcelona. Even if there is no proof that the great Catalan club's colours are taken from Basel, it is accepted that the Swiss club's kit did inspire Barcelona's now-classic claret and blue jerseys. In fact, this is partly what has made FC Basel famous. Another factor, of course, is their sporting prowess.

Historically the Zurich club Grasshoppers have dominated Swiss football. The team won the first domestic league in 1898, and up to 2001 had brought home the title 26 times, compared to Basel who at that point had not won the league since 1980. But then, at the start of the new millennium, things started to turn in Basel's favour as the club's new stadium, St. Jakob Park, was opened. During the first season in their new home, Basel won the league for the first time in 22 years. Thereafter the club established itself as number one in Switzerland with 12 titles in 17 seasons – a position of dominance underlined by the fact that they became champions eight years on the trot between 2010 and 2017. Their domestic supremacy was so emphatic that the club has appeared repeatedly in the Champions League.

The FC Basel club crest has changed very little in the club's long history and has long taken the form of a shield with the club intials shown in gold against the red and blue background.

1. 1893–1980. FC Basel kept its first club crest for a long time – 87 years, in fact. It consisted of the club colours, initials and a football. The colours mean a lot to the club and are referenced in the motto, *Rot isch unseri Liebi, Blau die ewigi Treui, Basel unseri Stadt* ('Red is our love, blue our eternal loyalty, and Basel our town').

2. 1980–2004. FC Basel and Barcelona share not only colours but also their initials. Furthermore the footballs in their respective club crests are virtually identical. In FC Basel's second emblem, the position of the ball has shifted and the letters and contours have been rendered in a more vivid yellow.

3. 2004–present. After the club's 10th league title, this badge was unveiled. The greatest change is the star, which symbolises that the club have been champions 10 times. Before the 2008/09 season, the histories of FC Basel and FC Barcelona were once again intertwined when the clubs changed match jerseys with each other. Basel's shirt, traditionally divided into two parts – half red, half blue – became striped like Barcelona's classic kit. At the same time the great Catalan club changed the design of their own match kit, dividing the colours into two fields, the way Basel's used to be.

CLUB: FC Basel 1893

NICKNAMES: FCB, Bebbi and RotBlau (Red and Blue)

FOUNDED: 1893

STADIUM: St. Jakob Park, Basel (38,512 capacity)

HISTORIC PLAYERS: Josef Hügi, Massimo Ceccaroni, Benjamin Huggel, Alexander Frei, Marco Streller and Mohamed Salah

1.

2.

3.

Numermous talented players have represented FC Basel, not least Egyptian striker Mohamed Salah in 2012-13. Interestingly, the club crest is worn in the centre of the shirt opposed to on the traditional left-hand side.

SL BENFICA

CURSED EAGLES

Football is not always easy to explain and therefore some odd myths can develop in the world's greatest sport. One of the best known is the one about Benfica and 'the curse of Béla Guttman'. In the early 1960s Benfica won two successive European Cup titles, and the football world was at their feet. Led by the famous Hungarian coach Béla Guttman, everything seemed possible for the great Portuguese club. But soon after they won the final against Real Madrid in 1962, there were some problems. Guttman left in protest after he was refused the pay rise he felt he deserved, and is supposed to have shouted, 'Benfica will not be European Champions for the next 100 years.' So far Guttman has been proved right, because since then the club has lost eight straight finals on the continent – five in the European Cup and three in the UEFA Cup/Europa League.

Even so, Benfica should never be underestimated – as both history and their fan base bear witness. Beyond the two European Cup triumphs, Benfica is Portugal's most successful club, taking into account the number of titles they've won and the size of their home support. The club crest has always shown an eagle called Vitória (Victory) and the only question is whether they can break Guttman's curse and be victorious again in Europe.

1. 1904–1908. Benfica was founded in 1904 under the name Sport Lisboa. The club's emblem was printed in red and white (the team colours) and crowned with an eagle. The great raptor is sitting on a scroll with the Latin text *E pluribus unum*, which translates as 'Out of many, one' – very fitting for a football team; it is, of course, also the unofficial motto of the United States.

2. 1906–1908. A contemporary of Sport Lisboa was Grupo Sport Benfica. Sport Lisboa was first and foremost a football club while Grupo Sport Benfica was a cycling club, which is seen in their crest with the bicycle wheel that supports the shield and the club initials.

3. 1908–1927. In 1908 the two clubs merged, forming Sport Lisboa e Benfica. Even the emblems were combined so that Sport Lisboa's crest lies in front of Grupo Sport Benfica's bicycle wheel. This crest remained like this with only small alterations for the next 20 years.

4. 1927–1999. Between 1927 and 1930 two new variations of the emblem were introduced, both of them including more colour. Between 1930 and 1939 there were no updates.

5. 1999–present. Before the turn of the millennium the club launched a new version of its emblem in which the eagle was given a more dominant place. The new design placed the bird above instead of in front of the wheel. The eagle, which is also the club mascot, is called Vitória (Victory). Since 2011 Vitória has flown around the Estádio da Luz before matches.

CLUB: Sport Lisboa e Benfica

NICKNAMES: Águias (the Eagles), Encarnados (the Reds) and Glorioso (the Glorious)

FOUNDED: 1904

STADIUM: Estádio da Luz, Lisbon (65,647 capacity)

HISTORIC PLAYERS: Eusébio, José Águas, Nené, José Torres, António Veloso, Mário Coluna, Rui Costa, Davd Luiz and Luisão

1.

2.

3.

4.

5.

Benfica icon Eusebio lashes home the first goal of the 1963 European Cup final. This is one of the 317 goals he scored for the Eagles in just 301 appearances.

BEŞİKTAŞ

THE LITTLE BROTHER IN ISTANBUL

It is easy to think that Turkish football is all about two clubs: the arch-rivals Galatasaray and Fenerbahçe. But that's to forget the country's oldest club, Besiktas. It's true that Galatasaray and Fenerbahçe have shared two-thirds of the titles since the establishment of the domestic league in 1959, but it's Besiktas that has presented the strongest challenge over the years.

Like Galatasaray, and unlike Fenerbahçe, Besiktas comes from the European side of the Bosphorus. In spite of their great successes the club has, in international terms, stood in the shadow of their local rivals. This does seem unfair because the club not only have the third most league titles but are also one of the three teams that have never dropped out of the top flight. (Galatasaray and Fenerbahçe are, of course, the other two.) Besiktas was also, after their league victory in 1960, the first Turkish team to take part in the European Cup.

In their black and white stripes, the Istanbul club have excelled off the pitch as well. The team's supporters are officially the world's loudest football fans. In a match against Manchester United in 2009, a volume of 132 decibels was recorded inside their then-stadium Inönü, a world record according to both UEFA and *The Guinness Book of Records*. Even so, Besiktas is seen as the little brother, not just in Istanbul but also more widely in Turkey. You wonder what they have to do to get proper recognition?

1. 1903–1930. According to myth and several written sources, Besiktas's first colours were red and white. After the Balkan War (1912–1913), when the Ottoman Empire lost vast stretches of land and an enormous number of soldiers, the club exchanged red for black to show its grief. The club deny this story and, in connection with their 100-year anniversary, presented proof that their colours had always been black and white. This is Besiktas's first crest. At the top is the name of the club in Arabic. On the right is the Arabic equivalent of the letter J, and on the left that of the letter K, the initials for Besiktas Jimnastik Kulübü (Besiktas Gymnastic Club).

2. 2000–present. In today's emblem the club's initials are at the top, and at the bottom is the year the club was founded. The half-moon and the star in the centre refer to the Turkish flag, a symbol with which the club was presented because it was the country's first sports association. There is also a hidden message in the crest. The white and black stripes form, together with the other elements in the logo, the year of the club's foundation in the Islamic calendar: the year 1319 in Islam corresponds to 1903 in the Gregorian calendar.

CLUB: Besiktas Jimnastik Kulübü

NICKNAMES: Kara Kartallar (the Black Eagles) and Siyah Beyazlilar (the Black and White)

FOUNDED: 1903

STADIUM: Vodafone Park, Istanbul (41,903 capacity)

HISTORIC PLAYERS: Rıza Çalımbay, Feyyaz Uçar, Les Ferdinand, Óscar Córdoba and Ricardo Quaresma

1.

2.

Beşiktas take on
Boluspor in Istanbul in
1981 on a very muddy
pitch. Such were the
conditions, the Beşiktas
club crest, with its
striking black and white
stripes, is barely visible.

CELTIC

THE IRISH HERITAGE

The emblem of Celtic is deeply connected to the Irish settlers in Scotland and to the country's Catholic population. During the first half of the 19th century, many Irish people moved eastwards, to Scotland and England. Between 1845 and 1852, emigration increased dramatically because of the famines in Ireland. The majority of the Irish immigrants to Scotland settled in Glasgow and there they became, as they were in the rest of the country, the new underclass.

Celtic was founded with the purpose of bringing some joy into the lives of the poverty-stricken Irish in Glasgow's East End. The immigrants were discriminated against because of their religion, their language and their origins, and Celtic quickly came to be an important part of their lives. Hence the Irish colours green and white and the Irish symbols. Celtic's first emblem consisted of the Celtic cross and this, along with the club's early successes, led to religious conflicts between the Catholic Celtic and their Protestant rivals, Rangers.

Today's club is linked above all to the four-leaf clover, but it wasn't until 1977 that the clover appeared on their jerseys. With the exception of the 100-year anniversary of the club's founding, when the Celtic cross made a welcome appearance, the four-leaf clover has remained Celtic's symbol ever since. The four-leaf clover, the Celtic cross, the Irish harp and the Irish flag are all symbols often to be seen at Celtic Park.

1. 1977–1995. Up to 1977 Celtic had been symbolised by the Celtic cross, the Irish harp and the three-leaf clover, which represents Christianity in Ireland. The Irish patron saint, St Patrick, is said to have used the three-leaf clover as a symbol for the holy trinity. The four-leaf clover is said to stand for luck and the four leaves represent faith, hope, charity and just luck. This emblem became the first one to be used continuously on Celtic's shirts.

2. 1987–1988. At the club's centennial the regular emblem was temporarily replaced with the Celtic cross, which was Celtic's original symbol and was said to have been created by St. Patrick. This crest was popular with the fans but was used for only one season.

3. 1995–present. In March 1994, the businessman Fergus McCann bought Celtic for £9 million and the club was modernised in various ways; the new home Celtic Park was built, and the club was turned into a limited company. The listing on the stock exchange brought with it the change of name: no longer 'The Celtic Football & Athletic Coy. Ltd.', but simply 'The Celtic Football Club'. The emblem also changed, and it also appears with the colours inverted.

CLUB: The Celtic FC

NICKNAMES: The Bhoys, The Hoops and The Celts

FOUNDED: 1887

STADIUM: Celtic Park, Glasgow (60,411 capacity)

HISTORIC PLAYERS: Billy McNeill, Pat Bonner, James McGrory, Henrik Larsson and Stiliyan Petrov

1.

2.

3.

3.

Roy Aitken wearing the 1986 version of the Celtic club crest. Roy Aitken ranks fourth in total number of appearances (682) for the Bhoys and won six league titles and six cups in his 15 years at the Glasgow club.

DYNAMO KYIV

THE TEAM WITH SECRETS

Dynamo Kyiv's history has been marked by political propaganda. Under the Soviet Union, several athletics clubs were created within the framework of various agencies: CSKA was the army team (CSKA Moscow); Lokomotiv was the transport ministry's team (Lokomotiv Moscow); and Dynamo was the intelligence service's team.

Emerging from Cheka, the Soviet secret police, the two Dynamo clubs, Kyiv and Moscow, soon became forces to be reckoned with alongside Dinamo Tbilisi. After the founding of the Soviet League in 1936, all of them were leading teams. It was not until 1961, however, that the league title came to the Ukrainian capital, a title that marked the beginning of the club's golden age. Between 1966 and 1981, Dynamo Kyiv won nine league titles. With these successes the club became the first Soviet club to take part in the European Cup – and a symbol for Ukraine. As a small part of the Soviet Union, it was difficult for the Ukraine to assert itself, but thanks to Dynamo Kyiv a significant proportion of the Soviet national team of the 1970s and '80s was Ukrainian. The club certainly helped put Ukraine on the map. After a total of 13 Soviet league titles, Dynamo Kyiv continued to dominate Ukrainian football following the country's independence in 1991.

Even if Dynamo has tougher domestic oppsition these days, the club has nurtured stars like Andriy Shevchenko, a player who walked in the footsteps of the legendary Oleh Blokhin and Valeriy Lobanovskyi.

CLUB: FC Dynamo Kyiv

NICKNAMES: Dynamo and Bilo-Syni (the White and Blues)

FOUNDED: 1927

STADIUM: Olympic Stadium, Kyiv (70,050 capacity)

HISTORIC PLAYERS: Valeriy Lobanovskiy, Oleh Blokhin, Andriy Shevchenko, Sergei Rebrov and Oleksandr Shovkovskiy

1. 1927–1939. When the first Dynamo clubs were founded in 1921, this emblem was created, one that was adopted by the Kiev club when it was founded in 1927.

2. 1972–1989. The club crest was radically changed in the early '70s. At the top they introduced the Cyrillic letters УРСР (for Ukrainian Soviet Socialist Republic). The original diamond shape was given a colourful background, which was actually the Ukrainian flag of the time, though sometimes the players displayed just the letter D.

3. 1989–1996. With the fall of the Soviet Union and newly won Ukrainian independence, the emblem was changed. The letter D remained but was now accompanied by the name of the city. The crest appeared in various colours; and yellow and blue were chosen as an homage to the new Ukrainian flag, which became official in 1992.

4. 1996–2003, 2003–2007 and 2008–2011. Under new leadership a new club crest was introduced in 1996. The diamond was changed to a circle and the year of the club's founding was added. The star was added in 2003 after 10 domestic league titles. Five years later the second star was added in memory of the 13 Soviet league titles.

5. 2011–present. 'We are returning to the basis of Dynamo Kyiv's history. When Ukraine became independent the club wanted to use yellow and blue in the emblem, but those are the colours of the national team,' said the club's owner Ihor Surkis when the new club crest was introduced in July 2011, a change opposed by a number of the legendary players.

1.

2.

3.

4.

Ukraine star Andriy
Shevchenko had two spells
at the Kyiv club (1994–1999
and 2009–2012) and won
the domestic league title
with Dynamo in each of
his first five seasons with
the club.

5.

FENERBAHÇE

THE GARDEN OF THE LIGHTHOUSE

The Strait of Bosphorus doesn't just connect the Black Sea to the Mediterranean, it also divides Europe from Asia. It cuts right through Istanbul, dividing the Turkish metropolis in two – and keeping the arch-rivals Fenerbahçe and Galatasaray apart. The academics' Galatasaray is to be found on the European side amid sights such as the Galata Tower, Hagia Sophia and the Blue Mosque, while the workers' club Fenerbahçe has the harbour area Kadiköy on the Asian side as their base. These roots in different social classes and parts of the world means that the rivalry between Fenerbahçe and Galatasaray seems inevitable.

Ever since the first national championship was organised in 1959, the atmosphere between the two Istanbul giants has been charged with animosity. Fenerbahçe were crowned the first national champions after beating Galatasaray 4-1 on aggregate. Then followed three consecutive titles, which laid the foundations for the club's successes.

But Fenerbahçe's history is not a wholly uncomplicated one. In 2011 the club won its 18th league title, but this would be overshadowed by a match-fixing scandal. The club was punished with a two-year ban from European competition instead of relegation – the correct punishment according to Turkish law. In October 2015, after a year in prison, Fenerbahçe's chairman Aziz Yıldırım and his colleagues were released on appeal. Fenerbahçe supporters rejoiced, but opposition fans around the country felt that the Istanbul club had been saved by Turkish President Recep Tayyip Erdogan, who had bent the rules in order to curry favour with the country's biggest group of fans – a huge addition to his electoral base.

1. 1910–1929. When the club was founded in 1907 in Kadiköy, its name and colours were taken from the local lighthouse: Fener means lighthouse and bahçe garden. Around the lighthouse grew daffodils, which are usually yellow and white, and these became the colours of the club's first kit. In 1910 Fenerbahçe player Topuz Hikmet designed the club's first crest.

2. 1929–present. After the Turkish language reform of 1928, when the Arabic alphabet was replaced with the European version, so the crests of several clubs were altered, among them Fenerbahçe's. The emblem was udpated in 1929 with Turkish writing (which has its origins in Latin), while the colours and symbols remained. The white circle, which carries the name, symbolises purity and openness. The red stands for love and the Turkish flag. Yellow represents the envy of their adversaries, and blue symbolises nobility. The oak leaf suggests the power within the club and the green bears witness to their success.

CLUB: Fenerbahçe SK

NICKNAMES: Sari Kanaryalar (the Yellow Canaries), Sari Lacivertliler (the Blue and Yellows), Efsane (the Legends) and Fener

FOUNDED: 1907

STADIUM: Sükrü Saracoglu Stadium, Istanbul (50,509 capacity)

HISTORIC PLAYERS: Zeki Rıza Sporel, Müjdat Yetkiner, Toni Schumacher, Rüstü Reçber and Alex

1.

2.

In terms of league titles, Fenerbahçe are Turkey's most successful club. Note the additional Turkish flag on Nicolas Anelka's shirt in 2005. This indicates that the Yellow Canaries are the reigning league champions.

GALATASARAY

THE ACADEMICS' CLUB

Istanbul, where the Bosphorus divides Europe from Asia, where cultures from different worlds collide, is also the seat of perhaps the greatest rivalry in world football. The eastern, Asian side of the straits, belongs to Fenerbahçe, the people's club. On the other, the European side, reigns Galatasaray, the academics' club, famous for welcoming its opponents to 'hell' (as their earlier home ground, the Ali Sami Yen stadium, was known) and which took Turkish football into the new millennium with their UEFA Cup triumph in 2000.

Galatasaray were born out of the university of the same name. This academic institution on the west bank of the Bosphorus has roots going back to the 15th century. Here Grand Viziers, prime ministers, diplomats, teachers and philosophers have studied. And this is where the sports club Galatasaray was founded in 1905, by the student Ali Sami Yen. The club grew and soon became a dominant force in Istanbul and thus Turkey. The domestic national league was first organised in 1959, by which time a rivalry was already well established between Galatasaray and Fenerbahçe – two clubs whose derby is considered one of the world's fiercest.

The yellow and red Istanbul club may have prospered at home, but European success was a long time coming. In the spring of 2000, Galatasary did at last secure their first European title. At the Parken Stadium in Copenhagen, before a capacity crowd and after a dramatic extra time, the Turks took Arsenal to penalties, which Galatasaray won 4-1 thanks to stars like Hakan Sükür and Cláudio Taffarel.

1. 1925-1929. During their early years, the club experimented with their emblem but were never really happy with it. Eventually in 1923 they proposed this badge, which shows the team colours and combines the Arabic letters gayn (in red) and šin (in yellow). The board approved and so this became Galatasaray's first official crest when it was adopted in 1925.

2. 1929-present. Some years later the club crest was updated. After the language reform in 1929, the Arabic alphabet was replaced with the European version, which opened the gates for Galatasaray to explore their academic origins. There is some confusion as to when the new emblem was first used and there have been a number of variations over the years. This is the current one. Even if the European letters have remained in the club crest since they were introduced, they echo the Arab version, emphasising Istanbul's geographical position between two worlds.

CLUB: Galatasaray SK

NICKNAMES: Sarı-Kırmızılılar (the Yellow and Reds), Aslanlar (the Lions), Avrupa Fatihi (Europe's Conquerors), Gala and Cimbom

FOUNDED: 1905

STADIUM: Türk Telekom Arena, Istanbul (52,652 capacity)

HISTORIC PLAYERS: Metin Oktay, Bülent Korkmaz, Gheorghe Hagi, Hakan Sükür, Didier Drogba and Wesley Sneijder

Arguabaly Galatasaray's greatest triumph to date, Hakan Sükür lifts the 2000 UEFA Cup trophy after the Aslanlar (the Lions) defeated Arsenal 4–1 in a penalty shoot-out.

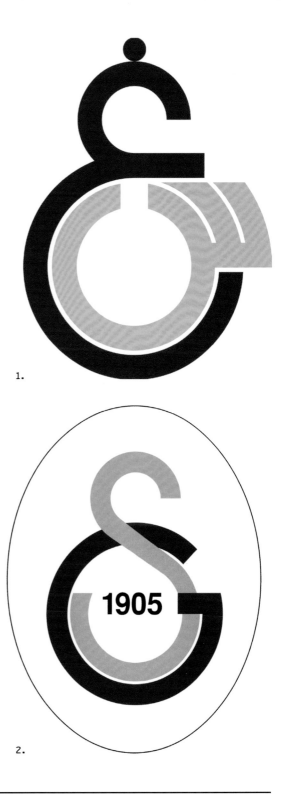

1.

2.

HEART OF MIDLOTHIAN

THE FOOTBALL BATALLION

Scottish football has been strongly defined by the rivalry between the two Glasgow clubs: Celtic and Rangers. But at the same time there have been other significant antagonisms in the country's rich footballing history, not least between the two great Edinburgh clubs: Hibernian and Heart of Midlothian.

As with the two Glasgow clubs, the rivalry between the two great sides in the country's capital city is rooted in their religious, ethnic and economic differences. The green and white Hibs is the club of the Irish Catholics, while Hearts is the team of the Protestant Scots – allegiances that are clearly evident in Hearts' emblem, the Scottish blue and white cross.

Beyond the Scottish colours, Hearts nurtures strong local connections. The name of the club and the emblem derive from a pavement mosaic in central Edinburgh. One of the capital's best known sites, it features the image of a heart, and bears witness to a grim historic location: the Old Tollbooth, the town's jail and place of execution. The prison was torn down in 1817 but lives on thanks to this mosaic and the football club Heart of Midlothian.

Historically, Hearts is one of Scotland's most successful clubs – despite suffering in modern times from relegations and threats of bankruptcy caused by foreign owners. Only the two Glasgow giants consistently better it.

1. 1995–present. From the founding of the club in 1874 until 1883, Hearts players wore a rust-coloured heart on their match shirts. In 1883 the emblem disappeared from their match kit and wasn't reintroduced until the 1977/78 season. A couple of modifications have been made since then, and today's emblem was unveiled in 1995.

2. 2014–2015. In time for the summer of 2014 and the the centennial of the outbreak of the First World War, Hearts introduced this emblem, a symbol honouring the Scottish army's sixteenth batallion, better known as McRae's batallion, an infantry force which largely consisted of volunteering sportsmen and their fans. Among them were 16 Hearts players and 500 club fans. McCrae's was the first of the war's so-called 'football batallions. The emblem adorned their home kit in the 2014/15 season and proved popular among Hearts supporters. Apart from the emblem, the sixteenth batallion was also voted into the Scottish Hall of Fame in October 2014.

CLUB: Heart of Midlothian FC

NICKNAME: Hearts, The Jambos and The Jam Tarts

FOUNDED: 1874

STADIUM: Tynecastle Park, Edinburgh (20,099 capacity)

HISTORIC PLAYERS: Gary Mackay, John Robertson, Jimmy Wardhaugh, Rudi Skácel and Craig Gordon

1.

2.

Reintroduced in 1977, Sandy Clark wears the Heart of Midlothian club crest in the 1986 Scottish Cup final against Aberdeen. While they lost on this occasion, the Jambos won the trophy in 1998, 2006 and 2012.

MALMÖ FF

FROM RED AND WHITE TO SKY BLUE

Malmö FF is Sweden's most successful club. MFF were at their peak in 1979, when they played in the final of the European Cup against Nottingham Forest. Along the way they had beaten AS Monaco, Dynamo Kyiv, Wisła Kraków and Austria Wien. In Munich the Englishmen were too strong and they won 1-0, but Malmö FF had shown what Swedish football can achieve. To date Malmö FF remain the only club from a Scandinavian country to have reached the final of the European Cup/Champions League.

This success is attributed to the English manager Bob Houghton, who revolutionised Malmö FF and Swedish football with new tactics and training methods. In 1985 another English manager, Roy Hodgson, led the club to five consecutive league titles. This was also the club that spawned stars such as Patrik 'Bjärred' Andersson, Stefan Schwarz and Martin Dahlin. Not to mention the greatest name in Swedish football: Zlatan Ibrahimovic.

In the distant past, Malmö have played in red and white, but the team is known for their famous sky blue kit. The present club crest made its debut in the 1940s and consists of a shield adorned with white and sky blue stripes and five towers. The club's full name was added when club chairman Eric Persson realised that people abroad were unable to identify the city form the club crest.

CLUB: Malmö FF
NICKNAMES: Di blåe (the Blues) and Himmelsblått (the Sky Blues)
FOUNDED: 1910
STADIUM: Swedbank Stadion, Malmö (24,000 capacity)
HISTORIC PLAYERS: Bo Larsson, Roy Andersson, Jan Möller, Patrik Andersson and Zlatan Ibrahimovic

1. 1910–unknown date. Malmö FF was founded in 1910 by members of the sports club BK Idrott, whose jerseys were blue and white. The emblem showed a football with the club's initials inscribed across it. The full name of the club, as well as the year they were founded, was written in the circle around the ball. It is unclear when this emblem was discarded.

2. At some point between 1910 and 1920 the emblem was changed. As with many other clubs at this time, a flag was chosen as the symbol. The ball from the previous crest was retained as well as the initials, even if now full stops had been introduced. The colours came from the team's kit; MFF played in red and white during the greater part of the 1910s.

3. 1920–1931. In 1920, MFF reverted to playing in blue and white and the emblem was given a makeover. The initials were still there, but this time they were placed within a shield. This crest would be used for a little over 10 years.

4. 1931–1970. At the start of the 1930s, the emblem was changed. The shield was given a new form and the colour became sky blue, the colour of the team's kit since 1920. A mural crown in silver also appeared at the top of the crest.

5. 1970–present. The club's legendary chairman Eric Persson, known as Hövdingen (the Chief), did not think the emblem was sufficiently recognisable abroad, so he added the name and the star below the shield. Zlatan Ibrahimovic began his career at Malmö, and when he joined PSG in the autumn of 2012, the emblem was projected onto Malmö's landmark building Turning Torso. The year before, a second star had been added as a symbol of the club's national league titles, something that provoked protest in some quarters as only 17 of these really counted. In Sweden, as in many other countries, one star resembles ten titles and therefore the upset.

1.

2.

3.

4.

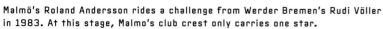

Malmö's Roland Andersson rides a challenge from Werder Bremen's Rudi Völler in 1983. At this stage, Malmo's club crest only carries one star.

5.

OLYMPIACOS

THE OLYMPIC IDEAL

Faithful to the history of its country, one of Greece's leading sports clubs was inspired by the basic values of Ancient Greece. The first Olympic Games were organised in 776 BC, in Olympia. The competition became a recurring tradition and would go on to inspire the modern Olympics, which were launched in 1896 in Athens. The Latin motto for the modern games is *Citius, Altius, Fortius*, meaning, 'Faster, Higher, Stronger'. Out of this motto emerged Olympiacos, one of Greece's foremost sports associations.

Olympiacos was founded in 1925 in the port of Piraeus, just outside Athens, after the merging of two former clubs. Although most of those present at that historic meeting were prosperous, the club soon gained popularity within Piraeus's working-class community. The team laid the foundations for their future dominance when they were undefeated for three consecutive seasons between 1926 and 1929 – an achievement that not only fostered the myth of Olympiacos but also provided the club with its nickname, *Thrylos* ('The Legend'). The early successes, including a further six league titles in the 1930s, set the tone for the remainder of the century. Today the red and white club is by some distance Greece's most successful in terms of league and cup titles.

While Olympiacos has struggled to match such domestic triumphs on the international stage, the club is one of five European teams who have made the most Champions League group stage appearances. But where the football section has so far failed, other parts of the association have stepped up and the club has won European titles in volleyball, water polo, wrestling and basketball – a breadth of achievement which fits well with the club's Olympic heritage.

1. When Olympiacos was founded, the club's first emblem portrayed a young athlete wearing a wreath of olive leaves that were awarded to winners in the ancient Olympic Games. The olive tree was associated with the god Zeus, while the athlete symbolised strength, morals, sportsmanship, the Olympic ideal and Ancient Greece. The precise years when these earliest emblems were used are vague, but it is certain that the club was given the emblem in 1925. This is one of the earlier versions.

2. 1995–2003 and 2003–2013. The club crest underwent a couple of changes, though the basic image, the wreathed Olympian, was retained. The look of the athlete, the placing of the year and the colours have all been subject to alteration, which we can see in these two versions.

3. 2013–present. The stars were introduced after Olympiacos' 40th league title in 2013, a star for every 10th championship. When the club was created, the colour red was chosen to convey courage and passion while the white represented innocence and morality. The name Olympiacos was adopted to honour Ancient Greece but also to attract supporters beyond Piraeus.

CLUB: Olympiakós Sýndesmos Filáthlon Peiraiós (Olympic Association of Piraeus Sportsmen)
NICKNAMES: Thrylos (the Legend), Erythrolefkoi (the Red and Whites) and Dafnostefanomenos (Those Wearing the Olive Wreaths)
FOUNDED: 1925
STADIUM: Georgios Karaiskakis Stadium, Piraeus (33,296 capacity)
HISTORIC PLAYERS: Giorgos Sideris, Giovanni, Predrag Djordjevic, Yaya Touré, Rivaldo, Javier Saviola, Esteban Cambiasso and Christian Karembeu

1.

2.

2.

3.

Olympiacos' Predrag Djordjevic under pressure from Juventus' Zinedine Zidane in the 1999 Champions League quarter-final. Having already recorded their best performance in the tournament to date, the Greek team narrowly missed out on a semi-final spot after conceding a goal in the final minutes of their second-leg match.

FC PORTO

THE UNVANQUISHED DRAGONS

For several years, the Champions League had been dominated by such giants as AC Milan, Real Madrid and Bayern Munich. As the riches grew within the sport, a surprise victory seemed ever more unlikely. On May 26, 2004, the tournament reached its finale at the packed Arena AufSchalke at Gelsenkirchen. The atmosphere within the venue was supercharged, perhaps because the final would not be contested by any of the usual titans of European football. Instead it was the suprise packages of AS Monaco and FC Porto who took to the field.

Didier Deschamps' Monaco took charge at once. The team created chances and put pressure on José Mourinho's Porto. But the Portuguese picked themselves up and Carlos Alberto scored the opening goal. A shocked Monaco, who had knocked out both Real Madrid and Chelsea en route to the final, saw themselves outmanoeuvred in the second half when Deco and Dmitri Alenichev added to the goal tally. The match finished 3-0 to the Portuguese club and the Champions League was well and truly shocked. Porto showed that success can not always just be bought, and at the same time they ushered in a new era for the footballing world – the era of José Mourinho. The charismatic coach had made his international breakthrough along with Deco, Ricardo Carvalho and Paulo Ferreira.

Porto are Portugal's second most decorated club and have won more than 75 major trophies, including 28 Primeira League titles. Known as *Dragões* (Dragons), from the mythical creature that is part of the club's crest, the club won five consecutive Primeiras between the 1994/95 season and the 1998/99 season.

1. 1900. Although FC Porto was founded in 1893 it took until the new century (the year 1900 is believed to be the correct date) before the club's first emblem was designed. It features the initials against a dark blue background. Blue and white became the club colours because they symbolise calm, innocence and serenity.

2. 1910–1922. The club crest was altered a couple of years later: for simplicity, a football was chosen as background to the club's initials.

3. 1922–2005. After a board meeting, a new version of the club crest was designed by the player Augusto Baptista Ferreira. He combined the club's earlier emblem with Portugal's national crest and what was then the city crest of Porto. The football was turned around and the initials were moved to make space for the new element. The long chain in the town crest represents a special Portuguese accolade, and frames the country's royal crest as well as Mary, who is holding the baby Jesus. At the top is the crown of the city crest, on which sits a dragon with a banner bearing the text *Invicta* (Unconquered).

4. 2005–present. The club crest was modernised at the beginning of the new millennium. The dragon remained, although it disappeared from the city crest in 1940. This is the mythological creature that has given the club their nickname Dragões (the Dragons), and the name of their stadium, Estádio do Dragão.

CLUB: Futebol Clube Porto

NICKNAME: Dragões (the Dragons) and Azuis e brancos (the Blue and Whites)

FOUNDED: 1893

STADIUM: Estádio do Dragão, Porto (50,035 capacity)

HISTORIC PLAYERS: Fernando Gomes, Rabah Madjer, Vítor Baía, Mário Jardel and Deco

1.

2.

3.

4.

With the club's joyously complex club crest on full dislay, Porto's Iker Casillas makes the decisive penalty save in a pre-season win over Valencia in 2015.

PSV EINDHOVEN

THE SUCCESSFUL FACTORY WORKERS

After being founded on the factory floor by workers at Philips, which was then a lightbulb company, PSV fought their way up to the very top of European football. With the electronics giant behind them and also lending them their name (Philips Sport Vereniging), little Eindhoven have become one of the great powerhouses of Dutch football. Alongside their rivals Ajax and Feyenoord, the club have dominated domestic football, an impressive achievement considering the challenges they have faced from the outset. Eindhoven has a population of around 220,000, a modest number compared to the millions living where their rivals play: Ajax in the capital Amsterdam and Feyenoord in Rotterdam, which is Europe's biggest port. PSV's greatest success came in 1988, when their team unexpectedly won the European Cup with players including Ronald Koeman, Hans van Breukelen and Eric Gerets. The manager was Guus Hiddink, no less.

After their triumph in Europe, PSV began buying up promising young talent, a strategy that would bring them a lot of success. Players like Romário, Ronaldo (Ronaldo Luís Nazário de Lima), Ruud van Nistelrooy and Arjen Robben all made their international breakthroughs here. As distinct from Ajax, who place great emphasis on producing their own talent, PSV are still investing in their scouting activities to find the stars of the future.

PSV and Philips have been inseparable since the club's birth in 1913. In the beginning only people from the firm could play for the team. When this rule was relaxed, new acquisitions were offered work for Philips alongside the football.

CLUB: PSV (Philips Sport Vereniging)
NICKNAMES: Boeren (the Farmers) and Rood-witten (the Red and Whites) and Lampen (lightbulbs)
FOUNDED: 1913
STADIUM: Philips Stadion, Eindhoven (35,000 capacity)
HISTORIC PLAYERS: Willy van der Kuijlen, Ralf Edström, Jan Heintze, Philip Cocu and Mark van Bommel

1. 1914–1917. PSV's first crest was created the year after the club was founded and featured its initials, PH, and 'SPORT' framed by the V – a design which, appropriately enough, is reminiscent of a light bulb.

2. 1917–1933. The design of the club crest was developed and in 1917 the club's roots were clarified. This time the light bulb couldn't be missed and within it the name of Philips is clearly visible. This emblem returned at the end of the 2015/16 season, when a special jubilee jersey was produced to celebrate the company.

3. 1933–2014. In the early 1930s, the emblem was created which would become closely associated with both PSV and Philips. The initials were placed in a flag, and this was in turn framed within a red and white shield. The colours were taken from the team kit. History suggests that one of the founders of the club, Jan-Willem Hofkes, liked the combination of his red raspberry drink and his white notebook – which is how they became PSV's colours. This emblem has been altered no fewer than eight times.

4. 2014–present. The year after PSV's centenary, the club crest was again updated, albeit modestly. The full stops between the initials were removed in 1990 and the year of the club's founding was introduced in 2013.

1.

2.

3.

PSV Eindhoven's Ronald Koeman battles for possession with Benfica's Rui Aguas in the 1988 European Cup final. The match ended 0-0 draw with the Dutch side eventually winning 6-5 on penalties to record their first European Cup success.

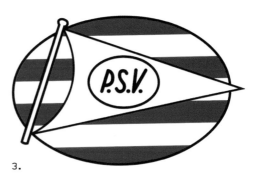

3.

3.

4.

RANGERS

ONE CLUB, TWO EMBLEMS

Scottish Premier League club Rangers is something of a rarity in football because it has two crests. One, in heraldic style with a lion rampant, is used on merchandise and official club documents; the second, a scroll version of intertwined club initials, is proudly worn on players' kit.

The scroll version is known to have been used with only minor changes from the 1881/82 season to the present day. This has been modified for special occasions such as in 2003, when Rangers won their 50th Scottish League title. Five stars, one for each 10 wins, were added.

On 5 April, 2016, four years spent in the wilderness were finally over for Rangers FC: they had beaten Dumbarton 1-0 before a packed and expectant Ibrox. James Tavernier became the hero who, with the crucial goal, ensured that Scotland's most successful club was back in the top league.

In July 2012 it had become obvious that the then 54-time league champions would be relegated for the first time ever. Money was the issue. Their debts amounted to well over £130 million and the club was being investigated for tax irregularities. Thus the holder of the world record in number of league titles had to make a fresh start in the country's fourth division.

In less than a year, Rangers went from playing against Manchester United at Old Trafford in the Champions League to away fixtures against Berwick Rangers and Annan Athletic. Even if Rangers broke records both in terms of points and attendances in the lower divisions, the club and Scottish football in general were damaged by the 2012 bankruptcy of this great footballing giant.

Therefore the return to the top tier of Scottish football was much desired. Celtic, who had won the title five times in a row, regained a challenger and the epic Old Firm derby was once more a feature of the league.

CLUB: Rangers FC
NICKNAMES: The Gers, The Teddy Bears, The Light Blues
FOUNDED: 1872
STADIUM: Ibrox Stadium, Glasgow (50,947 capacity)
HISTORIC PLAYERS: John Greig, Ally McCoist, Andy Goram, Brian Laudrup and Paul Gascoigne

1. 1968–present. There is no proof that Rangers' intertwined intials were included when the club was founded in 1872. The earliest evidence is a member's ticket from the 1881/82 season. In 1968, a modernised version of the club's original emblem made a comeback.

2. 1968–1991 and 1991–present. In 1959, Rangers changed the design and began to use the rampant red lion of Scotland's national crest, an important heraldic symbol for the region. Here it is shown against the background of a blue football. The motto 'Ready' was incorporated and the name of the club spelled out. The two versions here have represented Rangers since 1968 in media contexts and on various souvenirs; they have been used in parallel with the logo on club jerseys.

3. 1990–1994. In the first half of the 1990s, this badge was seen on the club shirts. It is a combination of the club's two emblems, where the initials from the one are linked with the name and motto from the other.

4. 2003–2012. In the spring of 2003, under the leadership of manager Alex McLeish, Rangers secured their 50th league title, which led to the club adding five symbolic stars to their emblem. This crest disappeared at the time of the bankruptcy, although a specially designed emblem with stars was used when the club, then in the fourth division, celebrated its 140th anniversary. Today the stars can be seen on the match kits once more, although the purer variant, with initials only, is the club's official emblem.

1.

2.

3.

4.

Rangers' Paul Gascoigne (front) celebrates with Davie Robertson after scoring against Aberdeen in 1996. His shirt club crest is the simpler design utilising the club's initials.

RED BULL SALZBURG

FOOTBALL AS A BRAND

Red Bull, the giant of energy drinks, knows the value of being visible. So the company has invested in extreme sports like rock diving and aerobatics as well as more conventional sports, owning stables, clubs and teams in horse racing, Formula 1, ice hockey and football. Dietrich Mateschitz, the Austrian founder and owner of Red Bull, discovered the value of football quite late. But once he did, the investment was dramatic. Within four years, between 2005 and 2009, Red Bull acquired five teams around the world: in the United States, Ghana, Brazil, Germany and Austria. The last two are particularly controversial.

In 2005, the great Austrian team SV Austria Salzburg were suffering financially. In spite of an illustrious history, with three league titles and a place in a UEFA Cup final, their money was running out. At this point Red Bull stepped in and bought the club. Austria Salzburg had previously carried sponsorship from Sparkasse, Casino and Wüstenrot, but this was something else. Under Red Bull, it was not only their name that was changed but also their colours and crest. The wild protests from the fans were ignored by the new owners. The name, logo and colours of Red Bull were now what it was all about – and the earlier purple and white of Austria Salzburg was just a memory. In protest the fans formed their own SV Austria Salzburg, a club that played in the second division as recently as 2016.

Even in Germany Red Bull has been criticised. There the company has not flouted a club's history in the same way but has instead been condemned for caring more about marketing than football. The organisation *Nein zu RB* ('No to RB') today includes supporter groups from across Germany.

1. 2008–present. Even though Red Bull's logo was introduced as late as 2005, it was updated only three years later to the design that we still see today. All the classic elements of the company are present in the form of the red bulls, the name in the same colour and the yellow sun.

2. 1998–2005. This is what Austria Salzburg's emblem looked like just before Red Bull changed it in 2005. The club was then playing under the sponsor name Wüstenrot. The emblem on the right was used in the UEFA Cup because of advertising regulations.

3. The fans' own club, SV Austria Salzburg, adopted an emblem based on the team's original emblem, which had been used from its formation in 1950 until 1978. The crest portrays the city centre and also appears in a version with the colours inverted.

4. In the United States, where franchising is commonplace, Red Bull did not provoke any criticism although the club got rid of anything relating to their predecessor, MetroStars. Like Salzburg, the New York branch has been using the same logo since 2008.

5. In Germany a club cannot be majority-owned by a company – rules from which Bayer Leverkusen and Wolfsburg, among others, are exempt. Red Bull has managed to circumvent these regulations, though. Neither Red Bull's name nor logo are featured, but the initials RB are included – standing, apparently, for *RasenBallsport*, which translates as 'Lawn-ball-sport'.

CLUB: Red Bull Salzburg
NICKNAME: Die Roten Bullen (the Red Bulls)
FOUNDED: 1933 or 2005 depending on how you see it
STADIUM: Red Bull Arena, Salzburg (31,895 capacity)
HISTORIC PLAYERS: Marc Janko, Eddie Gustafsson, Martin Hinteregger, Sadio Mané and Jonathan Soriano

1.

2.

3.

4.

5.

RED STAR BELGRADE

THE SYMBOL OF COMMUNISM

In the early 1990s, Eastern European football was still a force to be reckoned with. In the spring of 1991, war in the Balkans had not yet broken out and Red Star had made it to the European Cup final. The Belgrade club had gone through the tournament unbeaten, knocking out, among others, Rangers and Bayern Munich. The well-funded Marseille provided the opposition in the final at the Stadio San Nicola in the southern Italian town of Bari. Marseille were a team built around such global stars as Jean-Pierre Papin and Chris Waddle. Red Star consisted of unknown young players like Siniša Mihajlovic, Dejan Savicevic and Robert Prosinecki. The young Yugoslavs took the world of European football by surprise when they forced a penalty shoot-out, which they eventually won after Darko Pancev's decisive goal, an achievement that no other Eastern European side has managed since. The next year, 1992, the Champions League was formed and the war that was to see the break-up of Yugoslavia was already raging. The end of an era for Red Star.

In 1945, during the last months of the Second World War, a political anti-fascist group was formed, a sports association for young people. This would later become Red Star. At the end of the war the communist dictator Tito dissolved a number of football teams. Out of the ashes of one of these, SK Jugoslavija, Red Star rose to take over their stadium, premises and players. The club's name was chosen by the government. The communist symbol, the red star – which could also be found on the Yugoslavian flag – became the club's emblem.

CLUB: Red Star
NICKNAMES: Crveno-beli (the Red and Whites), Zvezda (the Star) and Delije (the Tough Guys)
FOUNDED: 1945
STADIUM: Rajko Mitic 'Maracana', Belgrade (55,538 capacity)
HISTORIC PLAYERS: Rajko Mitic, Dragan Dzajic, Vladimir Jugovic, Dejan Stankovic and Nemanja Vidic

1. 1945–1950. It was the Ministry for Sports that decided on Red Star's emblem. Hence the red star, which had symbolised communism since 1917. Alongside the hammer and sickle, the star was a powerful symbol for the Soviet Union. The crest was considered to be useful for the club, since it featured a symbol that also appeared in the national flag.

2. 1950–1995. When Red Star took over SK Jugoslavija, they also inherited their red and white colours, which were incorporated into Red Star's emblem five years after the club's founding. In Serbian, the team is called Fudbalski klub Crvena Zvezda and the two letters in the left-hand top corner are the Cyrillic versions of F and K. This emblem was used throughout the club's golden era.

3. 1995–2010. When countries like Croatia, Slovenia, and Bosnia and Herzegovina had declared their independence, only the name 'Yugoslavia' remained along with its colours – red, white and blue – with which Red Star clearly connected in this emblem.

4. 2010–present. The history of this great Serbian club is colourful and varied, having played over the years in the Yugoslav, the Serbia/Montenegro and Serbian leagues. All the titles count, however, which means that the club secured its 20th league victory in 1995. This was not noted in the emblem until 2010, when the two gold stars were added. By that time, they had managed to win five further titles. The club are far from the only one to wear the red star. Their sworn enemy and arch-rival FK Partizan use it, as do CSKA Moscow and the Paris team Red Star FC.

1.

2.

3.

4.

Red Star Belgrade's Robert Prosinecki running with ball in the 1991 European Cup final against Marseille. Red Star Belgrade won 5–4 on penalties.

SHAKHTAR DONETSK

THE MINERS FROM DONETSK

On 11 June, 2012 France played England at the Donbass Arena in Donetsk, the first of five matches in the European Championships to be played in the east Ukrainian city. It was a huge celebration for the locals and the matches were well attended. Two years later the stadium was in flames and the town's club, FC Shakhtar, was forced to flee. The Russian-Ukrainian War had broken out and redrawn the footballing map of the country. In the east, two separatist people's republics – both supported by Russia – were declared, including Donetsk. By contrast, the government in the west rejects the interference of Russia and insists that Ukraine should be united.

Life for the formerly pro-Russian club was untenable. The supporters were split. A majority of the fanbase belonged to the pro-Russian side: Donbass, the region where Donetsk is situated, historically looks towards Moscow. However, Shakhtar's owner, Rinat Akhmetov, somewhat unexpectedly expressed his support for a united Ukraine, and the club was forced into exile, basing themselves in the western city of Lviv.

To look beyond the club's precarious present state, Shakhtar have their origins in the Soviet coal industry. The first logo in 1936 incorporated a jackhammer, the miner's essential tool, lying diagonally across a red and blue hexagon. Later incarnations of the crest featured a drill tower, slag heaps and crossed hammers. From 2007, footballs have featured at the heart of the design.

This is a club with an impressive history – winning the UEFA Cup in 2009 – but it remains to be seen what the future holds for the Miners from Donetsk.

CLUB: FC Shakhtar Donetsk

NICKNAMES: Hirnyky (the Miners) and Kroty (the Moles)

FOUNDED: 1936

STADIUM: Donbass Arena, Donetsk (52,187 capacity) and Metalist Stadium, Kharkiv (40,003)

HISTORIC PLAYERS: Andriy Vorobey, Anatoliy Tymoshchuk, Darijo Srna, Willian and Luiz Adriano

1. 1936–1946. The first emblem of the Miners was created when the club was founded in 1936. As the club initially played under the name of Stakhanovets, in honour of the miner Alexey Stakhanov, the Cyrillic letter C (corresponding to our letter S) was placed in the middle of the shield.

2. 1946–1965. When, after ten years, the club changed its name to Shakhtar the crest was also changed. Again there was an obvious industrial reference with the drill-tower and the slag heaps, the latter looking like mountains at the base of the crest. 'WAXTEP' is the Cyrillic rendering of Shakhtar.

3. 1965–1989. In the mid-1960s, the classic miners' hammers were introduced into the emblem. Around them the whole name of the club is spelled out in Cyrillic lettering.

4. 1989–1997 and 1997–2007. When the club was reorganised in 1989 Viktor Savilov was hired to redesign the emblem. For the first time in Shakhtar's history an element was included which had something to do with sport. A football was placed at the centre of the crest and was framed in turn by a grass pitch. In 1997 the logo was updated and the colours from the match kit, which had been in use since the 1960s, were included.

5. 2007–present. In December 2007, Shakhtar introduced a new club badge. The miners' hammers, which had been absent for nearly 20 years, were brought back and for the first time the club name was written out in Ukrainian rather than Russian. Also included was the year of the club's founding. Shakhtar sought help from Interbrand (the same company that had earlier designed Juventus's emblem).

1.

2.

3.

4.

5.

Shakhtar's Brazilian midfielder Jadson celebrates after scoring against AS Roma in a 2011 Champions League match. The Miners reached the quarter-finals only to be beaten by the eventual tournament winners Barcelona.

SPORTING CLUBE DE PORTUGAL

THE LIONS OF LISBON

Luís Figo, Paulo Futre, Nani, João Moutinho, Ricardo Quaresma and Cristiano Ronaldo. These are just some of the international stars to be nurtured by Sporting Clube de Portugal. With such a successful youth academy, it is strange that Sporting haven't won more titles. The green and whites from the capital do count as one of the three greats of Portuguese football, alongside Benfica and FC Porto. However, rivals Benfica are the country's historically dominant club, while Porto has led Potugal into a new, more modern era of football – and Sporting have to make do with whatever's left.

Sporting has a haul of more than 40 domestic trophies, and yet this pales in comparison with the achievements of their rivals. The explanation is that up to 2018, with only two exceptions (Belenenses in 1946 and Boavista in 2001), the Portuguese league was only ever won by one of the Big Three: Benfica (36 wins), Porto (28) or Sporting (18). The same applies, pretty much, to the domestic cup.

Oddly enough, it's in modern times that Sporting has acquired its reputation as a loser. This in spite of the club having shaped world-class talents during the same period. After the league title of 1982, Sporting suffered their longest stretch without a title since the league was founded in 1934. It was 18 years before their next league triumph, in 2000. Since then the club, with a few exceptions, have played third fiddle on the west coast of the Iberian peninsula, a role that would have satisfied neither Luís Figo nor Cristiano Ronaldo.

NAME: Sporting Clube de Portugal
NICKNAMES: Leões (the Lions), Verde-e-Brancos (the Green and Whites), Sportinguistas and Sporting
FOUNDED: 1906
STADIUM: Estádio José Alvalade, Lisbon (50,095 capacity)
HISTORIC PLAYERS: Fernando Peyroteo, Hilário da Conçeicão, Héctor Yazalde, Luís Figo and Cristiano Ronaldo

1. 1907–1913. Sporting was founded in 1906 after a meeting that had taken place a year earlier in the seaside resort of Cascais. José Alvalade asked his fellow founder Fernando Castelo Branco if the club could adopt the lion rampant from the Branco family crest. Branco liked the suggestion with the proviso that the blue be changed. Thus green was chosen to symbolise hope.

2. 1913–1930. In 1910, Hugo Morais Sarmento moved from Germany to become Sporting's new goalkeeper, and brought with him a jacket decorated with various German badges. Three years later, the club chose to manufacture their new emblem in Germany. The lion was developed and framed by the name of the club. Who designed the new crest? Hugo Morais Sarmento.

3. 1930–1945. In 1923 the club started discussions to create a new logo. A special committee was formed to vote for the new crest, and seven years would pass before it was finally unveiled.

4. 1945–2001. After Sporting's second league title in 1944, a new club crest was created. Aside from a change in the shape of the shield, the club initials were moved to the top of the emblem like a crown. This emblem remained for 50 years and was popular with the fans.

5. 2001–present. To represent the club's efforts to achieve sporting and financial success, this emblem was unveiled in 2001. The club admits there was much debate about the name featured, because Sporting Lisbon is not the official name. To establish its correct name on the international stage the initials were retained at the top, and both 'Sporting' and 'Portugal' were spelled out on the shield. The white lion was made golden and the green and white colours were enhanced.

1.

2.

3.

4.

5.

Sporting's Beto celebrates after scoring in the quarter-final of the 2005 UEFA Cup. The Lions made the final, which was to be played at their home ground, Estádio José Alvalade, only to lose 3-1 to CSKA Moscow.

ZENIT SAINT PETERSBURG

THE ARROW FROM SAINT PETERSBURG

Russian national football got an international boost during the 2008 European Championships, partly thanks to the star from Zenit Saint Petersburg, Andrey Arshavin. The Russian national team, led by Arshavin, impressed, achieving success in their group and overcoming Holland in the quarter-final to reach the semi-final. Many of the players responsible for this success came from the reigning league champions – apart from Arshavin, there was Aleksander Anyukov, Konstantin Zyryanov, Roman Shirokov and Vyacheslav Malafeev, players who had shocked Europe earlier that spring by winning the UEFA Cup. Rangers had been easily brushed aside 2-0 in the final in Manchester, and Arshavin was named Man of the Match.

Between 2009 and 2015, the Northern Russian club won a further three league titles and never finished outside the top three. Hefty investments were made in the shape of established global stars like Hulk, Axel Witsel and Ezequiel Garay. Under coaches like Luciano Spalletti and André Villas-Boas, the team enjoyed several campaigns in the Champions League. But the life of the club hasn't always been so glamorous. Zenit was born out of the steel industry of Leningrad (as Saint Petersburg was then called) and for a long time they were unable to make an impact in the Soviet Union. The cup win in 1944 and the league title in 1984 were the only exceptions. After the fall of the Soviet Union, things improved thanks to money from Gazprom. The Russian gas giant took over Zenit in 2005 and has since then financed the club's successes.

CLUB: FC Zenit
NICKNAMES: Sine-Belo-Golubye (the Blue-White Sky-Blues) and Zenitchiki (the Anti-Aircraft Gunners)
FOUNDED: 1925
STADIUM: Krestovsky Stadium, Saint. Petersburg (64,468 capacity)
HISTORIC PLAYERS: Andrey Arshavin, Aleksandr Kerzhakov, Roman Shirokov, Anatoliy Tymoshchuk and Hulk

1. 1925–1936. Zenit's first emblem represented a flag with the club's colours, which symbolised the steel industry. Across the flag was written *Stalinets*, a word taken from the club's roots in the steel industry of Saint Petersburg.

2. 1940–1977 and 1978–1988. During the Second World War, the so-called Zenit arrow was introduced, alluding to the way the emblem was stylised. The crest was adopted when the club officially changed name to Zenit in 1939. Nearly 40 years later it was updated.

3. 1988–1991. When the winds of change blew in the Soviet Union, the club changed their emblem again. For the first time, a football appeared in the crest, and the golden ship on the Admiralty building of Saint Petersburg was depicted. From 1988 up to the fall of the Soviet Union in 1991, Leningrad was written on the emblem, but when the club won promotion to the top division, it read 'Saint Petersburg'.

4. 1998–2013. The club crest was updated in 1998 and the colours reverted to blue and white, while the ship was reduced in size.

5. 2013–present. On 11 July, 2013, Zenit's new emblem was unveiled at St Peterburg's steelworks, a symbolic act celebrating the club's origins. The new club crest was designed as a tribute to former times. A star was added in 2015 after the club's fifth league title. During the spring of 2015, Zenit got into a Twitter storm with the *Daily Mail* after the latter listed the team's logo as one of the 10 ugliest in the world. Zenit responded by declaring the *Daily Mail*'s emblem to be the ugliest in the world of newspapers.

1.

2.

2.

3.

4.

1925

5.

Andrey Arshavin celebrates after scoring against
Bayer Leverkusen in the 2008 UEFA Cup quarter-
finals. In a remarkable year, the Russian side won the
UEFA Cup and UEFA Super Cup, beating Rangers and
Manchester United in the respective finals.

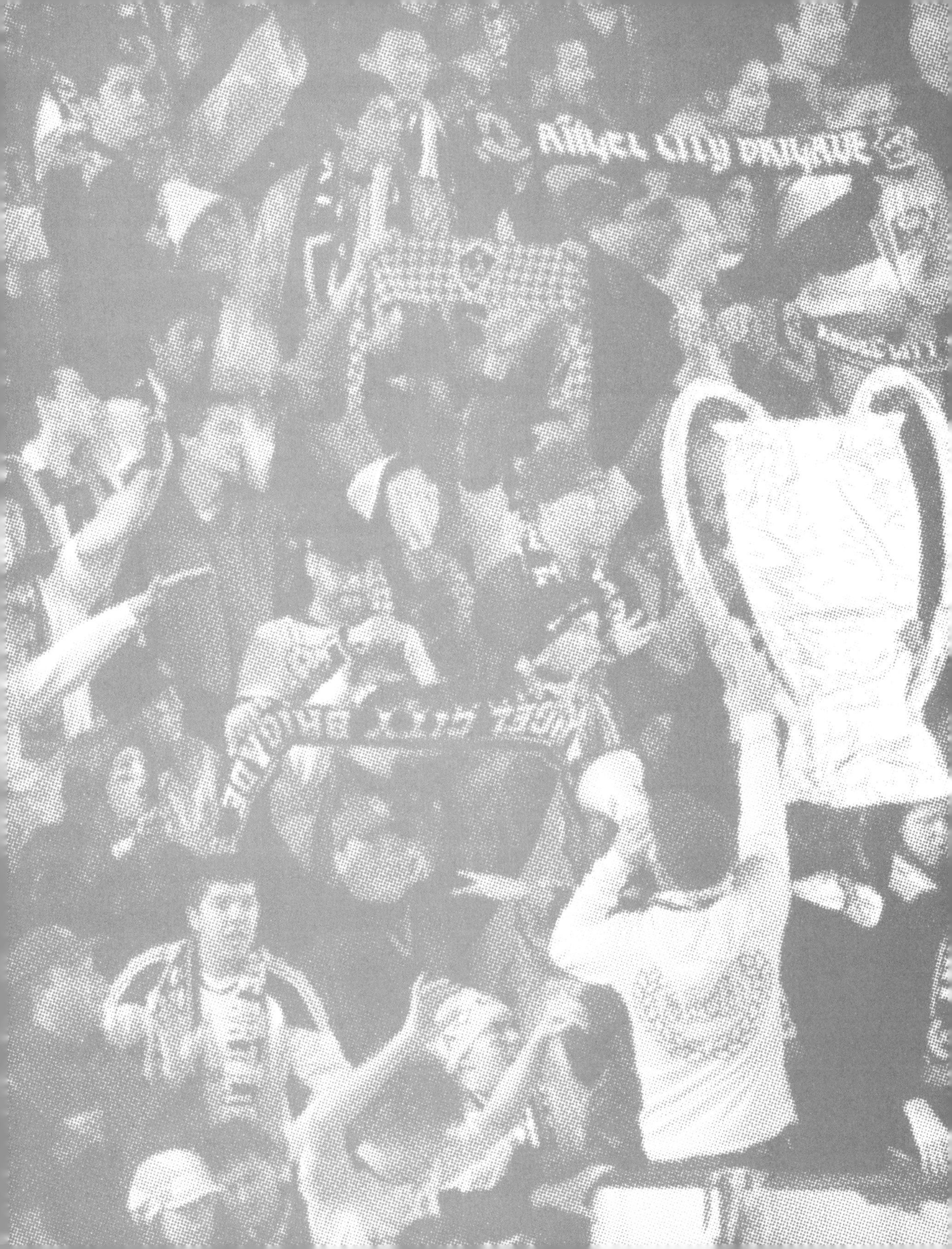

USA

CHICAGO FIRE

WHERE THE FIRE NEVER DIES

The football club and franchise Chicago Fire have taken their name, their theme and their inspiration from the great fire that devastated the city in the 19th century. Lasting from 8 to 10 October, 1871, it took nearly 300 lives. More than 7.76 square kilometres (3 square miles) of the city were destroyed and more than 100,000 inhabitants were left homeless. One popular theory is that a cow caused the tragedy by kicking over a burning lantern while it was being milked. Whether or not the cow was responsible for the fire is unclear, but Chicago Fire did not include her in their crest.

It was unveiled on the 126th anniversary of the fire: 8 October, 1997. The city of Chicago now had its own Major League Soccer (MLS) club, and early successes meant that Chicago Fire soon gained respect across the United States. In their first season, under Bob Bradley, Chicago Fire managed to win the double: the MLS and the US Open Cup, still the club's greatest success.

After these triumphs, and still with Bradley at the helm, the team produced such young talents as Carlos Bocanegra and DaMarcus Beasley, players who would become key international stars and help to stimulate interest in football in the United States.

1. 1998–2019. With the historical fire as inspiration, it was more or less inevitable that Chicago Fire would use an emblem similar to that of the city's fire brigade, a symbol also known as the St Florian's Cross. The timeless look of the C at the centre of the emblem represents Chicago and was inspired by some of the city's other sports clubs, like the Bears (American football) and the Cubs (baseball). The six white points surrounding the letter are taken from the six-pointed stars on the city emblem of Chicago. The stars represent four important events in the city's history: the Battle of Fort Dearborn in 1812, the fire of 1871 and the great fairs of 1893 and 1933.

2. 1998–2006. For eight years from the club's founding, this alternative emblem was also used – one that exaggerated the club's links to the city's firefighters.

3. 2017. In 2017 Chicago Fire played their 20th season in the MLS. This was celebrated with a specially designed emblem, in which the normal crest was framed by a red and white circle, these being colours of the team's home kit.

4. 2019–present. In an attempt to modernize the club, the board introduced a new club crest while they moved stadium by the end of 2019. In the centre of the badge is a so called "Fire Crown", an orange crown mirrored by red flames. A symbol of rising out of the ashes as the city once did. This against a navy blue background. The club's new visual identity was met with criticism and disbelief by the fans.

CLUB: Chicago Fire Football Club
NICKNAME: Men in Red
FOUNDED: 1997
STADIUM: Soldier Field, Chicago (61,500)
HISTORIC PLAYERS: Eric Wynalda, Piotr Nowak, Chris Armas, C.J. Brown, Logan Pause, Cuauhtémoc Blanco and Bastian Schweinsteiger

1.

2.

3.

Chicago Fire's Kevin Ellis (5) celebrates his goal against
Atlanta United FC at Toyota Park in 2018.

4.

COLUMBUS CREW SC

THE REBIRTH OF FOOTBALL

In the centre of Ohio, south of Cleveland and Detroit, and between Indianapolis and Pittsburgh, lies Columbus. The state capital, with more than 850,000 inhabitants, is two hours away from the Canadian border. This is where German and Irish immigrants came together to build a town around a number of industries – and this is where football in the United States was reborn.

Two years after the country had successfully hosted the World Cup in 1994, it was time to inaugurate the new top league, Major League Soccer. Columbus Crew was one of the 10 original clubs to take part in the first season, and were the first in the league to have their own stadium specially adjusted for football. Columbus Crew Stadium was completed and inaugurated in time for the 1999 season.

Since then the club have achieved a number of respectable placings in the Eastern Conference, and won the MLS Cup in 2008. During this period they have been role models of continuity, both on and off the pitch – something to which the relatively late updating of the club's emblem, and thereby its identity, bears witness.

CLUB: Columbus Crew SC
NICKNAME: The Black & Gold
FOUNDED: 1994
STADIUM: Mapfre Stadium, Columbus (19,968 capacity)
HISTORIC: Brian McBride, Jeff Cunningham, Guillermo Barros Schelotto, Chad Marshall, Jonathan Mensah and Federico Higuaín

1. 1996–2014. As the club grew out of the working man's culture of the city of Columbus and of the whole state of Ohio, the name 'Crew' was pretty well inevitable. After the public voted for it as the ideal name for the new franchise, an emblem in this same spirit was needed. 'It was necessary to represent society in a positive way. The name points to a hard-working team with a "show, don't tell" attitude. It suggests a team, people working together,' said Peter Moore of Adidas, who designed the emblem. It illustrates just what Moore is talking about: three determined, square-jawed builders in safety helmets, united below the franchise's nickname. But this emblem was often criticised, and it was one factor that led to a rebranding 18 years later.

2. 2014–present. It was in October 2014 that the club went through a process involving a change of both name and crest. At first sight today's emblem looks like any generic logo, but there is in fact a great deal of symbolism behind the colours and patterns. The form of the emblem represents the togetherness and values that the club shares with the players, the club officials, the supporters and society. The outer black circle was inspired by German emblems and is an homage to the city's German heritage. The inner circle represents the letter O from the state flag of Ohio. The number 96 refers to Crew being the first MLS franchise in that year. The nine diagonal lines in the background represent, generously, the other nine original MLS clubs. The diagonals also demonstrate the club striving onwards and upwards. The culture of the club's supporters is represented through the yellow and black chessboard squares, a common symbol at the team's matches.

Columbus Crew fans cheer on their team and display their allegiance in a second leg MLS Cup playoff match against the Colorado Rapids in 2010. A penalty kick shootout saw the Crew eliminated in the quarterfinals for the second consecutive year.

1.

2.

LA GALAXY

WHERE THE STARS SHINE

In March 2007, when LA Galaxy acquired a 31-year-old David Beckham from the mighty Real Madrid, the world of football gasped. The Englishman was still an important part of his national team and was at the end of his fourth season in the Spanish capital when the deal was announced. Beyond securing the biggest name and the best player that modern US football had seen up to that time, the club acquired a touch of glamour. So too did Major League Soccer (MLS): this was reminiscent of olden times, the halcyon days of the 1970s when icons like Pelé, Franz Beckenbauer and Johan Cruyff rounded off their careers in the west.

The difference was that Beckham still had many years at the top level ahead of him. Even so he chose the United States at this point, intending to return to Europe for the final years of his career. The whole business was of course carefully considered and well planned, and was the first huge step on the path to establishing MLS internationally. But Beckham was also a guiding star in the revolution at LA Galaxy, driven through by general manager Alexi Lalas. And, of course, the revolution succeeded. LA Galaxy, like the League, grew in international status while Beckham and the club celebrated several triumphs together, among them the MLS Cup in 2011 and 2012.

The greatest effect was that Beckham opened the door for others. In time, players like Giovani Dos Santos, Robbie Keane and Zlatan Ibrahimovic could make the same move, players who all live up to the name Galaxy. This is the club that has become the natural home for stars.

1. 1996–2007. When LA Galaxy was founded, the club took the name Galaxy as a kind of nod to Hollywood and its film stars. The colours were black, green and orange, the latter as a reference to the sun, forever associated with California. The fact that the emblem seems to be turning briskly is a reference to the noise of the town as much as the intensity of the sport. The font in which the club name is spelled out reflects the style of Art Deco, so closely identified with the golden age of Hollywood. However, both the colours and the crest disappeared in the course of the facelift performed in 2007.

2. 2007–present. When David Beckham landed at LAX in time for the 2007 season, he was very much part of the rebranding instigated by general manager Alexi Lalas. Apart from sending a signal to the whole of world football with the purchase of the megastar of the time, the club also modernised its whole facade. The new colours were navy blue and gold, the former illustrating space, and the latter representing stars, the club's history and California's nickname, 'the Golden State'. The world-famous abbreviation for Los Angeles, LA, dominated the emblem, exploiting its international brand value. The star at the top is, in fact, a quasar – a super-bright, distant and active core of a galaxy.

CLUB: LA Galaxy
NICKNAME: The Galaxy
FOUNDED: 1994
STADIUM: StubHub Center, Carson (27,000 capacity)
HISTORIC PLAYERS: Cobi Jones, Danny Pena, Carlos Ruiz, David Beckham, Landon Donovan, Robbie Keane, Ashley Cole and Zlatan Ibrahimovic

1.

2.

One of the Galaxy's brightest stars, Zlatan Ibrahimovic marks his debut with a 45-yard half volley and a stoppage time header that led to the Galaxy beating local rivals Los Angeles FC 4-3 in the El Trafico derby in 2018.

NEW YORK RED BULLS

THE FRANCHISING OF AN ENTERPRISE

The New York/New Jersey MetroStars were one of the 10 original clubs in Major League Soccer (MLS). But in spite of considerable advantages – one of the world's great metropolises as their catchment area and superstars like Roberto Donadoni and Lothar Matthäus – the club never managed to go any further than the semi-final in the MLS play-offs in the year 2000.

The owners AEG were disillusioned and Dietrich Mateschitz, the owner of Red Bull, saw his chance. On 9 March, 2006, the deal was announced. The 10-year-old MetroStars was bought by the energy drink company and the team totally redesigned in its colours. The red and black MetroStars were just a memory; the white and red New York Red Bulls were the future. Even if the rebranding didn't meet with the same wild protests as in Austria, and later even in Germany, it was still a franchise that provoked a strong emotional response. Americans are used to changes of clubs and names; that is the way franchising works. What they are not used to, however, are clubs being repainted completely in company colours and their players being transformed into walking billboards. A number of supporters abandoned the club.

In simple sporting terms, Red Bull's investment has borne fruit. Since the reborn club's first season in 2006, they have won the Eastern Conference several times and even got to the play-off finals – far more than their mismanaged predecessors achieved. And, as Mateschitz and Red Bull are only too aware, it is sporting achievements that develop a brand.

CLUB: New York Red Bulls
NICKNAMES: Red Bulls and The Metros
FOUNDED: 1994
STADIUM: Red Bull Arena, New Jersey (25,000 capacity)
HISTORIC PLAYERS: Tony Meola, Tim Howard, Juan Pablo Ángel, Rafael Márquez, Thierry Henry, Tim Cahill and Bradley Wright-Phillips

1. 1996–2002. MetroStars' first emblem showed a clear connection to the club's geographical home. An almost comic book-style rendition of a skyline formed the background of a crest that suggested the city's frenzied jostling. The sharp electric edges of the M illustrate the city that never sleeps, the never-waning energy of a metropolis.

2. 2003–2005. A more generic crest was introduced after a couple of years, this time clearly inspired by the traditional emblems found in Europe, and a rejection of the original, rather too naive logo. Red and black continued to be the club colours, as taken from the team kit. However, this crest was criticised by a number of fans, who said it was 'soulless'.

3. 2006–2007. When MetroStars became New York Red Bulls, the club went through changes on all levels, down to the club crest. The energy drink giant's idea about marketing itself through sport was exemplified when the company logo also became the emblem of the football team. All the important elements from the company were there: the bulls, the sun, and the unmistakable font in which 'Red Bull' is written.

4. 2008–present. It took just two years before the emblem was updated, and made cleaner by removing the speed lines of the bulls and simplifying the design of the sun. The irony in all this is that while Red Bull conquers the world through football, Formula 1 and extreme sports by rejuvenating teams, stables and clubs with its brand, they are doing so with a logo that is virtually unchanged from the original. The original drink, Krating Daeng (Red Bull in Thai), which is distributed right across the world, has been represented from the start by the red bulls and the yellow sun. Mateschitz clearly realises the value of hanging on to what already works.

1.

2.

Kaku (Alejandro Romero Gamarra) points to the New York Red Bulls club crest during a MLS Hudson River derby match against New York City FC in 2018.

3.

4.

PORTLAND TIMBERS

THE LUMBERJACKS FROM OREGON

Portland Timbers knows the value of a brand with a local connection: during its more than 40-year history, the franchise has never tried to disguise its origins. And why should it? The timber industry was a massive force in the town's economy during the 19th century, and continued as such well into the last decades of the 20th century.

This was, of course, a symbol which the original club exploited when it was founded in 1975. The name of the club was chosen on 8 March the same year, from more than 3,000 suggestions sent in by the public, and with this choice the club's identity was determined. Portland's proud lumberjacks would now represent the town even on the football pitch, and initially this worked out well. The fight for the title that same year, in front of 20,000 wildly cheering home fans, gave rise to the town's nickname, Soccer City USA – a name and an identity that have followed the club through various franchises, fresh starts and divisions since then. Today, the club's most visible inheritance is the mascot, Timber Joey (known as Timber Jim up to 2008).

Every time Portland score a goal, Timber Joey saws through a tree trunk with his chainsaw. This has become an internet phenomenon in football circles and, of course, references Portland's origins and identity.

CLUB: Portland Timbers
NICKNAME: The Timbers
FOUNDED: 2009
STADIUM: Providence Park, Portland (21,144 capacity)
HISTORIC PLAYERS: Clive Charles, John Bain, Jimmy Conway, Mikael Silvestre, Mick Hoban, Darlington Nagbe and Jack Jewsbury

1. 1975–1982. During the years in the North American Soccer League (NASL), various different club crests were used, all with the same basic message. The circle symbolises togetherness and the search for perfection; the diagonals represent the trees in and around Portland; and the axe, the emblem's main element, references the timber business that was invaluable for the town's development.

2. 2001–2004 and 2005–2010. When the Timbers figured in the American second division in the early 2000s, an updated crest was unveiled with a new shape and different colours. The three-pointed crest was neither popular nor long-lasting. The later crest, which reverted to the club's origins, was welcomed by the fans. Both marked a fresh start in Oregon's football heartland.

3. 2011–2014. Before Portland Timbers' first season in Major League Soccer (MLS) in 2011, a new, modernised version of the earlier emblem was introduced. The updates irritated a great number of Timbers fans. Superficially there are no great differences, but the axe, indeed the whole emblem has a more comic-book-style look than before. In addition 'Portland' has become much larger than 'Timbers', a change that again irked supporters, although this was a common device by clubs to show their attachment to their region. The fact that the axe extends beyond the borders of the circle suggests the club's strength, precision and attention to detail.

4. 2015–present. In the same year that the club won the MLS Cup, the emblem was changed. After representations from the fans, the time had come for an update. With this, the name disappeared. The design of the axe had already been somewhat toned down, and the fact that the axe is shaped like a T is, of course, no coincidence. The three lines on either side still represent the trees of the area, but also refer to the club's three epochs: NASL ('where we have our roots'), USL (the United Soccer League, 'where we started to flourish') and MLS. The club's colours – moss green and ponderosa pine – represent Oregon's forests.

1.

2.

3.

4.

SEATTLE SOUNDERS

A FORCE ON AND OFF THE PITCH

Ever since the franchise Seattle Sounders took its place in America's top tier, Major League Soccer (MLS), we have been able to witness the unfolding of a modern success story. The club had emerged from the team that played during the 1970s in the North American Soccer League (NASL), and from the second division outfit that played during the early years of the new millennium, but no one could foresee the glories that awaited this new MLS franchise.

Since 2009, the club's first season, Seattle Sounders have established themselves as a force within American soccer, both on and off the pitch. They secured successive top positions between 2009 and 2016 in the Western Conference (placing first on one occasion, and never lower than fourth), and the Sounders also became known as a cup team after winning three out of four US Open Cup Finals in their first four seasons. The highpoint, so far, came when the club beat Toronto FC on penalties to be crowned 2016 MLS Champions.

Internationally, however, it is events off the pitch which have made the headlines. The supporters have played a major role in the Sounders' success, a fact to which the club's average attendances bear testimony. Every season between 2009 and 2016, the club boasted the highest gate in the MLS. In 2015, they set a League record with an average gate of 42,247 for Seattle's home games. The fans and the club have also become known for fighting for LGBT rights and for their participation in fundraising for charity.

CLUB: Seattle Sounders

NICKNAME: Sounders

FOUNDED: 2007

STADIUM: CenturyLink Field, Seattle 72,000/41,000 capacity instead of 69,000

HISTORICA PLAYERS: Fredy Montero, Brad Evans, Zach Scott, Kasey Keller, Osvaldo Alonso, Obafemi Martins and Clint Dempsey

1. 1974–1982 and 2003–2008. The original emblem, which still represents Seattle Sounders for many people, was created soon after the club was founded in 1973, playing in the North American Soccer League (NASL). The connection to the city was clear, the waves referring to the port of Seattle. This crest would be used again in the American second division, when the owner Adrian Hanauer changed the stadium to Qwest Field in 2003.

2. 1983–1984. In 1983, Sounders was sold and the new owners rebranded the club. New colours were introduced – navy blue, light blue and white – to reflect more clearly the coast of Seattle. The landmark Space Needle was added next to the football. The waves were still there, though not for long because the club folded in 1984.

3. 1994–2002. When Seattle Sounders was recreated in the mid-'90s, the contemporary colours were kept in the new crest and a killer whale heading a football was added to the design.

4. 2008–present. When the franchise took its place in MLS in 2008, today's crest was introduced. The famous landmark, the Space Needle – the internationally recognised symbol for the city – had once more become the focus. The heraldically inspired shield consists of two parts, one green, one blue. This symbolises 'the cooperation between the owners, city, players and supporters'. The blue colour suggests the water around Seattle, specifically Puget Sound. Blue also stands for calm, strength and loyalty. Green is a reference to the forests of the Pacific Northwest, which surround Seattle. The colours also reflect the inhabitants' passion and optimism. The dark contours and the colour of the font suggest the Cascade range of mountains to the east of the city.

1.

2.

3.

Clint Dempsey has played more than 100 games for the Seattle Sounders. In 2017, ESPNFC and MLS named Dempsey the greatest-ever U.S. soccer player.

4.

AUSTRALIA

MELBOURNE CITY

PLAYING WITH HEART

When the owners of Manchester City bought Melbourne Heart in January 2014, this was part of City Football Group's ambitious project to go global. This was a project that also included the purchase of New York City FC. The English club was serious about the acquisition of their Australian little brother and showed clear intentions when David Villa left Atlético Madrid for New York City the same year and was shortly afterwards loaned to Melbourne.

Melbourne Heart now underwent a powerful transformation. The club, who had played in the A-League since 2010, suddenly changed name to Melbourne City FC and a new club brand was presented. In addition, the colours were modified: the red and white were now set against Manchester City's light blue – a decision that proved controversial. Sydney FC already played in sky blue, and filed an appeal with the Football Federation Australia (FFA) in April 2014. 'We are concerned about the proposal that they use sky blue. In a series of ten teams it is illogical to have two clubs with the same colours. Especially when the colour is so closely linked to New South Wales,' said Sydney FC president Scott Barlow. In 2016 the FFA issued an ambivalent ruling: Sydney FC had the right to the sky blue colour while Melbourne City had the right to integrate the colours of Manchester City. It's a diplomatic decision in a process that showed that rebranding is not always easy to implement.

1. 2010–2014. Just over half a year after Melbourne Heart was founded, the club's first emblem was presented in February 2010. The colours were taken from Melbourne's official flag and were chosen to represent the city as rivals to Melbourne Victory's blue. The shield assumed the form of a subtle heart composed of the club's initials, M and H, and was created by Elmwood Local Design Agency.

2. 2014–present. What do the symbols in the emblem stand for? The new branding was inspired by the history of the Heart, by Melbourne's heritage and by aspects of modern society in Victoria. The Merino sheep is indispensable to the state's agriculture. The cow reflects the region's dairy industry, while whales migrate every year to the coastal waters of Victoria. The ship is also found on Manchester City's emblem. The crown in the middle symbolises the link to the English mother club. The red and white cross in the city's colours reference the club's predecessor, as do the two little hearts located on either side.

CLUB: Melbourne City FC
NICKNAME: City, Heart and City Blues
FOUNDED: 2009
STADIUM: AAMI Park, Melbourne (30,050 capacity)
HISTORIC PLAYERS: Matt Thompson, Aziz Behich, Clint Bolton, Michael Marrone, Orlando Engelaar, Aaron Mooy, Tim Cahill and Bruno Fornaroli

1.

2.

With the controversy surrounding the club's renaming
in the past, Melbourne City's club record goalscorer
Bruno Fornaroli celebrates a goal against Central Coast
Mariners in 2018.

MELBOURNE VICTORY

A CONSTANT REMINDER OF THE SWEETNESS OF VICTORY

To adopt the word 'Victory' and use it in the name of a club could have devastating consequences: defeat makes the team an irresistible target for irony and sarcasm, and the ridicule of opposing fans. But that's precisely the risk the team took when they were founded in 2004, and Melbourne Victory have managed to live up to their name many times over.

Melbourne Victory was one of the eight original clubs who took part in the first season, 2005/2006, of the Australian league, the A-League. It took only one year before the club lived up to their name, winning both the Premiership and the Championship in 2006/07. Victory have built on those two triumphs since then, and today they are the team with the most titles. In addition, in every season since the A-League was founded, Melbourne Victory have been the club with the highest average attendances – just over 20,000 in recent years.

1. 2004–present. From the start, the colours of Melbourne Victory have been navy blue, white and silver. These are closely connected to Victoria, coming from the state's flag and crest. In fact, several of the state's teams, in various sports, use this colour combination, including Melbourne United (basketball) and Carlton Blues (Australian rules football). That the provocative name Victory is taken from the state itself is not difficult to deduce, but the background of the white V is rather harder to work out. It actually comes from Victoria's state team in Australian rules football, which traditionally have the letter V on their jerseys and are simply called Big V, a nickname also used for Melbourne Victory today. The crest has been noted internationally because it is very like that of the French team Bordeaux.

2. 2014–2015. For Melbourne Victory's 10th season in the A-League, this special commemorative emblem was unveiled, which proudly proclaims the club's history. The season ended with the club becoming the first to secure the treble: the Premiership, the Championship and Westfield FFA Cup.

CLUB: Melbourne Victory FC

NICKNAME: Victory and Big V

FOUNDED: 2004

STADIUM: AAMI Park, Melbourne (30,050 capacity) and Marvel Stadium, Melbourne (56,347 capacity)

HISTORIC PLAYERS: Kevin Muscat, Archie Thompson, Robbie Kruse, Mark Milligan, Harry Kewell, Leigh Broxham and Carl Valeri

1.

2.

For Melbourne Victory's inaugural season the use of the letter V was restricted to the club badge. It has since been incorporated into the shirt design. Here, Harry Kewell celebrates scoring against the Central Coast Mariners in 2012.

PERTH GLORY

THE RAYS OF SUNSHINE

Perth Glory, the pride of Western Australia, is today one of the best known football clubs in the country.

Although the domestic National Soccer League began in 1977, it wasn't until the 1996 season that Perth Glory made their entrance. And how! During the eight seasons that followed, the club from Australia's west coast reached six play-offs, played four finals and won two. A new football dynasty was born. But all dynasties have problems sooner or later.

When the NSL was replaced by the A-League, Glory was one of just three clubs that survived the transition (Adelaide United and Newcastle Jets were the other two). Even so, this was followed by some unsuccessful years. The club needed a fresh start, which came when Tony Sage became sole majority owner in 2008. His takeover would eventually allow the team to live up to their name, but in the shorter term it meant the third change to the club's crest in 13 years.

'Our sponsors, partners, members and supporters have a strong connection with and loyalty to Perth Glory's emblem and associate it with progress, passion and innovation. The new logo will strengthen this link,' said the owner Tony Sage when the club was rebranded and the emblem updated. Sage realised the value of Perth Glory's history, something that has made the club live up to their fame today.

CLUB: Perth Glory FC

NICKNAME: The Glory

FOUNDED: 1995

STADIUM: nib Stadium, Perth (20,500 capacity)

HISTORIC PLAYERS: Scott Miller, Bobby Despotovski, Alistair Edwards, Jamie Harnwell, Robbie Fowler, Shane Smeltz and William Gallas

1. 1996–2003. When Perth Glory was founded, it was essential, given Australia's history, to create an identity that was appealing for everyone, without ethnic undertones, an identity that could represent the rebirth of football in Western Australia. Perth Glory fought for a multicultural country, and to this end the club broke away from traditional European football design by avoiding names like 'United', 'City' and 'Wanderers'. Instead they chose the suffix 'Glory', and the colours orange and purple also represented a departure from tradition. The rays of sunshine represent the famously warm summers on Australia's west coast.

2. 2005-2008. When the A-League was created, a new era was ushered in. The harbinger of this new age was the updated emblem, which focused still more on the word 'Glory' than on its home town of Perth. This was a monument to times past and to hope for the future. The football itself inherited the club's orange colour.

3. 2009–present. After a couple of lean seasons, Perth Glory could sense a new optimism when Tony Sage became the club's sole owner in 2008. 'We have set out on a journey of renewal,' said Sage when the new crest was unveiled. In response to concerns from the supporters, the emblem kept both its colours and its name as the club moved into a new era. Two design agencies (KURV and Whitekite) collaborated on the logo for several months. The result was a recognisable but modernised image that retained the ball, the rays of sunshine and the colours from before. The biggest change was that the form was now a traditional heraldic shield. The home city of the team was also enlarged, for commercial reasons, and silver was added to the palette.

4. 2011–2012. Like many other clubs, Glory created a special jubilee emblem to celebrate its rich history. This was used in the club's 15th season.

1.

2.

4.

3.

SOUTH AMERICA

BOCA JUNIORS

THE SWEDISH-INSPIRED MEGA-CLUB

In Argentina's capital city Buenos Aires is a district shrouded in myth. Located in the south-east corner of the city, by the delta of the river Río Matanza, La Boca is a harbour area that is nowadays much visited by tourists, not least because of the Caminito, an alley closely associated with the tango and world-famous thanks to the composition of the same name. La Boca is also well known for its political past. This is where new Italian immigrants proclaimed their independence from Argentina in 1882. It is also where the first socialist member of Congress was elected, and during the economic crisis of 2001 the demonstrations spilled out into its streets. It was in this impoverished part of the city that players like Carlos Tévez, Juan Román Riquelme and Diego Maradona made their breakthrough, all players who made the game sizzle in the club's stadium, La Bombonera.

The stadium, which is actually called Estadio Alberto J. Armando, is known for its fantastic atmosphere, particularly when there is a local derby with their arch-rivals River Plate. The Superclásico is ranked among the world's great derbys, a contest in which, historically speaking, Boca has the upper hand.

Along with River Plate, Boca Juniors is Argentina's most successful club. It has also done dramatically well across South America and indeed globally. As far as international titles go, the blue and yellow team from Buenos Aires are mentioned in the same breath as FC Barcelona, Real Madrid and AC Milan – a quartet that makes up the world's most successful clubs on the international stage, which is reflected in the stars appearing on Boca's crest.

CLUB: Club Atlético Boca Juniors

NICKNAMES: Xeneizes (the Genovese), Azul y Oro (the Blue and Gold) and La Mitad Más Uno (the Half Plus One)

FOUNDED: 1905

STADIUM: La Bombonera, Buenos Aires (49,000 capacity)

HISTORIC PLAYERS: Roberto Mouzo, Diego Maradona, Martín Palermo, Juan Román Riquelme and Carlos Tévez

1. 1922–1955. The first emblem represented Boca's initials, CABJ, and was adopted 17 years after the club's founding. In 1906, so the story goes, Boca were playing a match against Nottingham de Almagro. The kits of the two teams were incredibly alike, and therefore it was decided that the loser would have to change colours. Boca lost the match and chose to take their new colours from the port; the boat that first sailed into the harbour would give the club their new strip. It turned out to be a Swedish vessel and thus yellow and blue became the colour of this great Argentine club.

2. 1955–1960. When the club reached its 50th birthday, the emblem was changed. The shield adopted the same colours as the club strip and the initials were written in black to show up more clearly. The laurel leaves were introduced as a symbol of the jubilee.

3. 1960–1970. After five years the branches disappeared, and the name was spelled out.

4. 1970–1996. On the advice of the club president, Alberto J. Armando, the shield was altered again in 1970. The initials returned and 30 stars were added, one for each League title, a gesture that was to become legendary.

5. 1996–present. After further successes it was time to update the emblem: 30 titles had become 50, so the number of stars was changed accordingly. To make room, the yellow central stripe was removed. Another alteration was the darkening of the yellow tone. Since 1996 they have updated the crest a couple of times with stars for each new title.

1.

2.

3.

4.

Argentina's Diego Maradona in action for Boca Juniors in 1997, his second spell with the club. He won the league with Juniors in 1981 and has therefore contributed to one of the many stars that adorn the club crest.

5.

CORINTHIANS

BRITISH-INSPIRED HERITAGE

Corinthians have won all there is to win: regional championships, the national League, the domestic Cup, the Brazilian Supercup, Copa Libertadores (South America's Champions League) and the FIFA club teams' World Cup. Global footalling artists like Sócrates, Rivelino and Ronaldo (Ronaldo Luís Nazário de Lima) have played in the team. Considered the people's club in São Paulo, Corinthians are the second most beloved club in the country. Only Flamengo, from Rio de Janeiro, have more supporters. In 2013 Corinthians also became the first non-European club to be ranked as one of the 20 most valuable clubs in the world by Forbes. But what connects this giant to a club of amateurs in England?

In 1882 Corinthian FC was founded in London, a club that kept the amateur rules when others were professionalised. Instead of joining the Football League, which was launched in 1888, Corinthian FC went on several tours abroad, among them to Brazil in 1910. This was a journey that inspired five railway workers to start a Brazilian version in São Paulo. In those days football was something reserved for the elite and the upper classes, and Corinthians became the first club to be open to the general public.

The Brazilian and English Corinthians have developed in different directions. The former is one of South America's biggest clubs while their forerunners are still playing amateur football under the name of Corinthian-Casuals FC. This did not stop the clubs from meeting in a friendly match as late as 2015. Thanks to the support of the Brazilian fans, the English amateur club has more than 140,000 followers on Facebook.

The Brazilian club's crest has changed over time and evolved from relatively simple badges featuring the club's initials through to a more intricate design inspired by the São Paulo's federal state flag via additional designs celebrating the sports club's success in rowing.

CLUB: SC Corinthians Paulista
NICKNAMES: Timão (the Big Team), Time do Povo (the People's Team), Todo Poderoso (the All-Powerful) and Coringão
FOUNDED: 1910
STADIUM: Arena Corinthians, São Paulo (49,205 capacity)
HISTORIC PLAYERS: Cláudio, Wladimir, Rivellino, Jo, Sócrates, Dunga, Deco, Carlos Tévez and Ronaldo

1. 1913–1914 and 2010. For the sake of simplicity, the Corinthians' first emblem contained only the letters C and P, standing for Corinthians Paulista. The crest was revived for the club's centennial.

2. 1914–1916, 1916–1917 and 1917–1920. The emblem was designed by the lithographer Hermogenes Barbuy, the brother of one of the players. It made its first appearance in a training match against Torino in São Paulo. A third initial, S, was added, for 'Sport'.

3. 1920–1926. Big changes occurred in 1919, when São Paulo's federal state flag was introduced into the emblem. The year the club was founded and its name are written in the circle.

4. 1926–1939 and 1939–present. In spite of the opposition of the Brazilian dictator Getúlio Vargas to the regional symbols, the Corinthians managed to keep their flag and to update their emblem. Thanks to the club's great successes in water sports, two oars and an anchor were added. This was unusual: several football clubs have grown out of rowing clubs, but rarely has this happened the other way round. The crest was designed by the artist Francisco Rebolo. Since then the crest has been modernised a couple of times, as in 1990 and 2011, when the club introduced stars above the emblem.

1.

Sport Club Corinthians Paulista
100 anos de Glórias

2.

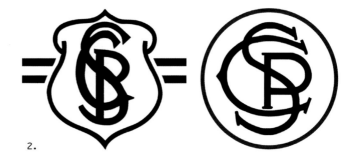

3.

4.

Jadson pays tribute to the club crest after scoring
a goal against Atlético Mineiro as Corinthians triumph
with their seventh title in 2017.

FLAMENGO

WHEN THE INITIALS ARE MORE IMPORTANT THAN THE CREST

Brazilian football rests on several big clubs and classic names, among them the Rio de Janeiro team Clube de Regatas do Flamengo. This is the club that gave Zico to the world and which offers the annual Fla-Flu derby (one of the world's greatest, against Fluminense). This is the club that is said to be the property of the people in the homeland of football: they have around 40 million fans, a figure large enough for four Brazilian papers to suggest as late as 2008 that this is the biggest in the world. That may not be a qualified truth but, whatever, successes don't lie.

With recurring titles in the domestic league and international triumphs in the shape of Copa Libertadores and the Intercontinental Cup, Flamengo are one of Brazil's most consistently victorious outfits. The question for the club today, however, is this: will they ever live up to the golden generation? That was how the global magician Zico and his teammates were known when they won the treble: Campeonato Carioca, Copa Libertadores and the Intercontinental Cup (3-0 against the mighty Liverpool) in 1981. Apart from Zico the team consisted of such personalities as Júnior, Nunes and Adílio, all stars of the national team.

Not so bad for a team that started out as a rowing club in the early 19th century.

CLUB: Clube de Regatas do Flamengo
NICKNAMES: Mengão (Big Mengo) and Rubro-Negro (Scarlet-Black)
FOUNDED: 1895
STADIUM: Maracaña, Rio de Janeiro (78,838 capacity)
HISTORIC PLAYERS: Henrique Frade, Adílio, Zico, Júnior and Dejan Petkovic

1. 1895. Flamengo's first crest was, unsurprisingly, a boat club emblem. The oars and the anchor suggest the club's rowing origins. The initials stand for Clube de Regatas do Flamengo, which is still the name of the club in spite of their footballing successes.

2. 1896. The crest was altered early on to look like this, an emblem that represents Flamengo as a club for rowing and other water sports. It also exists with gold-coloured details instead of white. The colours were initially blue and gold to symbolise Guanabara Bay and the natural resources of Brazil.

3. 1912. More than 15 years after the founding of the club, a new emblem was created, which would become famous throughout the world. The reason for the new crest was that deserters from the future arch-rivals Fluminense founded their own team with neighbouring Flamengo. In the top left-hand corner were the by now familiar initials. Traditionally Flamengo have often played with just their initials on their match jerseys instead of the crest, as they were doing as far back as 1916, when the club's first red and black kit was used.

4. 1981-present. The crest has gone through various subtle changes throughout the years and this is the latest version. The shape of the shield comes out of traditional European heraldry.

5. 1895–1944. Like Rangers in Scotland, so Flamengo have largely set aside the emblem on their match shirts and replaced it with just the club initials. This became a common practice in the 1960s and '70s in England, but it remains uncommon in Brazil.

6. 1981. This version of the initials, inspired by the original shield, was used in the 1981 season, the club's golden year, when they won the Copa Libertadores, the Intercontinental Cup and the Campeonato Carioca. In this variant, like the current one, the letters' serif has been subtly altered from the original.

1.

2.

3.

5.

4.

6.

FLUMINENSE

RIO DE JANEIRO'S ELITE CLUB

Fluminense FC is that rare thing: a club for the upper classes and the aristocracy in Brazil. How this came about reflects the era when the club was founded.

Fluminense was not the very first club in Brazil, but it was the first in Rio de Janeiro. Founded on 21 July, 1902 by the English-born Oscar Cox, who had brought back the game of football from Europe, Fluminense quickly became a club for the aristocracy. Based in Laranjeiras, one of the smartest areas of Rio de Janeiro, Fluminense expanded through Brazilian society. As more clubs were founded, among them their arch-rivals Flamengo, the appeal of football itself became broader even while Fluminense was firmly anchored in the upper echelons of society. Through the years members of Brazil's cultural elite have supported the club, among them the composer Cartola, the musicians Chico Buarque and Ivan Lins, and the former President of FIFA João Havelange.

Today the stereotype of Fluminense as an upper class club is only partly accurate: the fan base has been shaken up and now contains more of a social mix. Even so, the club's white, green and claret tricolour (the colours representing, respectively, peace, hope and vigour) is still connected to the Brazilian elite, both on and off the pitch.

1. 1902–1905. On October 17, 1902, three months after Fluminense had been founded, the club's first emblem was created. The board met to choose a simple design: the club's initials written over a grey and white shield. The colours were taken from the team kit.

2. 1905–present. After just three years Fluminense's crest was updated to the original version of today's emblem. The form of the crest was modified to look more like the Swiss heraldic shields of the 18th and 19th centuries. It's not surprising that the club took inspiration from Europe because the founder Oscar Cox had discovered football when he studied in Lausanne in Switzerland. To match the shape of the shield, the initials were also changed. They were now written in gothic style, which also has its origins in central Europe. The colours were also changed. The new colours represented peace (white), hope (green) and vigour (claret), a combination that gave rise to the club's nickname, Tricolor. The crest has been subtly modernised several times since 1905 but it remains fundamentally the same.

CLUB: Fluminense FC
NICKNAMES: Tricolor and Pó de arroz (rice powder) and Flu
FOUNDED: 1902
STADIUM: Maracanã Stadium, Rio de Janeiro (78,838 capacity)
HISTORIC PLAYERS: Castilho, Waldo Machado, Telê Santana, Rivellino and Fred

1.

2.

Resplendent in their famous colours of white, green and claret, the Fluminense players celebrate after a fourth goal against Argentina's Arsenal at the 2008 Libertadores.

SANTOS FC

THE SANTÁSTICOS

When you discuss Brazilian football, you cannot escape the name of Pelé, the striker who scored 77 goals in 92 appearances for the national team, the icon who guided his country to three World Cups, including Brazil's first. This took place in Sweden in 1958, when he was just a teenager – a 17-year-old who had emerged from Santos FC.

Pelé put Santos on the map, and vice versa. When he made his debut for the club, he was just 15, and part of the team that would come to be known as Os Santásticos (The Santastics). Alongside other future legends such as Zito, Coutinho and Pepe, Pelé led Santos to unimagined heights. Victory in the regional championship in 1958, Campeonato Paulista, was the first of many titles that Pelé and the club would win together. That season they scored 143 goals, 58 of them Pelé's – a record that still stands. And so it went on for the unbeatable duo.

Brazilian champions six times, 10 regional titles, two Copa Libertadores titles, and two Intercontinental Cup victories was the final tally for Pelé and Santos when he left the team in 1974. In 1,106 matches he scored 1,091 goals, and with that he has, like Santos, inspired successive generations of world football.

The club have not been quite that successful since then, but another player from the Santos academy, in the shape of Neymar, is now making his own mark on football. A player in the same mould as Pelé, guided by the legend himself, he has again put Santos on the international football map.

NICKNAMES: Peixe (Fish), Alvinegro Praiano (The Black-and-Whites from the Beach) and Santástico
FOUNDED: 1912
STADIUM: Éstadio Vila Belmiro, Santos (16,068 capacity)
HISTORIC PLAYERS: Pelé, Pepe, Coutinho, Toninho Guerreiro and Neymar

---

1. 1915. Although the club was founded in 1912 under the name Santos Foot-Ball Club, it would be another three years before they got their first emblem, under the name União FC – initials reflected in the club's crest. The reason for the temporary change of name was to allow the club to take part in a tournament in another town. Initially the team colours were white, blue and gold in tribute to Concordia Club, whose premises they had borrowed to found Santos. The colours were soon exchanged for today's black and white combination because the club experienced problems with the original colour scheme. White was chosen to suggest peace, while black symbolises nobility.

2. 1925–1968. The first version of today's emblem was created in the 1920s. The 11 black and white stripes represent the team's 11 players. Like previous logos, the complete name was not spelled out, initials being preferred. The ball in the top left corner is said to come from a crest at the time that the club was founded. This emblem is supposedly an homage to Concordia Club.

3. 1968–present. At the end of the 1960s, the club crest was updated: the font was changed, the ball had sharper contours, and two stars were added at the top. These stars illustrate the team's successes in the Intercontinental Cup of 1962 and '63, the same years that they won I Copa Libertadores. All this guided by Pelé, of course. Since then, the club crest has undergone minor, superficial changes to move with the times.

4. 1942–1944. Since today's crest was introduced in 1925, it has been set aside for only two years and then with this emblem. The focus is on the initials, but here they are interwoven, a style that has always been popular with a number of Brazilian clubs. The supporters didn't accept the new symbol and it quickly disappeared.

1.

2.

4.

3.

Santos' most famous son, Pelé in action for the team in 1969. In his 18 years with the club he made 638 appearances and scored 619 goals.

NOTABLE CRESTS

1.

2.

3.

4.

5.

6.

7.

8.

9.

1. <u>CLUB</u>: FC Santa Claus Arctic Circle
   <u>NICKNAME</u>: Santa
   <u>FOUNDED</u>: 1993
   <u>COUNTRY</u>: Finland
   <u>STADIUM</u>: Keskuskenttä, Rovaniemi
   (4,000 spectators)

2. <u>CLUB</u>: Bohemians Prague 1905
   <u>NICKNAME</u>: Klokani (The Kangaroos)
   <u>FOUNDED</u>: 1905
   <u>COUNTRY</u>: Czech Republic
   <u>STADIUM</u>: Dolicek, Prague
   (5,000 spectators)

3. <u>CLUB</u>: FC Avenir Beggen
   <u>NICKNAME</u>: Wichtelcher (The House elfs)
   <u>FOUNDED</u>: 1915
   <u>COUNTRY</u>: Luxembourg
   <u>STADIUM</u>: Stade rue Henri Dunant, Beggen
   (4,830 spectators)

4. <u>CLUB</u>: Asante Kotoko SC
   <u>NICKNAME</u>: Porcupines
   <u>FOUNDED</u>: 1935
   <u>COUNTRY</u>: Ghana
   <u>STADIUM</u>: Kumasi Sports Stadium, Kumasi
   (40,528 spectators)

5. <u>CLUB</u>: Benevento Calcio
   <u>NICKNAME</u>: Stregoni (The Witches)
   <u>FOUNDED</u>: 1929
   <u>COUNTRY</u>: Italy
   <u>STADIUM</u>: Stadio Ciro Vigorito, Benevento
   (18,975 spectators)

6. <u>CLUB</u>: Hereford FC
   <u>NICKNAME</u>: The Bulls, The Whites & The Lilywhites
   <u>FOUNDED</u>: 2014
   <u>COUNTRY</u>: England
   <u>STADIUM</u>: Edgar Street, Hereford
   (4,913 spectators)

7. <u>CLUB</u>: R.S.C. Anderlecht
   <u>NICKNAME</u>: Paars-wit/Les Mauves et Blancs
   (Purple & White), Sporting & RSCA
   <u>FOUNDED</u>: 1908
   <u>COUNTRY</u>: Belgium
   <u>STADIUM</u>: Constant Vanden Stock, Brussels
   (28,063 spectators)

8. <u>CLUB</u>: Aalesunds FK
   <u>NICKNAME</u>: Tangotrøyene (Tangoshirts),
   Tango & De oransje og blå (Orange and blue)
   <u>FOUNDED</u>: 1914
   <u>COUNTRY</u>: Norway
   <u>STADIUM</u>: Color Line Stadion, Ålesund
   (10,778 spectators)

9. <u>CLUB</u>: FC Lokomotiv Moscow
   <u>NICKNAME</u>: Krasno-zelonyye (Red-Greens),
   Zheleznodorozhniki (Railroaders) & Parovozy
   (Steam Locomotives)
   <u>FOUNDED</u>: 1923
   <u>COUNTRY</u>: Russia
   <u>STADIUM</u>: RZD Stadium, Moskva (27,320 spectators)

1.

2.

3.

4.

5.

6.

7.

8.

9.

1 **CLUB:** Club Atlético Huracán
NICKNAME: Globo (Balloon) & Quemeros (Burners)
FOUNDED: 1908
COUNTRY: Argentina
STADIUM: Tomás A. Ducó, Buenos Aires
(48,314 spectators)

4. **CLUB:** Morecambe FC
NICKNAME: The Shrimps, Red and White Army
& Seasiders
FOUNDED: 1920
COUNTRY: England
STADIUM: Globe Stadium, Morecambe
(6,476 spectators)

7. **CLUB:** SC Freiburg
NICKNAME: Breisgau-Brasilianer
(Brazilians of Breisgau)
FOUNDED: 1904
COUNTRY: Germany
STADIUM: Schwarzwald-Stadion, Freiburg
(24,000 spectators)

2. **CLUB:** FC Bunyodkor
NICKNAME: Qaldirg'ochlar (the Swallows)
FOUNDED: 2005
COUNTRY: Uzbekistan
STADIUM: Bunyodkor Stadium, Tashkent
(34,000 capacity)

5. **CLUB:** FC Sheriff
NICKNAME: The Sheriff
FOUNDED: 1997
COUNTRY: Moldova
STADIUM: Sheriff Stadium, Tiraspol
(12,746 spectators)

8. **CLUB:** Virtus Entella
NICKNAME: Biancocelesti (The White-Light-Blues)
& Diavoli neri (The Black Devils)
FOUNDED: 1914
COUNTRY: Italy
STADIUM: Stadio Comunale, Chiavari
(5,535 spectators)

3. **CLUB:** P.A.O.K.
NICKNAME: Dikéfalos (Double-headed) & Asprómavi
(White-blacks)
FOUNDED: 1926
COUNTRY: Greece
STADIUM: Toumba Stadium, Thessaloniki
(28,703 spectators)

6. **CLUB:** Kilmarnock FC
NICKNAME: Killie
FOUNDED: 1869
COUNTRY: Scotland
STADIUM: Rugby Park, Kilmarnock
(18,128 spectators)

9. **CLUB:** New York City FC
NICKNAME: The Pigeons, The Bronx Blues, The Blues
& The Boys in Blue
FOUNDED: 2013
COUNTRY: USA
STADIUM: Yankee Stadium, New York City
(47,422 spectators)

1.

2.

3.

4.

5.

6.

7.

8.

9.

1. **CLUB:** Coventry City FC
NICKNAME: The Sky Blues
FOUNDED: 1883
COUNTRY: England
STADIUM: Ricoh Arena, Coventry
(32,609 spectators)

4. **CLUB:** Defensor Sporting Club
NICKNAME: El Violeta (The Violet one), La Viola,
Tuertos (The One eyed ones), El Defe & La Farola
y La Cometa (The Streetlight and the Comet)
FOUNDED: 1913
COUNTRY: Uruguay
STADIUM: Estadio Luis Franzini, Montevideo
(18,000 spectators)

7. **CLUB:** Brentford FC
NICKNAME: The Bees
FOUNDED: 1889
COUNTRY: England
STADIUM: Griffin Park, London
(12,573 spectators)

2. **CLUB:** Club Universidad de Chile
NICKNAME: La U (The U), Los Azules (The Blues), El
Chuncho (The Owl), El Bulla (The Noise), El Romántico
Viajero (The Romantic Traveller) & El León (The Lion)
FOUNDED: 1927
COUNTRY: Chile
STADIUM: Estadio Nacional Julio Martínez Prádanos,
Santiago (48,665 spectators)

5. **CLUB:** Orlando Pirates FC
NICKNAME: Buccaneers, Bucs, Sea Robbers,
the Ghost, Happy People & Amabhakabhaka
Ezimnyama Ngenkani (The Black Ones)
FOUNDED: 1937
COUNTRY: South Africa
STADIUM: Orlando Stadium, Johannesburg
(40,000 spectators)

8. **CLUB:** Stade Malherbe Caen
NICKNAME: SMC
FOUNDED: 1913
COUNTRY: France
STADIUM: Stade Michel d'Ornano, Caen
(21,500 spectators)

3. **CLUB:** Nagoya Grampus
NICKNAME: Grampus
FOUNDED: 1939
COUNTRY: Japan
STADIUM: Toyota Stadium, Nagoya
(45,000 spectators)

6. **CLUB:** Espérane Sportive de Tunis
NICKNAME: Mkachkha, Blood & Gold & Taraji
FOUNDED: 1919
COUNTRY: Tunisia
STADIUM: Stade Olympique de Rades, Tunis
(60,000 spectators)

9. **CLUB:** ADO Den Haag
NICKNAME: The Hague, De Residentieclub (Home Club)
& De Ooievaars (The Storks)
FOUNDED: 1905
COUNTRY: Netherlands
STADIUM: Cars Jeans Stadion, The Hague
(15,000 spectators)

1.

2.

3.

4.

5.

6.

7.

8.

9.

---

1. CLUB: Ipswich Town FC
NICKNAME: The Blues & The Tractor Boys
FOUNDED: 1878
COUNTRY: England
STADIUM: Portman Road, England
(30,311 spectators)

2. CLUB: SC Heerenveen
NICKNAME: De Superfriezen (The Superfriezes)
FOUNDED: 1920
COUNTRY: Netherlands
STADIUM: Abe Lenstra Stadium, Heerenveen
(26,100 spectators)

3. CLUB: Vitória SC
NICKNAME: Os Vimaranenses (the ones from Guimarães)
& Os Conquistadores (the Conquistadors)
FOUNDED: 1922
COUNTRY: Portugal
STADIUM: Estádio D. Afonso Henriques, Guimarães
(30,165 spectators)

4. CLUB: Partick Thistle FC
NICKNAME: The Maryhill Magyars, The Harry Wraggs,
The Thistle & The Jags
FOUNDED: 1876
COUNTRY: Scotland
STADIUM: Firhill Stadium, Glasgow (10 102 spectators)

5. CLUB: Charlotte Independence
NICKNAME: The Jacks
FOUNDED: 2014
COUNTRY: USA
STADIUM: Sportsplex at Matthews, Matthews
(2,300 spectators)

6. CLUB: MFK Ružomberok
NICKNAME: Ruža (The Rose)
FOUNDED: 1906
COUNTRY: Slovakia
STADIUM: Štadión pod Čebraťom, Ružomberok
(4,876 spectators)

7. CLUB: ND Gorica
NICKNAME: Vrtnice (The Roses) & Plavo-beli
(The blue and whites)
FOUNDED: 1947
COUNTRY: Slovenia
STADIUM: Nova Gorica Sports Park, Nova Gorica
(3,100 spectators)

8. CLUB: Club Tijuana Xoloitzcuintles de Caliente
NICKNAME: Los Xolos & La Jauría
(The Pack of hounds)
FOUNDED: 2007
COUNTRY: Mexico
STADIUM: Estadio Caliente, Tijuana
(27,333 spectators)

9. CLUB: Halmstads BK
NICKNAME: HBK
FOUNDED: 1914
COUNTRY: Sweden
STADIUM: Örjans Vall, Halmstad
(15,500 spectators)

1.

2.

3.

4.

5.

6.

7.

8.

9.

1. CLUB: FC Hansa Rostock
   NICKNAME: Hansa, Hanseaten, Kogge, Hansa-Kogge
   & Ostseestädter (People by the Baltic sea)
   FOUNDED: 1965
   COUNTRY: Germany
   STADIUM: Ostseestadion, Rostock
   (29,000 spectators)

4. CLUB: Aberdeen FC
   NICKNAME: The Dons, The Dandies & The Reds
   FOUNDED: 1903
   COUNTRY: Scotland
   STADIUM: Pittodrie Stadium, Aberdeen
   (20,866 spectators)

7. CLUB: Portsmouth FC
   NICKNAME: Pompey
   FOUNDED: 1898
   COUNTRY: England
   STADIUM: Fratton Park, Portsmouth
   (20,620 spectators)

2. Club: AFC Bournemouth
   Nickname: The Cherries & Boscombe
   Founded: 1899
   Country: England
   Stadium: Dean Court, Bournemouth
   (11,360 spectators)

5. CLUB: Club Universitario de Deportes
   NICKNAME: Cremas (The Cream), Los Merengues
   (The Meringues) & La U
   FOUNDED: 1924
   COUNTRY: Peru
   STADIUM: Estadio Monumental "U", Lima
   (80,093 spectators)

8. CLUB: Scunthorpe United FC
   NICKNAME: The Iron
   FOUNDED: 1899
   COUNTRY: England
   STADIUM: Glanford Park, Scunthorpe
   (9,088 spectators)

3. CLUB: KAA Gent
   NICKNAME: De Buffalo's (The Buffalos)
   FOUNDED: 1864
   COUNTRY: Belgium
   STADIUM: Ghelamco Stadium, Gent
   (20,000 spectators)

6. CLUB: Hannover 96
   NICKNAME: Die Roten (the Reds)
   FOUNDED: 1896
   COUNTRY: Germany
   STADIUM: HDI-Stadium, Hannover
   (49,000 spectators)

9. CLUB: Rochester Rhinos
   NICKNAME: Raging Rhinos
   FOUNDED: 1996
   COUNTRY: USA
   STADIUM: Capelli Sport Stadium, Rochester
   (13,768 spectators)

1.

2.

3.

4.

5.

6.

7.

8.

9.

1. CLUB: Palmeiras
   NICKNAME: Verdão (Big Green) & Porco (Pig)
   FOUNDED: 1914
   COUNTRY: Brazil
   STADIUM: Allianz Parque, São Paulo
   (47,500 spectators)

2. CLUB: FC Vaduz
   NICKNAME: Residenzler (The Resident) &
   Fürstenverein (The Princes Club)
   FOUNDED: 1932
   COUNTRY: Liechtenstein
   STADIUM: Rheinpark Stadion, Vaduz
   (7,838 spectators)

3. CLUB: Tout Puissant Mazembe
   NICKNAME: Les Corbeaux (The Ravens)
   FOUNDED: 1939
   COUNTRY: Democratic Republic of Congo
   STADIUM: Stade TP Mazembe, Lubumbashi
   (18,500 spectators)

4. CLUB: Kaizer Chiefs FC
   NICKNAME: Amakhosi (The Chiefs) & Glamour Boys
   FOUNDED: 1970
   COUNTRY: South Africa
   STADIUM: FNB Stadium, Johannesburg
   (94,796 spectators)

5. CLUB: Rosenborg BK
   NICKNAME: Troillongan (The Troll Children)
   FOUNDED: 1917
   COUNTRY: Norway
   STADIUM: Lerkendal Stadion, Trondheim
   (21,405 spectators)

6. CLUB: Burton Albion FC
   NICKNAME: Brewers
   FOUNDED: 1950
   COUNTRY: England
   STADIUM: Pirelli Stadium, Burton upon Trent
   (6,912 spectators)

7. CLUB: FC Metz
   NICKNAME: Les Grenats (the Maroons), Les Messins
   & Les Graoullys (The Dragons)
   FOUNDED: 1919
   COUNTRY: France
   STADIUM: Stade Saint-Symphorien, Metz
   (25,636 spectators)

8. CLUB: Hartlepool United FC
   NICKNAME: Pool & Monkey Hangers
   FOUNDED: 1908
   COUNTRY: England
   STADIUM: Victoria Park, Hartlepool
   (7,858 spectators)

9. CLUB: FC Augsburg 1907
   NICKNAME: Fuggerstädter (Fugger City Dwellers)
   FOUNDED: 1907
   COUNTRY: Germany
   STADIUM: WWK Arena, Augsburg
   (30,660 spectators)

1.

2.

3.

4.

5.

6.

7.

8.

9.

1. <u>CLUB:</u> Nottingham Forest FC
<u>NICKNAME:</u> The Reds, Forest & Tricky Trees
<u>FOUNDED:</u> 1865
<u>COUNTRY:</u> England
<u>STADIUM:</u> City Ground, Nottingham
(30,445 spectators)

4. <u>CLUB:</u> Oxford United FC
<u>NICKNAME:</u> The U's, Yellows & The Boys from Up the Hill
<u>FOUNDED:</u> 1893
<u>COUNTRY:</u> England
<u>STADIUM:</u> Kassam Stadium, Oxford
(12,500 spectators)

7. <u>CLUB:</u> 1. FSV Mainz 05
<u>NICKNAME:</u> Die Nullfünfer (the 0-Fives)
& Karnevalsverein (Carnival club)
<u>FOUNDED:</u> 1905
<u>COUNTRY:</u> Germany
<u>STADIUM:</u> Opel Arena, Mainz (34,034 spectators)

2. <u>CLUB:</u> Dundee United FC
<u>NICKNAME:</u> The Tangerines & The Terrors
<u>FOUNDED:</u> 1909
<u>COUNTRY:</u> Scotland
<u>STADIUM:</u> Tannadice Park, Dundee
(14,223 spectators)

5. <u>CLUB:</u> D.C. United
<u>NICKNAME:</u> Black-and-Red
<u>FOUNDED:</u> 1994
<u>COUNTRY:</u> USA
<u>STADIUM:</u> Audi Field, Washington D.C.
(20,000 spectators)

8. <u>CLUB:</u> IFK Göteborg
<u>NICKNAME:</u> Blåvitt (Blue-white), Änglarna
(The Angels) & Kamraterna (The Comrades)
<u>FOUNDED:</u> 1904
<u>COUNTRY:</u> Sweden
<u>STADIUM:</u> Gamla Ullevi, Gothenburg (18,416 spectators)

3. <u>CLUB:</u> Go Ahead Eagles
<u>NICKNAME:</u> The pride of the Ijssel & Kowet
<u>FOUNDED:</u> 1902
<u>COUNTRY:</u> Netherlands
<u>STADIUM:</u> Adelaarshorst, Deventer
(10,000 spectators)

6. <u>CLUB:</u> Hibernian FC
<u>NICKNAME:</u> Hibs, Hibees & The Cabbage
<u>FOUNDED:</u> 1875
<u>COUNTRY:</u> Scotland
<u>STADIUM:</u> Easter Road, Edinburgh
(20,421 spectators)

9. <u>CLUB:</u> New England Revolution
<u>NICKNAME:</u> Revs
<u>FOUNDED:</u> 1994
<u>COUNTRY:</u> USA
<u>STADIUM:</u> Gillette Stadium, Foxborough
(20,000 spectators)

1.

FK Haugesund

2.

3.

4.

5.

6.

7.

8.

9.

---

1. CLUB: Orlando City SC
NICKNAME: The Lions
FOUNDED: 2013
COUNTRY: USA
STADIUM: Orlando City Stadium, Orlando
(25,527 spectators)

2. CLUB: FK Haugesund
NICKNAME: FKH & Araberne (The Arabs)
FOUNDED: 1993
COUNTRY: Norway
STADIUM: Haugesund Stadion, Haugesund
(8,754 spectators)

3. CLUB: Cambridge United FC
NICKNAME: United & The U's
FOUNDED: 1912
COUNTRY: England
STADIUM: Abbey Stadium, Cambridge (8,127 spectators)

4. CLUB: AFC Wimbledon
NICKNAME: The Dons & The Wombles
FOUNDED: 2002
COUNTRY: England
STADIUM: Kingsmeadow, London (4,850 spectators)

5. CLUB: Linfield FC
NICKNAME: The Blues
FOUNDED: 1886
COUNTRY: Northern Ireland
STADIUM: Windsor Park, Belfast
(18,167 spectators)

6. CLUB: RC Strasbourg Alsace
NICKNAME: Racing, RCS & RCSA
FOUNDED: 1906
COUNTRY: France
STADIUM: Stade de la Meinau, Strasbourg
(29,371 spectators)

7. CLUB: Dynamo Dresden
NICKNAME: SGD & Dynamo
FOUNDED: 1953
COUNTRY: Germany
STADIUM: Stadion Dresden, Dresden
(32,085 spectators)

8. CLUB: Colorado Rapids
NICKNAME: Rapids
FOUNDED: 1995
COUNTRY: USA
STADIUM: Dick's Sporting Goods Park, Commerce City
(18,061 spectators)

9. CLUB: Cheltenham Town FC
NICKNAME: The Robins
FOUNDED: 1887
COUNTRY: England
STADIUM: Whaddon Road, Cheltenham
(7,066 spectators)

1.

2.

3.

4.

5.

6.

7.

8.

9.

1. **CLUB:** Oldham Athletic AFC
   NICKNAME: Latics
   FOUNDED: 1895
   COUNTRY: England
   STADIUM: Boundary Park, Oldham
   (13,512 spectators)

4. **CLUB:** Club de Deportes Iquique
   NICKNAME: Los Dragones Celestes
   (The Sky Blue Dragons)
   FOUNDED: 1978
   COUNTRY: Chile
   STADIUM: Estadio Municipal de Cavancha, Iquique
   (3,500 spectators)

7. **CLUB:** St Mirren FC
   NICKNAME: The Buddies & The Saints
   FOUNDED: 1877
   COUNTRY: Scotland
   STADIUM: St Mirren Park, Paisley
   (8,023 spectators)

2. **CLUB:** Philadelphia Union
   NICKNAME: The U
   FOUNDED: 2008
   COUNTRY: USA
   STADIUM: Talen Energy Stadium, Chester
   (18,500 spectators)

5. **CLUB:** 1. FC Union Berlin
   NICKNAME: Die Eisernen (The Iron Ones)
   FOUNDED: 1906
   COUNTRY: Germany
   STADIUM: Stadion An der Alten Försterei, Berlin
   (22,012 spectators)

8. **CLUB:** Notts County FC
   NICKNAME: The Magpies, County & Notts
   FOUNDED: 1862
   COUNTRY: England
   STADIUM: Meadow Lane, Nottingham
   (19,841 spectators)

3. **CLUB:** Minnesota United FC
   NICKNAME: The Loons
   FOUNDED: 2015
   COUNTRY: USA
   STADIUM: TCF Bank Stadium, Minneapolis
   (50,805 spectators)

6. **CLUB:** Cork City FC
   NICKNAME: Rebel Army & City
   FOUNDED: 1984
   COUNTRY: Ireland
   STADIUM: Turners Cross, Cork
   (7,485 spectators)

9. **CLUB:** Yeovil Town FC
   NICKNAME: The Glovers
   FOUNDED: 1895
   COUNTRY: England
   STADIUM: Huish Park, Yeovil
   (9,565 spectators)

1.

2.

3.

4.

5.

6.

7.

8.

9.

1. CLUB: Vancouver Whitecaps FC
   NICKNAME: Caps & Blue and White
   FOUNDED: 1974
   COUNTRY: Canada
   STADIUM: BC Place, Vancouver
   (22,120 spectators)

2. CLUB: Atlanta United FC
   NICKNAME: The Five Stripes
   FOUNDED: 2014
   COUNTRY: USA
   STADIUM: Mercedes-Benz Stadium, Atlanta
   (71,000 spectators)

3. CLUB: GD Estoril Praia
   NICKNAME: Canarinhos (Canaries), Equipa da Linha
   & Estorilistas
   FOUNDED: 1939
   COUNTRY: Portugal
   STADIUM: Estádio António Coimbra da Mota,
   Cascais (8,015 spectators)

4. CLUB: FK Partizan
   NICKNAME: Crno-beli (The Black-Whites) &
   Parni valjak (The Steamroller)
   FOUNDED: 1945
   COUNTRY: Serbia
   STADIUM: Partizan Stadium, Belgrade
   (32,710 spectators)

5. CLUB: Dinamo Zagreb
   NICKNAME: Plavi (The Blues)
   FOUNDED: 1911
   COUNTRY: Croatia
   STADIUM: Stadion Maksimir, Zagreb
   (35,123 spectators)

6. CLUB: Sporting Kansas City
   NICKNAME: Wizards
   FOUNDED: 1995
   COUNTRY: USA
   STADIUM: Children's Mercy Park, Kansas City
   (18,467 spectators)

7. CLUB: Mansfield Town FC
   NICKNAME: The Stags & Yellows
   FOUNDED: 1897
   COUNTRY: England
   STADIUM: Field Mill, Mansfield (9,186 spectators)

8. CLUB: Dunfermline Athletic FC
   NICKNAME: The Pars
   FOUNDED: 1885
   COUNTRY: Scotland
   STADIUM: East End Park, Dunfermline
   (11,480 spectators)

9. CLUB: MSV Duisburg
   NICKNAME: Die Zebras (The Zebras)
   FOUNDED: 1902
   COUNTRY: Germany
   STADIUM: Schauinsland-Reisen-Stadium, Duisburg
   (31,514 spectators)

1.

2.

3.

4.

5.

6.

7.

8.

9.

1. <u>CLUB:</u> Plymouth Argyle FC
<u>NICKNAME:</u> The Pilgrims
<u>FOUNDED:</u> 1886
<u>COUNTRY:</u> England
<u>STADIUM:</u> Home Park, Plymouth (17,800 spectators)

4. <u>CLUB:</u> Club The Strongest
<u>NICKNAME:</u> Tigre , Gualdinegro, El Decano & Aurinegro
<u>FOUNDED:</u> 1908
<u>COUNTRY:</u> Bolivia
<u>STADIUM:</u> Estadio Hernando Siles, La Paz
(42,000 spectators)

7. <u>CLUB:</u> Dundalk FC
<u>NICKNAME:</u> Lilywhites & The Town
<u>FOUNDED:</u> 1903
<u>COUNTRY:</u> Ireland
<u>STADIUM:</u> Oriel Park, Dundalk
(4,500 spectators)

2. <u>CLUB:</u> Real Salt Lake
<u>NICKNAME:</u> Claret and Cobalt, Royals & RSL
<u>FOUNDED:</u> 2004
<u>COUNTRY:</u> USA
<u>STADIUM:</u> Rio Tinto Stadium, Sandy (20,213 spectators)

5. <u>CLUB:</u> FC Anzhi Makhachkala
<u>NICKNAME:</u> Orly (Eagles) & Zhelto-zelyonye
(Yellow-Greens)
<u>FOUNDED:</u> 1991
<u>COUNTRY:</u> Russia
<u>STADIUM:</u> Anzhi-Stadium, Kaspiysk (26,400 spectators)

8. <u>CLUB:</u> Panathinaikos
<u>NICKNAME:</u> To Trifýlli (The Shamrock) & I Prásini
(The Greens)
<u>FOUNDED:</u> 1908
<u>COUNTRY:</u> Greece
<u>STADIUM:</u> Apostolos Nikolaidis Stadium, Athens
(16,003 spectators)

3. <u>CLUB:</u> Toronto FC
<u>NICKNAME:</u> The Reds
<u>FOUNDED:</u> 2005
<u>COUNTRY:</u> Canada
<u>STADIUM:</u> BMO Field, Toronto (30,991 spectators)

6. <u>CLUB:</u> FC Nordsjælland
<u>NICKNAME:</u> The Tigers
<u>FOUNDED:</u> 2003
<u>COUNTRY:</u> Denmark
<u>STADIUM:</u> Right to Dream Park, Farum
(10,300 spectators)

9. <u>CLUB:</u> FC Dallas
<u>NICKNAME:</u> Toros, Hoops & Burn
<u>FOUNDED:</u> 1995
<u>COUNTRY:</u> USA
<u>STADIUM:</u> Toyota Stadium, Frisco (20,500 spectators)

1.

2.

3.

4.

5.

6.

7.

8.

9.

1. CLUB: Montreal Impact
   NICKNAME: The Impact
   FOUNDED: 2010
   COUNTRY: Canada
   STADIUM: Saputo Stadium, Montreal
   (20,801 spectators)

2. CLUB: Helsingborgs IF
   NICKNAME: Di Röe (The Reds) & Skånes stolthet
   (The Pride of Scania)
   FOUNDED: 1907
   COUNTRY: Sweden
   STADIUM: Olympia, Helsingborg (16,500 spectators)

3. CLUB: Werder Bremen
   NICKNAME: Die Werderaner (The River islanders)
   & Die Grün-Weißen (The Green-Whites)
   FOUNDED: 1899
   COUNTRY: Germany
   STADIUM: Weserstadion, Bremen (42,100 spectators)

4. CLUB: Luton Town FC
   NICKNAME: The Hatters
   FOUNDED: 1885
   COUNTRY: England
   STADIUM: Kenilworth Road, Luton
   (10,356 spectators)

5. CLUB: Shamrock Rovers FC
   NICKNAME: Hoops & Rovers
   FOUNDED: 1899
   COUNTRY: Ireland
   STADIUM: Tallaght Stadium, Tallaght
   (6,000 spectators)

6. CLUB: St Johnstone FC
   NICKNAME: The Saints
   FOUNDED: 1884
   COUNTRY: Scotland
   STADIUM: McDiarmid Park, Perth
   (10,696 spectators)

7. CLUB: Valenciennes FC
   NICKNAME: VA & Les Athéniens (the Athenians)
   FOUNDED: 1913
   COUNTRY: France
   STADIUM: Stade du Hainaut, Valenciennes
   (25,172 spectators)

8. CLUB: KV Oostende
   NICKNAME: De Kustboys
   FOUNDED: 1904
   COUNTRY: Belgium
   STADIUM: Versluys Stadium, Ostend
   (8,432 spectators)

9. CLUB: US Salernitana 1919
   NICKNAME: I Granata (The Grenades)
   FOUNDED: 1919
   COUNTRY: Italy
   STADIUM: Stadio Arechi, Salerno
   (31,300 spectators)

1.

2.

3.

4.

5.

6.

7.

8.

9.

1. CLUB: Leyton Orient FC
   NICKNAME: The O's & Orient
   FOUNDED: 1881
   COUNTRY: England
   STADIUM: Brisbane Road, London (9,271 spectators)

2. CLUB: Motherwell FC
   NICKNAME: Well & The Steelmen
   FOUNDED: 1886
   COUNTRY: Scotland
   STADIUM: Fir Park, Motherwell (13,677 spectators)

3. CLUB: Houston Dynamo
   NICKNAME: Dynamo
   FOUNDED: 2005
   COUNTRY: USA
   STADIUM: BBVA Compass Stadium, Houston
   (22,039 spectators)

4. CLUB: Accra Hearts of Oak S.C.
   NICKNAME: Continental Club Masters & Phobia
   FOUNDED: 1911
   COUNTRY: Ghana
   STADIUM: Accra Sports Stadium, Accra
   (40,000 spectators)

5. CLUB: MŠK Žilina
   NICKNAME: Sosoni (The Shoshons) & Zlto-Zeleni
   (The Yellow-Greens)
   FOUNDED: 1908
   COUNTRY: Slovakia
   STADIUM: Štadión pod Dubnom, Žilina
   (11,258 spectators)

6. CLUB: Associação Chapecoense de Futebol
   NICKNAME: Verdão (Big Green), Furacão do Oeste
   (Western Hurricane), Chape & Chape terror
   FOUNDED: 1973
   COUNTRY: Brazil
   STADIUM: Stadium Condá, Chapecó
   (22,600 spectators)

7. CLUB: Montpellier HSC
   NICKNAME: MHSC & La Paillade
   FOUNDED: 1919
   COUNTRY: France
   STADIUM: Stade de la Mosson, Montpellier
   (32,939 spectators)

8. CLUB: FC Groningen
   NICKNAME: Pride of the North & Green-White Army
   FOUNDED: 1971
   COUNTRY: Netherlands
   STADIUM: Noordlease Stadion, Groningen
   (22,579 spectators)

9. CLUB: Zulte Waregem
   NICKNAME: Essevee
   FOUNDED: 2001
   COUNTRY: Belgium
   STADIUM: Regenboogstadion, Waregem
   (12,500 spectators)

1.

2.

3.

4.

5.

6.

7.

8.

9.

1. CLUB: Fortuna Düsseldorf
   NICKNAME: Flingeraner
   FOUNDED: 1895
   COUNTRY: Germany
   STADIUM: Esprit Stadium, Düsseldorf
   (54,600 spectators)

2. CLUB: Celta de Vigo
   NICKNAME: Célticos (The Celtics), Celestes
   (The Sky Blues) & Celtiñas (The Little Celta)
   FOUNDED: 1923
   COUNTRY: Spain
   STADIUM: Balaídos, Vigo (29,000 spectators)

3. CLUB: AC Cesena
   NICKNAME: Cavallucci Marini (The Seahorses)
   & Bianconero (Black and white)
   FOUNDED: 1940
   COUNTRY: Italy
   STADIUM: Stadio Dino Manuzzi, Cesena
   (23,900 spectators)

4. CLUB Boavista Futebol Clube
   NICKNAME: Os Axadrezados (The Chequered Ones)
   & As Panteras (The Panthers)
   FOUNDED: 1903
   COUNTRY: Portugal
   STADIUM: Estádio de Bessa, Porto (28,263 spectators)

5. CLUB: HJK Helsinki
   NICKNAME: Klubi (The Club)
   FOUNDED: 1907
   COUNTRY: Finland
   STADIUM: Telia 5G-areena, Helsinki
   (10,770 spectators)

6. CLUB: San Jose Earthquakes
   NICKNAME: Quakes & The Goonies
   FOUNDED: 1974
   COUNTRY: USA
   STADIUM: Avaya Stadium, San Jose
   (18,000 spectators)

7. CLUB: FC København
   NICKNAME: Byens Hold (The Team of the City)
   & Løverne (Lions)
   FOUNDED: 1992
   COUNTRY: Denmark
   STADIUM: Telia Parken, Copenhagen (38,065 spectators)

8. CLUB: Hammarby IF
   NICKNAME: Bajen
   FOUNDED: 1897
   COUNTRY: Sweden
   STADIUM: Tele2 Arena, Stockholm
   (30,000 capacity)

9. CLUB: Djurgårdens IF
   NICKNAME: Blåränderna (the Blue Stripes) &
   Järnkaminerna (The Iron Furnaces)
   FOUNDED: 1891
   COUNTRY: Sweden
   STADIUM: Tele2 Arena, Stockholm
   (30,000 capacity)

ACKNOWLEDGEMENTS

With special thanks to:

All the participating clubs. For your help, understanding and support.

Mattias Nykvist. For your belief and advice.

Anton Boström, Adam Nilsson and *John Witt*. For our Bundesliga hours.

Martin Älveby. Because, no interest is too niche.

Bosse Petersson. Because you believed in me.

Suheyb Sinan Kandemir, Deng Yun, Seung Hwan Hwang and *Kieran Chumun*. For the French football we shared.

Hampus Collén, Ludwig Lindebratt and *Erik Westerlund*. For your never-ending support.

Jakob Lotz. For the most beautiful crest out there.

Sjökrickan. For our friendship.

My grandfather, Stig. For making me dream.

Mum and Dad. For all your love and support.

Marie, my love. Because you read each crest, every note and every letter in this book with the same glow, spark and passion as you take care of me.

ABOUT THE AUTHOR

Leonard Jägerskiöld Nilsson is a Swedish sports journalist who has worked as a producer, commentator and reporter for TV channels such as Eurosport, Discovery Networks and Viasat Sport. He has covered the UEFA Champions League, Europa League, Premier League, Bundesliga, Serie A, La Liga, Ligue 1 and the Swedish national team. He has also featured in Swedish sports papers such as *Sportblade*t and international football magazines such as *11Freunde* and *The Blizzard*.

His interest in football club crests and badges goes a long way back and as a child he enjoyed the team badges far more than the football itself. Twenty years on and he still has the same passion for these important symbols of sporting identity.

Of the 200+ football club crest designs found in this book, he has a special admiration for the following:

Sampdoria: What's not to like about a pipe-smoking sailor who also happens to be the local patron saint?

Ajax: The simplicity of eleven lines that illustrate the ancient hero Ajax is simply stunning.

Blackburn Rovers: Because the club's motto summarises football in the best possible way *Arte et Labore* 'By skill and labour' and is the very essence of football.

@worldclubcrests

@LeonardJN